*The Facts of Causation*

# International Library of Philosophy

EDITED BY TIM CRANE AND JONATHAN WOLFF
University College London

The history of the International Library of Philosophy can be traced back to the 1920s, when C. K. Ogden launched the series with G. E. Moore's *Philosophical Papers* and soon after published Ludwig Wittgenstein's *Tractatus Logico-Philosophicus*. Since its auspicious start, it has published the finest work in philosophy under the successive editorships of A. J. Ayer, Bernard Williams and Ted Honderich. Now jointly edited by Tim Crane and Jonathan Wolff, the ILP will continue to publish works at the forefront of philosophical research.

Related titles in the ILP include:

REAL TIME II
D. H. Mellor

A MATERIALIST THEORY OF THE MIND
D. M. Armstrong

MIND, METHOD AND CONDITIONALS
Frank Jackson

G. E. MOORE: SELECTED WRITINGS
Edited by Thomas Baldwin

THE SCEPTICAL CHALLENGE
Ruth Weintraub

# The Facts of Causation

D. H. MELLOR

London and New York

First published 1995
by Routledge
11 New Fetter Lane, London EC4P 4EE

Simultaneously published in the USA and Canada
by Routledge
29 West 35th Street, New York, NY 10001

First published in paperback 1999

Typeset in Times by the author

Printed and bound in Great Britain by
TJ International Ltd, Padstow, Cornwall

*British Library Cataloguing in Publication Data*
A catalogue record for this book is available from the British Library

*Library of Congress Cataloguing in Publication Data*
Mellor, D. H.
    The facts of causation/D. H. Mellor.
        p. cm. – (International library of philosophy)
    Includes bibliographical references and index.
    1. Causation. I. Title. II. Series.
    BD531.M39 1995                     95–5708
    122–dc20                           CIP

ISBN 0–415–09779–7 (hbk)
ISBN 0–415–19756–2 (pbk)

*For the Vikings, and the Wizards of Oz*

# Contents

# *Preface*

This book has grown over many years and survived several false starts and adjournments. Although self-contained, it uses the conclusions of my *The Matter of Chance* (1971) and *Real Time* (1981), while making corrections to the latter [now incorporated in my *Real Time II* (1998)]. On causation itself I first linked my two principal claims – that causation links not events but facts, and that causes must raise the chances of their effects – in print in my 'Fixed past, unfixed future', in *Michael Dummett: Contributions to Philosophy*, ed. B. Taylor, 166–86, © 1987 Martinus Nijhoff Publishers, Dordrecht, parts of which are reprinted here by permission of Kluwer Academic Publishers. I argued these claims more fully in my 1987 'The singularly affecting facts of causation', *Metaphysics and Morality: Essays in Honour of J. J. C. Smart*, ed. P. Pettit et al., Oxford: Blackwell, 111–36, and my 1988 'On raising the chances of effects', *Probability and Causality*, ed. J. H. Fetzer, 229–39, © 1988 D. Reidel Publishing Company, Dordrecht; parts of which are reprinted here by permission respectively of Blackwell and Kluwer Academic Publishers.

However, only while writing this book did I come to see and work out many of the consequences of my claims: how causing things differs from affecting them, and why it matters; how causation is embodied, why it is not a relation and why it entails laws; what fixes what causal properties and kinds of facts there are; how spacetime embodies laws; how our experience of time, as well as its linearity and direction, depends on causation. Most of this material, in chapters 12 to 17, is new and, I believe, original. (In particular, the arguments that causation is what gives time its direction and makes it linear, given in chapter 17, supersede the arguments for these claims given in chapter 10 of *Real Time* and developed in my 1991 'Causation and the direction of time', *Erkenntnis* **35**, 191–203.)

This new work has not of course been done all on my own. Besides the works listed in the Bibliography (especially Tooley 1987), I owe most to the colleagues and students in Cambridge and elsewhere with whom, individually and collectively, I have discussed these matters in the last few years. I am especially grateful to those taking part in lectures and seminars on some of this material which I have given recently at Cambridge University, University College London and the Universities of Keele and Frankfurt. Those from whose private comments on these matters I have learned most include Tom Baldwin, Alexander Bird, Jeremy Butterfield, Max Cresswell, Dick Jeffrey, Arnold Koslow, David Lewis, Peter Lipton, Peter Menzies, Paul Noordhof, Graham Oddie, Alex Oliver, David Owens, Fred Schick, Peter Simons, Jack Smart, Paul Teller and Jamie Whyte.

I owe five special debts of gratitude. The first is to Nils-Eric Sahlin (a friend and fellow fan of F. P. Ramsey) and his students at Lund University, notably Johannes Persson, who for much of 1991 discussed early drafts of the first part of the book and showed me both that I must rewrite it and how. The second is to the members of the Philosophy Department at the University of Uppsala, who invited me to give the 1993 Hägerström Lectures on causation. Their comments on these lectures, and especially those of Wlodek Rabinowicz, fired me to finish the job properly at last. The third is to my ex-student Chris Daly, whose Ph.D. thesis work on laws and properties has taught me a great deal. My fourth debt is to Tim Crane, for his friendship and his help, especially with the treatment of mental causation, and for reading my penultimate draft and showing me how to improve it. My last debt I share with all serious writers on this subject: to Hans Reichenbach, our century's greatest metaphysician of causation and time, and a prophet whose work is still too little honoured both in Germany and abroad.

*Cambridge*
*March 1995*

Now my *Real Time II* has superseded *Real Time*, all references here to the latter have been replaced. The only other noteworthy change is in chapter 16.8. I originally said there that the structure of most 'facta' (my term for the truthmakers of statements) about things is $Jdt$, where $t$ is the time at which $d$ has the intrinsic property $J$. Now, however, for reasons given in chapter 8.6 of *Real Time II*, I think that $t$ is not a constituent of a factum $Jdt$, but is merely the temporal location of one of many facta whose only constituents are $J$ and $d$. This enables all non-relational facta about both things and events to share the structure $Jd$. Thus the claim in chapter 14.5, that $Jd$ is the structure of all singular causal facta, no longer needs the qualification made in chapter 16.8, which has therefore been deleted.

*Cambridge*
*August 1998*

# Introduction

Everyone relies on causation all the time. We eat and drink because, among other things, we believe (truly) that not doing so will cause us to die. A climber, Don, takes a rope because he believes (perhaps falsely) that it will cause him to survive if he slips. Bill wants to stop smoking because he believes it may cause him to get cancer, which eventually it does. Invalids take medicine which they believe, truly or falsely, will cause them to recover. Motorists buy petrol because they believe that running out of it will cause their cars to stop. And so on, and so on. And these activities too exemplify causation, all of them being, among other things, caused by our belief in it.

Given our reliance on causation, a surprising number of philosophers (no names, no pack drill, though where the cap fits it is worn with pride) deny that it exists. I cannot see why. I know that educated and otherwise sensible people, even philosophers who have read Hume, can hold bizarre religious beliefs. I know philosophers can win fame and fortune by gulling literary theorists and others with nonsense they don't themselves believe. But nobody, however gullible, believes in *no* causation. On the contrary: the objection to most religions, as to parapsychology, astrology and the relativist view that science (like Tinkerbell) only works because we believe in it, is that these views postulate causal links which manifestly do not exist, not that they deny links which manifestly do.

Why then do some serious philosophers say there is no causation? We should not after all deny in our work what our every action shows we believe: philosophy is not a branch of fiction. There are two possible excuses. First, what is denied may be not causation itself but a false doctrine about it: for example, that we can know *a priori* what causes what. Second, something that everyone assumes about causation may turn out to be false. This has happened, e.g. with time, which McTaggart (1908) showed cannot 'flow' (i.e. take events from the future to the past *via* the present), even though we may still think of it as doing so. Those who realise this – some still haven't – may then ask if what we call 'time' still deserves the name. McTaggart thought it did not, which is why he claimed to have shown that time does not exist. I think it does, but I also think the question overrated. For the main job of metaphysics is to increase our understanding of the world, as McTaggart did by proving that nothing can flow as we thought time did: that is what matters, not how much, if at all, accepting his proof changes our concept of time.

But however much or little that question matters, we do not face it here, since no one has shown that causation as we conceive it cannot exist. The indeterminism of modern physics may show that not everything has a cause, certainly not a deterministic one. But most events can have causes even if some do not; and showing that causes need not determine their effects is not like showing that time cannot flow. Why then should anyone deny that causation exists?

I can think of only three reasons, all bad. First, there is the bad habit of asking, of an obviously real X, 'how is X possible?' without any reason to think it otherwise. Given a seemingly good argument that we cannot, for example, know what other people think, this question makes sense, namely 'what's wrong with the argument?'. But without such an argument the only answer to the question of what makes X possible is that X exists. Suppose for example we ask how mental events, like my deciding to move, can have physical effects, like my moving. Since no theory of causation says they cannot, the only good reply, as to 'how is death possible?', is 'it happens'. Yet some philosophers take the lack of any other answer to cast doubt on the existence of mental causes that are not physical – though not, oddly enough, on mortality.

Second, there are the so-called *counterfactual* implications of causation, for example that, had I opted to stay put, I would have done so. That claim seems to be about the world not as it is but as it would be without the cause (my opting to move) of the effect (my moving). Some philosophers say therefore that in *this* world, and near me, there is only the cause and the effect: my decision and my movement. The causation which seems to link them lies elsewhere: in other possible worlds, or in general facts, for example that everyone who chooses to move (and can) does so. And either way there is still no causation: only people in this and other worlds (if any) choosing to move (or not) and acting accordingly.

This, on the face of it, is absurd. The idea that what makes *my* decision cause *me* to move is the fact that other people who decide to move also happen to do so is credible only if there is no alternative. And there is an alternative: facts about my mind and muscles can make my deciding to move cause me to move, just as my mass being what it is can make my stepping on my bathroom scales cause them and me to be as depressed by it as we are. And if such facts about me *can* give these causes the effects they have, then obviously they do: the obvious way to account for causation is to show how it is embodied in causal facts like the inertial masses of things. Only if we cannot do that can we credibly deny the existence of causation. But we can do that, as I shall show in this book by doing it.

This brings me to the third bad reason for denying that causation exists, namely that we never see it: that our senses never make a causal fact, like a thing's mass, cause us to have a true belief about it. But they do, as when the mass of what I carry causes me to feel how heavy and thus how massive it is. In reality we perceive causal facts all the time, in a perfectly straight-forward way, as we shall see in chapter 9.

Why then does the myth that causation is unobservable persist? One reason is a sceptical circle: the myth both supports and is supported by professions of disbelief in causation. For without causation our senses could not make *any* fact cause us to believe in it. But how then could our senses tell us anything – we end in a wholesale scepticism that is even less credible than the scepticism about causation which engenders it. We can therefore dispose of both at once by showing how causation lets our senses tell us the facts we all think they do tell us – including, as we shall see, the causal facts our senses need, thus turning a vicious sceptical circle into a virtuous non-sceptical one.

It would not however be worth devising an account of causation just to defeat a scepticism that no one really believes. There are better reasons for wanting to show how causation is embodied in facts about this world. One is that causation is increasingly invoked throughout philosophy: in theories of mind and language, of explanation, of decision making and of action, and of knowledge. Yet it is rarely either obvious or shown that what these theories assume about it is true. All too often crucial but contentious assumptions (e.g. that causation is physical, extensional or law-based, or involves necessity) are backed only by unargued intuitions. That is not good enough: the more we need to invoke causation, the more we need a full and fully argued account of it to tell us what it is, what it entails and what it can and cannot do.

The other, more direct, reason for wanting an account of causation is that it is itself a basic feature of our world, which we need to understand. And what makes it both important and hard to understand is also what makes it basic, namely its intimate links with other such features: necessity and chance, laws of nature, the properties of things, events, change and time. But this means that no proper account of causation can be self-contained, since it must say enough about these other matters to show how they bear on causation itself.

That is my real excuse for adding this book to the vast literature on the subject. For all their merits, none of the accounts of causation I know of seems to me full enough, a defect that is not just one of incompleteness. For we shall see that explaining causation's links with necessity, chance, facts, things and events, properties, laws and time requires unorthodox accounts of some of them as well. But if that makes a full account of causation harder to construct, it also makes it more worth constructing, since it will tell us something new about these other matters too; while its doing so will both affect and recommend what it says about causation.

So much for the purpose of this book, whose success in achieving it readers must judge for themselves. But before starting I should note an important assumption I shall make about time. This is the view, mentioned above, that time does not flow, a view I have defended elsewhere (Mellor 1998 chs 1–7) on grounds quite independent of causation. Although this view remains contentious (see Oaklander and Smith 1994), in what follows I shall take it for granted. I shall therefore ignore all accounts of causation which, like Mackie's (1974), invoke time's flow, e.g. by using the way in which it 'fixes' events as they become present to say how causes fix their effects and why they must precede them (see Mellor 1991 ch. 11). For, since time does *not* flow, this cannot really be how causes fix or why they precede their effects. We need other answers to those questions, answers which I shall give in chapters 2 and 17.

Four other aspects of the book should also be noted briefly before we start. First, keeping track of all the links between the aspects of causation I discuss requires a fair number of cross-references. I try to keep these as undistracting as possible by referring to other sections in the same chapter thus: [§3], and to other chapters thus: [6; 7.2–4]. I avoid footnotes for that reason too, putting asides in parentheses and, as here, using the author–date system to refer in the text to works listed in the Bibliography.

Second, I refer to existing literature almost as rarely as I do in my (1998) book on time, and for the same reason: it is too vast and varied for me to discuss it properly while developing my own views. So while I refer to some works from which I recall getting points that I make or attack, my object is not to survey and assess existing accounts of causation but to devise and defend my own; and the book must be read in that light. But if I have missed a due acknowledgement I apologise and will be glad to be told of it.

Third, while I use examples of mental causation, and make points about it in passing, I give no separate account of it. This is not an accidental omission. Indeed it is not an omission at all, as there is in a sense no mental causation, only mental causes and effects. But nor in this sense is there physical causation: there are only physical causes and effects. The causation is the same in both cases, and the facts that embody it may as easily be mental as physical. I stress this because many philosophers think causation is physical, which is like taking truth or chance to be physical. Of course some truths are truths of physics, and some chances are chances of something physical happening. But this does not make truth and chance the subject matters of special physical sciences, as light is the subject matter of optics, and they are not; and nor is causation. In short, while nothing in this book contradicts physicalism, the view that everything mental is really physical, nor does anything in it support that view, whose supposed importance and truth Tim Crane and I have disputed elsewhere (Mellor 1991 ch. 5).

Last, a remark about my way of doing metaphysics. Some philosophers reduce their metaphysics to physics, others to logic and semantics. I reduce mine to neither, while taking account of both. So while I will accommodate the relevant results of modern physics, I will not for example leave it to quantum physics to tell me whether causation can act immediately across spacelike intervals. On the contrary: only when our metaphysics has told us what causation is can we see if physics *could* reveal unmediated action at a distance (it couldn't).

Similarly, while I use logical concepts and devices – reference and truth, possible worlds, particulars, properties and facts, transparency and opacity, quantification – to express and test my account, logic alone cannot tell us what causation is. Nor can semantics, if what concerns us is what causation really is, not what those who never think about the matter think it is, i.e. not the everyday concept of causation but what causation is in the world. What follows is thus not an analysis of causation but a substantive metaphysical theory of it. And to any physicist, positivist or philosopher of language who asks how such a thing is possible when there is no reason to think it otherwise, the only sensible reply is, as above: here it is – try it.

# 1   *Deterministic causation*

## 1   Singular and general causation

To understand causation we need to answer three distinct questions. First, what kinds of entities can be causes and effects? Second, when entities of those kinds are causes and effects, what makes them so? And third, what follows from their being so: what are the consequences of causation? But although these questions are distinct, their answers will obviously affect each other. What causation is, and what it entails, will depend on what causes and effects are, and *vice versa*.

We therefore cannot expect to treat these questions entirely separately. But we must start somewhere, and I will start by saying something about what causes and effects are. First, whatever they are, they must be entities of the same kinds, since most if not all causes are also effects. Suppose for example that a climber, Don, is killed by falling while climbing. The cause here, Don's falling, is also an effect, of whatever made him fall; and his dying, the effect, is also a cause, for example of grief in others. Thus finding out what causes are will also tell us what effects are.

Second and more important, causes and effects appear at first sight to include two very different sorts of entity. One sort are general properties. Suppose smoking causes cancer. The causation here seems to link two properties, being a smoker and having cancer, regardless of who has these properties or when. Causation which links such properties, unlocalised in space or time, we may call *general* causation.

Don's falling causing him to die, by contrast, is a piece of what I shall call *singular* causation. Here the cause and effect are both local. Neither is everywhere in space and time, only where and when Don falls and dies. This is the kind of causation that concerns me in this book. However, much of what I shall say will apply also to general causation, since the two sorts of causation, although different, must be linked: it cannot be a coincidence that smoking causes cancer and that Don's son Bill's smoking causes him to get cancer. The link is indeed disputed, but as the dispute only concerns the nature of general causation, which is not my business, I shall simply state my view of it: namely, that general causation is a generalisation of singular

6

causation. Smoking causes cancer iff (if and only if) smokers' cancers are generally caused by their smoking.

If this is so, the real mark of general causation is generalisation, not lack of location. General causal facts can be as local as singular ones. I might for example claim not that smoking causes cancer everywhere and always but only that it causes cancer in Britain this century. My claim is local, but is still a general claim about the British this century. Localising the scope of a general claim does not make it singular.

This distinction between general and singular causation does not imply a distinction between general and singular causes and effects. For if general causation is just singular causation generalised, then it links the same kinds of entities: not general properties like being a smoker or having cancer, or types of events like falling or dying, but one or more instances of such properties or event-types, like Britons smoking and getting cancer, or Don's falling and dying.

I shall therefore take it for granted in what follows that all causes and effects are singular. This does not however mean that the causal links between them must be singular. The causation that links Bill's smoking to his getting cancer might be general. It might for example be the statistical fact that everywhere and always (or at least in Britain this century), among people relevantly like Bill, the fraction who get cancer is higher among those who smoke than among those who do not. Or it might be a law of nature that people like Bill have a greater chance of getting cancer if they smoke than if they do not: a law of which the statistical fact would then be a highly probable consequence. In neither case would there be a singular causal link between Bill's smoking and his getting cancer. The two might still be linked by a chain of intermediate causes and effects, such as a build-up of tar in his lungs and chemical changes in his cells. But this intermediate causation would also reduce to statistical correlations, or probabilistic laws, linking inhaled smoke with tar absorption, absorbed tar with cell changes, and so on.

There might therefore be no more to singular causation than individual instances of general laws or correlations. In fact, as we shall see, there is more to it: singular causation really is as singular as the causes and effects it links. But that question is not begged by taking causes and effects to be singular.

## 2  Two sorts of cause

Taking causes and effects to be singular is innocuous largely because it says almost nothing about what causes and effects are. They are at first sight very varied, as the following examples show. People and other animals affect each other, are caused by their parents and cause their offspring. Medicines cause our illnesses to go away. There are inanimate things like icebergs, which are caused by cooling water and cause ships to sink. There are instances of properties, like a tyre's high pressure, caused by inflating it, and which causes it to be rigid. My lighting a fire, thus causing a temperature difference between it and me, is an action causing an instance of a relation (hotter than). A spark causing the fuel and air in a car engine cylinder to ignite, thus causing the engine to run and the car to move, is one inanimate event causing another, which in turn causes a change.

Fortunately all these seemingly diverse causes and effects can be reduced to two basic sorts. The first of these is a species of what I shall call *states of affairs*, by which I mean what are stated by sentences, statements or propositions like 'Don falls', whether they are true or false: Don's falling is a state of affairs whether he falls or not. How sentences, statements and propositions relate to each other and to states of affairs is a complex and contentious question, whose answer fortunately does not matter here. (In particular, as the differences between sentences, statements and propositions will rarely matter in what follows, I shall mostly use one of these terms to stand for all of them.) What does matter here is the difference between *true* statements (etc.) and *false* ones, i.e. between those states of affairs that are *actual* and those that are not. Actual states of affairs, corresponding to true statements, I shall call *facts*, like the fact that Don falls, which exists iff 'Don falls' is true. Facts, so understood, are one of my two basic sorts of causes and effects.

Many objections have been raised to the idea of causes and effects as facts. The answers to most of them will have to wait until we learn more about what causation entails, but two of them can be answered now. The premise of the first objection is that statements of cause and effect, if true at all, are true everywhere and at all times. This makes it look as if facts, which correspond to truths, cannot have the restricted locations in space and time with which I have credited singular causes and effects.

Although the premise of this objection is contentious, I accept it. This does not of course mean that we can only use sentences which are true at all times to state causes and effects. We can perfectly well use tensed sentences like 'Don died', a sentence which, because it implies that Don's death is past, was not always true. But as I (1998 chs 2–3) and others have shown, we can always say in tenseless terms what makes tensed sentences true. We can do this in English by using the present tenses of verbs *atemporally*, by which I mean using them as a speaker does who, as the 1979 *Collins English Dictionary* puts it, 'does not wish to make any explicit temporal reference'. Thus we may say atemporally that any utterance of 'Don died' is true iff it is made after Don dies, and similarly in all other cases.

In short, replacing 'Don died because he fell' and 'Don's fall caused his death' with the atemporal 'Don dies because he falls' and 'Don's fall causes his death', loses nothing but the implication that this piece of causation occurs before I write or you read this sentence. But as we are concerned with all causation whenever it occurs, that implication is irrelevant. This is why, at the cost of some occasional inelegance, I shall from now on report all causation atemporally.

But then 'Don falls' and 'Don dies', if true at all, are true everywhere and always. How then can the facts that correspond to these truths have a restricted location in space and time? To see how, note first that we can and often do identify facts by their location. Thus 'it rains in Paris on 1 March 1998' and 'it rains in London on 9 July 2001', if atemporally true, state different facts, located at those places and times. And whether we say so or not, the fact is that Don dies somewhere and at some time: say in the Lake District in June 1988 – not in London and not in May. Similarly for any other located fact P. Even if its location is not stated in 'P', 'P at $s$ at $t$' will still be true, everywhere and always, for some but not all places $s$ and times $t$, with a smallest such $s$ and $t$ (e.g. the foot of Castle Rock, 2.23 pm on 4 June), included in all the others, which is P's location.

(This has the obvious and obviously true consequence that non-actual states of affairs have no location: for if 'P' is false then 'P at $s$ at $t$' will also be false for all $s$ and $t$. Thus while the fact that Shakespeare wrote *Hamlet* is located in London in about 1600, the state of affairs of Marlowe writing *Hamlet*, since it is not a fact, is not located anywhere.)

The other objection to facts is to the so-called *correspondence* theory of truth, i.e. to the thesis that statements are made true by corresponding facts. The objection is that only by definition can facts correspond to all true statements, thus making the theory either vacuous or false. With this objection I agree: facts, as I use the term 'fact', cannot be used to define truth. But I am not using facts to define truth: I am using truths to define facts. In so doing I am taking for granted some other account of what in the world, if anything, makes sentences like 'Don dies' and 'Don dies because he falls' true. We shall see later what the answers to those questions are: here all that matters is that they will not be 'the fact that Don dies' and 'the fact that Don dies because he falls'. This being so, the vacuity or falsity of correspondence theories of truth is no reason to deny that causes and effects can be facts, i.e. entities that correspond by definition to truths.

So much, for the time being, for facts. But we need more than facts, plentiful though they are. Some causes and effects cannot be facts because they cannot even be states of affairs: they do not correspond to anything which can be true or false. Hence the other sort of causes and effects, which correspond to names and other referring terms, like 'Don' and 'Don's fall', that cannot be used on their own to make any statement, true or false. These non-factual causes and effects are *particulars*, and they come in two sorts. There are what I shall call *things*, including people, animals, plants and inanimate objects ranging in size from quarks to galaxies; and there are *events*, like Don's fall and his death. Although the nature and even the existence of events is disputed, they are in fact the commonest kind of causal particulars, which is why I shall make them my exemplars. How they are related to things that are also causes and effects is a complex question, for whose answer we shall again have to wait [10].

This division of causes and effects into facts and particulars is not only exclusive, it is also exhaustive. All singular causes and effects are either facts or particulars. If this is not at once obvious, it will I hope become so as we tackle more and more cases. Meanwhile I shall recommend the idea by showing how to represent some of the causes and effects listed at the start of this section in one or other of these two ways. Thus parents (things) cause an offspring (thing) by an action of theirs (an event) causing its conception (an event). We affect others when our actions (events) cause some change in them (event or fact). We can also affect ourselves in the same way. Thus Bill's wife Kim causes herself to recover from an illness (fact) by taking her medicine (event or fact). And so on: as the reader may easily verify, all my other examples can be put in terms of causation linking facts or particulars or both.

How these two basic sorts of cause and effect are related, and which if either is the more basic, are questions whose answers must again await more information about causation [11]. Fortunately we can avoid the issue for the present, because most causation can be represented equally well either way. Thus we may say 'Don dies because he falls', which represents the cause and the effect as facts. Or we may say 'Don's fall causes his death', which represents them as particular events. For the moment it does not matter which way we put it.

However, to discuss causation generally without begging the answers to these questions, I need a single way of representing causation of both sorts. To get it I propose for the time being to represent causal particulars as facts, namely as the facts that those particulars exist (if they are things) or occur (if they are events) somewhere in the past, present or future of the actual world. And since the difference between things and events, and thus between existing and occurring, is not relevant here, I shall for brevity say of both kinds of particulars that they 'exist'. (Those who think that possible but non-actual particulars exist, in other possible worlds, should read my 'exists' as 'is actual'.)

Putting all this more generally and formally, we may use the following form of sentence to report all causation between facts:

(1)    'E because C'.

Instances of (1), like 'Don dies because he falls' are *molecular* sentences, so-called because they contain other sentences 'C' ('Don falls') and 'E' ('Don dies') linked by the sentential connective 'because'.

(I realise of course that 'because' is not an exclusively causal connective, being used also to give proofs – 'There is no greatest prime number, because if there were ...' – and explanations of non-causal kinds. There are thus many non-causal instances of (1), which I must exclude. I could exclude them by using an exclusively causal connective, like 'the fact that ... causes it to be the case that ...'. But I would rather avoid such turgid locutions if I can, and fortunately I can. For since these locutions exist, we can make (1) causal by fiat, i.e. by restricting its instances to those that do have exclusively causal equivalents. This for brevity I hereby do.)

The form of sentence I shall use to report causation between any two particulars *c* and *e* is

(2)    '*c* causes *e*'.

This form, unlike (1), needs no restriction to make it causal, being clearly causal to start with. On the contrary, (2) is itself only a restricted form of the more general but equally causal

(2′)    '*c* causes or affects *e*'

to be discussed later [12]. Since however, as we shall see, the difference between causing and affecting something is not a causal one, we shall beg no question here by using the simpler (2).

(2) differs radically in form from (1) in that its instances, like 'Don's fall causes his death', since they contain no other sentences, are not molecular. They are *atomic* sentences, containing only the referring terms '*c*' ('Don's fall') and '*e*' ('Don's death'), linked by the relational predicate 'causes'. Nevertheless, despite this difference, we can always turn them into equivalent sentences of form (1) by letting 'C' and 'E' be '*c* exists' and '*e* exists', to give

(2″)    '*e* exists because *c* exists',

a form which is, by definition, to mean whatever (2) means.

Thus 'Don's death exists because Don's fall exists' means 'Don's fall causes his death'. Whether this means the same as 'Don dies because he falls' remains to be seen. Meanwhile (2″) lets us waive that question without begging it by making (1) the form of all causal statements.

## 3 Causation's incomplete truth table

When is 'E because C' true? Part of the answer we know already. For to say that causation links facts is really just to say that 'E because C' entails 'C' and 'E'. No one will deny this: no one will deny that 'Don dies because he falls' entails both that Don falls and that he dies. To die because he falls he must fall and he must die; and similarly for all other cases of causation. Only actual states of affairs have actual causes and effects.

Put formally, this means that 'E because C' is at least a partial truth function of 'C' and 'E'. That is, the truth values (true or false) of 'C' and 'E' determine the truth value of 'E because C' in three of the four possible cases: 'E because C' is false whenever (i) 'C' and 'E' are both false, (ii) 'C' is true and 'E' is false and (iii) 'C' is false and 'E' is true.

But when 'C' and 'E' are both true 'E because C' does not always have the same truth value. If 'E because C' were always false then too, causation would link no facts at all: there would be no causation. While if it were always true, causation would link every pair of facts both ways round, making it universal and hence symmetrical, since 'E because C', *via* 'C' and 'E', would entail 'C because E'. But that is absurd: Don's dying because he falls does not entail that he falls because he dies! So 'E because C' is neither always true nor always false when 'C' and 'E' are true. The truth table of the causal connective 'because' must therefore be incomplete, as shown in Figure 1: 'E because C' is not a complete truth function of 'C' and 'E'.

| 'C'   | 'E'   | 'E because C' |
|-------|-------|---------------|
| True  | True  | ?             |
| True  | False | False         |
| False | True  | False         |
| False | False | False         |

Figure 1: Truth table for 'E because C'

The basic question about causation therefore is this: what more, besides the truth of 'C' and 'E', is needed to make 'E because C' true? Many conditions have been proposed, for example that causes must precede their effects, or be next to them in space and time. These we shall look at later. But the most important, obscure and contentious condition is that causes must somehow *necessitate* or *determine* their effects. We shall see in the end that this condition is too strong; but first we must see what it is. That is the main business of this chapter.

## 4 Deterministic causation

By causes that determine their effects I shall mean ones that are in the circumstances both *sufficient* and *necessary* for them. 'Sufficient' here means that the existence of the cause ensures, in a sense yet to be made clear, that its effects also exist. 'Necessary' here means that its non-existence ensures in the same sense that its effects do not exist.

These two conditions are clearly independent, and not all philosophers require deterministic causes to satisfy both of them. It is indeed more usual to read 'determinism' as requiring only that causes be sufficient for their effects. So before going on I should say why I also require deterministic causes to be necessary for their effects. It is really only a matter of convenience. For it will eventually turn out that causes need not, in my sense, determine their effects [5], and my account of indeterministic causation will then cover causes that are sufficient but not necessary, or necessary but not sufficient. This being so, it is simpler to tackle sufficient and necessary causes together, since they raise the same key question: in what sense does a sufficient cause's existence ensure that its effects exist and a necessary one's non-existence ensure that they do not?

Before tackling this question, however, I should say again what I mean, when causes and effects are facts, by saying that they 'exist'. All I mean is this: the cause C and effect E reported by 'E because C' exist iff 'C' and 'E' are true, i.e. if the states of affairs C and E are actual [§2]. Thus the facts that Don falls and that he dies exist iff 'Don falls' and 'Don dies' are true, i.e. iff Don falls and dies. If Don neither falls nor dies, i.e. if 'Don falls' and 'Don dies' are false, then the states of affairs those sentences report are not facts: the facts that Don falls and that he dies do not then exist.

This is all my talk of facts existing means. In particular, it implies nothing about the nature of facts, e.g. whether we can identify them with true propositions, and thus states of affairs with propositions generally [§2]. All I mean by 'the fact C exists' is that 'C' is true. And one advantage of this weak sense of 'fact' is that, without begging any questions about what facts are, I can use 'C' both as a sentence and also, as above, to abbreviate 'the fact that C' or 'the state of affairs that C' – and similarly for 'E' – provided of course I make it clear which of these things I mean.

This double use of 'C' and 'E' lets me turn (1) into

(1′)    'C causes E',

which is an abbreviation of 'the fact that C causes it to be a fact that E'. (1′) has the form of (2), '*c* causes *e*', while by definition meaning 'E because C', a device that will greatly simplify later discussion of factual causes and effects [9]. Meanwhile, to reduce the risk of ambiguity between instances of (1′) and of (2), I shall use phrases like 'Don's falling' to refer to the fact that he falls, as opposed to the event, his fall. Thus where it matters I shall use 'Don's falling causes his dying' to mean 'Don dies because he falls' as opposed to 'Don's fall causes his death'.

Given this terminology, we can now turn to deterministic causation, i.e. to true causal instances of 'E because C' where C is in the circumstances both sufficient and necessary for E. Suppose then that Don's falling is in the circumstances – he is brittle-boned and fifteen metres above rocks but otherwise alive and well – sufficient and necessary for his dying. (That is, for his dying roughly then, there and as he does. How much the time, place and manner of his dying could vary without it being a different fact is a question we can waive for now.) In other words, in the circumstances, Don's falling ensures that he does die, and his not falling would ensure that he did not die. What does 'ensure' mean here?

Whatever it means, it must not be entailed by the truth table for 'E because C' shown above in Figure 1. This says that 'E because C' entails 'E': the fact that C causes E is logically sufficient for E. But as we have seen, all this means is that only actual effects have actual causes: Don's falling cannot cause Don's dying unless he actually dies. But this truism applies to all causation, whether deterministic or not. It cannot be what makes C itself, as opposed to the fact that C causes E, sufficient for E. So what does make C sufficient for E?

## 5  Causal conditionals

The sufficiency and necessity of causes for their effects is usually expressed by conditional statements. It is usually said that for C to be sufficient for E is for E to exist if C does; and that for C to be necessary for E is for E not to exist if C does not. Or, writing '~' for negation, C is sufficient for E iff 'if C then E' is true, and necessary for E iff 'if ~C then ~E' is true. Let us for the time being call these conditionals *causal conditionals*.

We shall eventually have to redefine causal conditionals since, as we shall see, no reading of 'if C then E' and 'if ~C then ~E' will capture the sufficiency and necessity of causes for their effects [2.4]. But to see why not, we must first give these conditionals a fair run for their money. The obvious way to do this is to read them as so-called *counterfactual* or *subjunctive conditionals*, like 'if Don had fallen he would have died' and 'if

Don had not fallen he would not have died'. This is certainly the most natural way to express causal conditionals in English.

Unfortunately this fact does not tell us what we need to know, since causal conditionals lack several features commonly ascribed to these English conditionals. For a start, they lack the features suggested by calling them 'counterfactual' and 'subjunctive'. 'Counterfactual' suggests that 'if Don had fallen ...' implies that Don does not fall. But no causal conditional can imply this. For if 'if C then E' implied '~C', no actual cause could be sufficient for its effects, which is absurd. So this implication must go. And so must the grammatical implications of the term 'subjunctive': causal conditionals rarely use the English subjunctive mood, especially when they refer to the future, as in 'if Don falls he will die'. Calling causal conditionals 'subjunctive' tells us nothing about what makes them true.

Nor will better accounts of English conditionals, like Dudman's (1991), help us much. This should not surprise us. We cannot rely on grammarians to do our metaphysics for us: they have other fish to fry. It may for example matter to them that 'if ... (then) ...' is often not a sentential connective, since the clauses it connects often do not mean what they would mean on their own. (In 'if Don fell he would die', 'Don fell' no more refers to the past than 'he would die' states an intention to commit suicide!) But it does not matter to us. The 'if ... then ...' in a causal 'if C then E' and 'if ~C then ~E' must be a sentential connective, because we require it to link the sentences 'C' and 'E' that say what the cause C and the effect E are.

If English grammar will not tell us what makes causal conditionals true, nor will formal logic. In particular, we cannot read our conditionals as so-called *material conditionals*, symbolised by the connective '⊃'. 'C⊃E' cannot possibly capture C's sufficiency for E, and '~C⊃~E' cannot capture its necessity. The reason is that 'C⊃E' is by definition a complete truth function of 'C' and 'E': false if 'C' is true and 'E' is false, and otherwise true. So whenever 'C' is false or 'E' is true, 'C⊃E' is true. So in particular 'C⊃E' is true whenever 'E' is true, and '~C⊃~E' is true whenever '~C' is false, i.e. whenever 'C' is true. From this it follows that whenever 'C' and 'E' are both true, 'C⊃E' and '~C⊃~E' are also both true, as indeed are 'E⊃C' and '~E⊃~C'.

In other words, if causal conditionals were material, every fact would be both sufficient and necessary for every other fact, which again is absurd. The mere fact that Don both falls and dies does not make his falling sufficient and necessary for his dying, any more than it makes his dying sufficient and necessary for his falling. Material conditionals are far too weak to capture the sense in which deterministic causes are sufficient and necessary for their effects.

## 6 Strict conditionals

If the material reading of a causal 'if C then E' is too weak, the so-called *strict conditional*, which I shall write 'C⊰E', is too strong. 'C⊰E' is by definition true iff 'C⊃E' is necessarily true, i.e. iff it is impossible for 'C' to be true and 'E' false. This reading makes 'if C then E' and 'if ~C then ~E' true only when 'C' entails 'E' and '~C' entails '~E'. In other words, C is sufficient and necessary for E only if C cannot exist without E and E cannot exist without C: C ensures E and ~C ensures ~E necessarily.

To see why this condition is too strong, we must distinguish two quite different senses of the word 'necessary'. In 'sufficient and necessary' the word has what we may call its *without-which-not* sense: causes are necessary for their effects just in case their effects do not exist without them. But this could be a contingent fact. That is, it could be a fact in our world but not in every possible world: that being another, *not-possibly-not*, sense of 'necessary'. Necessity in the sense of holding in all possible worlds I follow Kripke (1980 Lect. 1) in calling *metaphysical*.

This distinction, between without-which-not and metaphysical senses of 'necessary', matters here because a cause may be necessary for its effects in the first sense without being necessarily so in the second sense. The strict reading of 'if ~C then ~E' is thus not entailed by our using this conditional to express the without-which-not necessity of a cause for its effects. The strict reading needs arguing for, just as it needs arguing that a cause is only sufficient for its effects if they exist in every possible world where it exists.

To make the strict reading of causal conditionals at all credible, we must eliminate the obvious contingency of the circumstances required for causes to determine their effects. For example, Don could have had a heart attack as he fell, and then his falling would not have been necessary for his dying; or he could have fallen onto something soft, and then it would not have been sufficient. To make the actual cause of his dying determine it in all possible worlds we must exclude all such contingencies.

To do this we must build into E's cause all the local *circumstances*, or surroundings, S, that are required to make C determine E. We must say that Don dies, not because he falls, but because he falls in such-and-such a way and in such-and-such surroundings. That is, what causes E is not C but what we might call 'C-in-S', meaning that C&S necessitates E and ~C&S necessitates ~E. Let us call C-in-S a *total* cause of E. Then since C-in-S by definition includes all the local facts on which E depends, its causation of E is not contingent on any of them. So perhaps it is not contingent on anything: perhaps E is entailed by C&S and ~E by ~C&S?

If so, there will be a price to pay for these entailments, namely that most apparent causes, not being total, will no longer be causes at all. Don's falling will no longer cause him to die, Bill's smoking will no longer cause him to get cancer and Kim's taking her medicine will not cause her to recover. Most apparent causation will become illusory. This is a high price to pay for trying to make deterministic causes entail their effects, even if the attempt succeeds. The price is certainly not worth paying if the attempt fails; and it does fail.

To see why, let us start with Hume's (1748 sect. IV pt I) undisputed thesis that we cannot know *a priori* of any cause that it determines its effects. Neither Don's dying, Bill's getting cancer, nor any other effect is deducible *a priori* from any cause of it; and no one thinks it is. Nor is the non-existence of any effect ever deducible *a priori* from the non-existence of any cause of it. In other words, 'E' is never derivable from 'C&S', nor is '~E' derivable from '~C&S', in any logic which can be known *a priori* to preserve truth.

This at once rules out self-causation, since both 'C' and 'C&S' are of course deducible *a priori* from 'C&S'. So if Hume is right, 'C causes E' entails 'C≠E'. This of course is no objection, since no one thinks that anything can cause itself, and with good reason. For causation has connotations, e.g. that causes provide evidence for, explain and are means of bringing about their effects [5.4; 7.1], none of which 'C causes C' can satisfy, since nothing can be evidence for, explain or be a means to itself.

No one then will defend self-causation. Yet ruling it out might rule out this reading of causal conditionals, since some views of facts make 'C⊸E' and 'E⊸C' entail 'C=E'. And if they do, then to stop any C causing itself, C's sufficiency and necessity for E *must* depend on a contingent S, in order to rule out C⊸E and ~C⊸~E, which entails E⊸C. However, for any cause or effect P, causation itself is arguably the best test of identity: P=P′ iff P and P′ have all the same causes and effects [9.3]. But then the claim that 'C⊸E' and 'E⊸C' entails 'C=E' begs the question against the mutual entailment of causes and effects. For this reason I shall not take the impossibility of self-causation to rule out a strict reading of causal conditionals.

Nor will I take the fact that cause and effect are never deducible *a priori* from each other to rule this reading out. For even if we cannot prove it, there may still be no possible world where Don falls just as he does but survives, none where Bill smokes just as he does but fails to get cancer. Metaphysical necessity may conceivably, as Kripke (1980 Lect. 1) has argued, not always be provable *a priori*. So Hume's thesis may not after all make all causation contingent. Deterministic total causes may still all entail their effects, despite our inability to prove that they do.

In fact however they do not all entail their effects, because as we shall see it takes laws of nature to link even total causes to their effects [15.2], and few if any laws are metaphysically necessary. Imagine for example a law that would make Don's falling as he does a sufficient cause of his dying. This would be, roughly, the law that all equally massive and brittle living things who fall as Don does, about fifteen metres under earth's gravity onto rocks, die. This law is not metaphysically necessary, if only because the laws which make bones brittle are not necessary: there are possible worlds in which bone is less brittle than it is in ours. So there are possible worlds in which Don, or someone just like him in all relevant respects, falls precisely as he does here but does not die. And as in this case, so in general. Most if not all of the laws that give total causes their effects are contingent. So most and perhaps all total causes do not entail their effects.

## 7  Closest-world conditionals

Causal conditionals can thus be neither material nor strict. They must be something in between, something stronger than a material conditional and weaker than a strict one. The best candidate is what I shall call the *closest-world conditional* and write 'C⇒E'. By this I mean a conditional which by definition satisfies something like Lewis's (1973) theory of counterfactual conditionals. Whether English counterfactuals satisfy this theory is a nice question, but one I shall not discuss, since it does not concern us. All that concerns us is whether *causal* conditionals satisfy the theory, i.e. whether Lewis's definition of '⇒' enables 'C⇒E' and '~C⇒~E' to express the sufficiency and without-which-not necessity of deterministic causes for their effects. In fact it does not, but seeing why not will enable us to see what will.

The relevant part of the definition runs as follows. For all 'P' and 'Q', 'Q⇒P' is true iff either 'Q' is true in *no* possible world or 'P' is true in all the closest Q-worlds, i.e. the worlds where 'Q' is true that are most like the actual world or, more precisely, not less like it than some other Q-world. So in particular any 'C⇒E' will be true in our world iff E exists in the closest C-worlds, and any '~C⇒~E' will be true iff E does not exist in the closest ~C-worlds. This reading of causal conditionals makes Don's falling sufficient for his dying iff he dies in the closest worlds where he falls, and necessary iff he survives in the closest worlds where he does not fall; and similarly in all other cases.

Will this reading of causal conditionals do? Many philosophers think it will, and it certainly does better than material or strict readings. For unlike the strict reading, it lets causes be contingently sufficient and necessary for their effects. And unlike the material reading, it does not make every fact sufficient and necessary for every other fact. On the other hand, the definition of '⇒' does make a controversial appeal to possible worlds other than our own. But that controversy can wait. There is a more pressing problem.

The problem is that 'C⇒E' is entailed by 'C&E'. This follows from the fact that 'C⇒E' is true iff 'E' is true in all the closest C-worlds. For on any measure of similarity, our world must be closer to itself than any other possible world. So whenever 'C' is true, i.e. is true in our world, the truth value of 'C⇒E' is fixed by that of 'E': it is true whenever 'E' is true, false whenever 'E' is false. Like 'E because C', 'C⇒E' is a partial truth function of 'C' and 'E', as shown below in Figure 2.

| 'C' | 'E' | 'C⇒E' |
|-------|-------|-------|
| True | True | True |
| True | False | False |
| False | True | ? |
| False | False | ? |

Figure 2: Truth table for 'C⇒E'

The problem with Figure 2 lies in the first row. The second row is no problem: there is nothing wrong with 'C' and '~E' being incompatible with 'C⇒E'. Indeed, since we need this to make *modus ponens* valid – i.e. to make 'C' and 'C⇒E' entail 'E' – it is arguably essential for any conditional connective. The problem is that the first row makes any true 'C' and 'E' entail both 'C⇒E' and 'E⇒C'. In other words, the closest-world reading of causal conditionals makes every fact sufficient for every other fact.

This is not quite as bad as the material reading's making every fact both sufficient and necessary for every other fact [§5]. But it is quite bad enough. For the whole point of invoking a causal 'if C then E' is to give the sense of saying that sufficient causes 'ensure' the existence of their effects. And whatever this sense is, it cannot let every fact ensure the existence of every other, or it will fail to distinguish pairs of facts that are causally linked from pairs of facts that are not, causes from effects, and those causes that are not sufficient for their effects from those that are.

Like 'C⊃E', therefore, 'C⇒E' as defined above is too weak a reading of the causal conditional. Its definition can indeed be strengthened to stop 'C&E' entailing it, e.g. by requiring 'E' to be true not only in our world but also in all others that are very like it (Lewis 1973 p. 29). But this, besides relying even more contentiously on non-actual worlds, is too *ad hoc*. It may give 'C⇒E' the truth values of certain English conditionals, but this, as we have seen, does not explain why causal conditionals should have those truth values.

In short, we need more than the simple 'C$\Rightarrow$E' to give the sense in which a deterministic cause C is sufficient and necessary for its effect E. This does not however make the closest-world reading of conditionals useless to us. The conditional I shall propose in place of 'C$\Rightarrow$E' is still a closest-world conditional: only what its consequent states is not the effect E but that the *chance* of E is 1. But before we can assess this proposal I must first say what I mean in general by 'chance' and in particular by 'the chance of an effect'. That is the business of the next three chapters.

# 2 *The chances of effects*

## 1 Chances

Chances measure a contingent and quantitative kind of possibility. An atom of a radioelement like radium, for example, has a fifty-fifty chance of decaying into an atom of a different element in a time that is, for this reason, called its *half life*. This does not mean that half the atoms in a piece of radium will decay in this time: all may decay, or none, or any fraction in between. No radium atom must decay, or must not decay, in any given time: it is merely possible for it to decay, a possibility that is both contingent and comes by degrees. The possibility is contingent on the structure and state of the atom's nucleus, and its degree is measured by the chance of the decay. Thus it is equally possible for an atom to decay and not to decay in its half life; in longer times the former is the greater possibility and in shorter times the latter is.

The kind of possibility that chance measures yields a corresponding sense of not-possibly-not necessity: the sense in which it is *not* necessary for a radioactive atom to decay, or not to decay, in any given time. This I maintain is the sense in which a sufficient cause C necessitates the existence of an effect E: C gives E no – i.e. zero – chance of not existing. It is also the sense in which a necessary cause's non-existence necessitates the non-existence of its effect: ~C gives E a zero chance of existing.

Taking chance to measure a contingent kind of possibility, as I do, is contentious. In the next chapter I shall defend this reading of chance by examining its implications to see what interpretation of the mathematics of chance is needed to make sense of it. But first we must see how chances, so understood, are involved in deterministic causation.

The first point I must make about chances is that they are *probabilities*. My other claims about chance may be contentious, but not this one: everyone measures chances by numbers which satisfy the standard calculus of probabilities. And this is all I mean by calling them 'probabilities'. It says almost nothing about what they are, since the probability calculus has several applications, demanding very different interpretations. Which of them we need in order to make sense of chance we shall see in chapter 3.

Meanwhile, the fact that chances are probabilities does tell us something about them. It tells us, for one thing, that their values are never greater than 1 or less than 0. It also tells us that the chance of any proposition 'P' being false, and so of '~P' being true, is 1 minus its chance of being true. In symbols, writing '$ch(P)$' for the chance that P, i.e. that P is a fact:

(3)     $ch(\sim P) = 1 - ch(P)$.

Thus in any given circumstances Don's chance of surviving is 1 minus his chance of dying, Bill's chance of avoiding cancer 1 minus his chance of getting it, Kim's chance of recovering 1 minus her chance of not doing so, and so on.

The next point I must make is that most if not all contingent facts that have any chances have several of them. By this I do not mean that an effect E would have a different chance without its cause C: I mean that many facts have more than one actual chance. Suppose for example that a coin $j$ is fairly tossed, so that its chance of landing heads, $Hj$, is 1/2: $ch(Hj)=0.5$. But just before $j$ lands, falling heads up, it is almost certain to land heads: $ch(Hj) \approx 1$, say 0.99. And in between, $Hj$ will have many other chances.

How can a single fact like $Hj$ have more than one chance? Obviously by having them at different times: $ch(Hj)$ is 0.5 when $j$ is tossed and 0.99 just before $j$ lands. But this does not make $ch(Hj)$ a changeable property of $Hj$ in the sense in which, say, Kim's temperature is a changeable property of her. Why not? How does a changing temperature differ from a changing chance?

One difference is that things can only have temperatures while they exist: Kim can have no temperature before she is conceived. But all $Hj$'s chances exist before it does, i.e. before $j$ lands heads – if it does land heads. And here lies the real difference: Kim cannot have a temperature without existing, whereas the fact $Hj$ can easily have a chance (less than 1) without existing. For all '$Hj$ exists' means is that '$Hj$' is true [1.2], and '$Hj$' can easily have a chance of being true even if it is actually false: the coin $j$ can have a 0.5 chance of landing heads and actually land tails.

There is of course nothing problematic about this fact, that the state of affairs $Hj$ can have a chance of being a fact and yet not be one. This is no more puzzling than the fact that beliefs can be false, as when I believe falsely that $Hj$ is a fact, i.e. believe that $j$ lands heads when it does not. But it does mean that $ch(Hj)$ cannot be a property, changeable or otherwise, of the fact $Hj$, since this fact may well not exist for $ch(Hj)$ to be a property of, just as it may not exist for my belief in $Hj$ to be a property of. So even if $Hj$ *is* a fact, neither its chance nor my belief in it is a property of it.

In short, we must not be misled by the fact that 'P's chance' looks like 'Kim's temperature'. This apparent grammatical similarity does not force $ch(P)$ to be a property or relation of P. It can be a property of something quite different, just as my belief that P can be and is a property of something quite different, namely me. In the same way, I maintain, every chance that any 'P' is true is a property of, i.e. a fact about, a different fact. $j$'s 0.5 chance of landing heads is a property of the fact, $Fj$, that it is tossed in a certain way; its 0.99 chance of landing heads is a property of the fact, $Lj$, that it faces heads up as it lands; and so on.

Such facts, of which the chances of other facts are properties, have many names ('trials', 'set-ups') in writings on chance, and they come in all shapes and sizes. But they all share two features: restricted locations in space and time, and the fact that, without them, the chances which are their properties would not exist. If the fact $Fj$ did not exist, i.e. if $j$ was not fairly tossed, nor would the $ch(Hj)=0.5$ that is a property of $Fj$; if the fact $Lj$ did not exist, i.e. if $j$ did not fall heads up, nor would the $ch(Hj)=0.99$ that is a property of $Lj$; and so on.

This is what lets a proposition like '$Hj$' have different actual chances of being true: its different chances are properties of different facts, such as $Fj$ and $Lj$. So in order to distinguish these chances of $Hj$, and to stop them seeming incompatible, I shall index them by the facts of which they are properties: $ch_{Fj}(Hj)=0.5$, $ch_{Lj}(Hj)=0.99$, etc.

To all this it may be objected that facts, such as $Fj$ and $Lj$, do not have properties in the same sense in which people and other things have temperatures. I agree, and will later reserve the term 'properties' for so-called *universals*, like temperatures, which cannot be properties of facts but only of particulars [13.2], and arguably of other universals [16.4]. But for the present it is more useful to count any fact about anything as a property of it. And in this sense there are certainly properties of facts, e.g. their locations. Thus suppose $j$ lands heads at a place $s$ and time $t$. Then '$Hj$' states a fact and so does '$Hj$ at $s$ at $t$': a fact which is about, i.e. contains as a constituent, the fact $Hj$. And if a location can in this sense be a property of $Hj$, then in the same sense it can be, and obviously is, a property of the fact $Fj$ that $ch_{Fj}(Hj)=0.5$, of the fact $Lj$ that $ch_{Lj}(Hj)=0.99$, and so on.

Seeing what chances are properties of is important, because it raises questions whose answers will help to tell us what chances are and so what causation is. There is the question of why some facts and not others have a chance of P as a property: it is not for example a property of *every* other fact that $j$ has some chance of landing heads. In particular, no $ch(P)$ is ever a property of a fact later than the fact P – or, if P is not a fact, the fact ~P

[17]. Why not: why can a *ch*(*Hj*) only be a property of facts which, like *Fj* and *Lj*, precede *Hj* or ~*Hj*?

Another question we face is what in the world gives the chances of *Hj* that are properties of *Fj* and *Lj* the values they have. Something must, since these values too are contingent. For even if the fact *Fj* that *j* is *fairly* tossed *has* to give *j* a 0.5 chance of landing heads, that is only because this is what 'fair' means: it is still contingent that *j* is tossed, *Tj*, in such a way that '*Fj*' and hence '*ch*(*Hj*)=0.5' are true. But contingent on what, and how?

We shall get answers to both these questions in due course. All we need do meanwhile is mark the dependence of P's chances on the existence of facts which are logically independent of P. This is all I mean by saying that P's chances are properties not of P but of other facts, in the same way as my belief that P is a property not of P but of me.

## 2  The chances of an effect

If all chances of facts are properties of other facts, then in particular the chances of effects must be. As with *j*'s chance of landing heads if tossed, so with Don's chance of dying if he falls. This chance cannot be a property of the fact that Don dies, since it can exist (if less than 1) even if he does not die. Don's chance of dying must be a property of other facts – that Don falls, that he falls such-and-such a distance, that his bones are brittle, that the ground he falls towards is hard, and so on. Similarly, Bill's chance of getting cancer if he smokes must be a property of that and other facts, about what and how much he smokes, his other activities and his health; Kim's chance of recovering if she takes her medicine must be a property of that and other facts, about what the medicine is, how much she takes, her illness and her metabolism; and so on.

The facts of which the chances of effects are properties are usually complex, as these examples show. Don's chance of dying if he falls is a property of a conjunction of facts, and similarly in the other cases. But not any conjunction will do. In particular, every conjunct in a conjunction of which a chance is a property must have more or less the same location: Don's chance of dying if he falls cannot, for example, depend directly on facts about things or events remote in space or time from his fall. We shall see why not later, when we see why causes must precede their effects, and why no fact can cause another at a distance without being linked to it by intermediate causes and effects [17.4]. For the time being we can just take for granted the approximate coincidence of these conjuncts in space and time.

When the chance of an effect E is 1, the complex fact of which this is a property may be like what in chapter 1.6 I called a 'total' cause of E. That is, it may be a fact whose sufficiency for E is not contingent on what I there called 'the circumstances' S in which C causes E. To cater for the possibility of indeterministic causation, I propose now to call *any* cause of E of which some $ch(E)$ is a property a total cause of E, even if it is not sufficient for E. For even among indeterministic causes it is useful to distinguish as total causes those that do not depend on their circumstances to give their effects a chance. And the point here, as in chapter 1.6, is that most causes are not total causes. C will usually be only one of several conjuncts in a total cause of E.

It nevertheless still makes sense to talk of the chance that any cause C gives its effect E, whether C is a total cause of E or not. This chance, which again I shall write '$ch_C(E)$', is a property of a fact that is either C itself or a conjunction of C with a fact S comprising all the relevant circumstances in which C causes E. Then my first claim about causation and chance is this. For every cause C with an effect E, there is such a chance:

$ch_C(E)$ exists.

For Don to die because he falls, the fact that he falls must either be, or be a conjunct in, a fact of which it is a property that he has a chance, 1 or less, of dying.

So far so good. It is easy enough to see what Don's chance of dying if he falls is a property of: for this, since Don actually does fall, is one of his actual chances of dying. It is harder to see what Don's chance of dying if he does *not* fall is a property of: for this, since Don actually does fall, is *not* one of his actual chances of dying. Yet there must be such a chance, and it must be a property of some actual fact. This is my second claim about causation and chance. Every effect E has a chance, which may be zero, of existing in the circumstances S without C:

$ch_{\sim C}(E)$ exists.

For Don to die because he falls, there must in the circumstances S be a chance, zero or greater, of his dying if he does not fall.

Of what actual fact can this chance be a property? By analogy with $ch_C(E)$, $ch_{\sim C}(E)$ should be a property of ~C, or of a conjunction of ~C with the circumstances S. But this it cannot be, because Don falls: '~C' is false. So ~C is not a fact, and nor therefore is any conjunction containing ~C. No fact containing ~C exists for $ch_{\sim C}(E)$ to be a property of.

Failing a conjunction containing ~C, the obvious fact for $ch_{\sim C}(E)$ to be a property of is S. Is it not a fact about the actual circumstances in which Don falls that, had he not fallen, his chance of dying would have been

$ch_{-C}(E)$? But if it is, then – again by analogy – it should also be a property of these circumstances that if Don *does* fall, his chance of dying is $ch_C(E)$. In other words, if $ch_{-C}(E)$ is a property of the circumstances S in which Don falls, so should $ch_C(E)$ be.

This is roughly right, but it needs qualifying in two ways. First, S as originally defined does not contain all the local facts, only those that make C-in-S a total cause of E [1.6]. That is, S is a fact such that one of Don's actual chances of dying, $ch(E)$, is a property of C&S. The relevant circumstances if Don did not fall should similarly be a conjunction S′ of local facts such that Don's chance of dying would then be a property of ~C&S′. And S′ may differ from S, for two reasons.

One reason is that C and ~C might conjoin with different facts to give Don a specific chance of dying. But they need not, and we can simplify what follows without begging any questions by assuming that they do not. The other reason is that some facts in a conjunctive S might not *be* facts if Don did not fall: he might, for example, not have the heart attack which contributes to his actual chance of dying. But this too we can ignore, since we want the *actual* fact of which $ch_{-C}(E)$ is a property; and this can be S even though, if Don did not fall, $ch_{-C}(E)$ would then be a property of a somewhat different S′.

We shall see later just what in the world makes $ch_C(E)$ and $ch_{-C}(E)$ exist and gives them their values [14.3]. For now we may simply assume that both these chances are properties of S. But what if there is no S, as there will not be if C is itself a total cause of E: since, by our definition of 'total cause', the relevant $ch(E)$ will then be contingent only on C? Of what can it then be a property that $ch(E)$ *is* contingent on C, i.e. that $ch_{-C}(E)$ differs from $ch_C(E)$?

The answer can only lie in the laws which are needed to link even total causes to their effects [1.6]. These are the laws that make C give E one chance and ~C give it another, laws like those that give radioactive atoms their chances of decaying in various times [§1]. But these laws are facts too in my weak sense of 'fact' [1.2], since all this means is that, by definition of 'law', a law statement must be true. And although no law N has any location, since 'N at $s$ at $t$' is true for *all* $s$ and $t$ [1.2], its instances, such as N at any specific $s$ and $t$, do have locations, namely $s$ and $t$ [16.7]. For example, the fact that any given atom of radium conforms at any given time to the laws of radioactivity is a local fact, entailing nothing about whether other atoms elsewhere, or even this atom at other times, conform to those laws. Similarly, the fact that any given $ch_C(E)$ and $ch_{-C}(E)$ conform to laws that fix their values is also a local fact.

In short, when C is a total cause of E, the facts of which $ch_C(E)$ and $ch_{\sim C}(E)$ are properties are local instances of laws, which we can then always include in the circumstances S. From now on therefore I shall take the circumstances of Don's fall to include not only the facts cited earlier – 'he is brittle-boned and fifteen metres above rocks but otherwise alive and well' [1.4] – but also the fact that he conforms to the laws that link such facts to people's chances of dying if they do fall and if they do not. This means that even when C is a total cause of E, there will still be a local fact S for $ch_C(E)$ and $ch_{\sim C}(E)$ to be properties of: namely the fact that C and E conform to some law or laws which fix these chances.

## 3  Closest-world chances

We may take it then that $ch_C(E)$ and $ch_{\sim C}(E)$ are always facts about some circumstances S, the facts being that S would conjoin with C to give E the chance $ch_C(E)$ and with ~C to give E the chance $ch_{\sim C}(E)$. What in the world makes these chances facts about S we shall see later [14.3]. What we need to see now is what these chances are.

It will simplify the answer to this question if from now on we restrict '$ch(E)$' to the chance that E gets in S from C or from ~C: for example, to the chance that Don's dying gets in the circumstances from his falling or from his holding on. We may ignore all the earlier and later chances of Don's dying, e.g. as he starts his climb and as he hits the ground. These are all equally real chances, and each of them may well relate Don's dying to some other cause of it, such as his climbing without a rope or his landing on rock. But they do not relate his dying to the cause that concerns us, which is his falling.

This is why what I shall mean by '$ch(E)$' in future is an actual chance of E that is a property of the conjunction of C or of ~C with the relevant circumstances S. Thus if 'C' is true, $ch(E)$ is $ch_C(E)$, E's chance in S with C, and if '~C' is true, $ch(E)$ is $ch_{\sim C}(E)$, E's chance in S with ~C. This restriction on '$ch(E)$' makes it much easier to state the hypothesis I shall now propose about what $ch_C(E)$ and $ch_{\sim C}(E)$ are.

By definition of the connective '$\Rightarrow$' [1.7], E's chances in the closest C-worlds and ~C-worlds – the possible worlds most like ours where 'C' is true and where '~C' is true – are the chances $p$ and $p'$ such that

(4)    '$C \Rightarrow ch(E)=p$' and
(4~)   '$\sim C \Rightarrow ch(E)=p'$'

are true. (These chances will of course rarely if ever have precise values, any more than temperatures or lengths do [3.1]. $p$ and $p'$ should therefore usually be given as intervals of numbers, like the interval $0.990\pm0.005$

implicit in my saying that $ch_{Lj}(Hj)$ is 0.99 [§1]. But it is simpler, and will affect nothing in what follows, to treat $p$ and $p'$ as if they were precise.)

Then my hypothesis is that $ch_C(E)$ and $ch_{\sim C}(E)$, E's chances in the circumstances S with and without its cause C, are the $p$ and $p'$ such that (4) and (4~) are true. In symbols, writing '$(\imath p)(\ldots)$' for 'the $p$ such that ...':

(5)     $ch_C(E) = (\imath p)(C \Rightarrow ch(E)=p)$;
(5~)    $ch_{\sim C}(E) = (\imath p')(\sim C \Rightarrow ch(E)=p')$.

In other words, $ch_C(E)$ and $ch_{\sim C}(E)$ are E's chances in the closest worlds to ours where 'C' and '~C' respectively are true.

Thus whatever makes (4) and (4~) true for some $p$ and $p'$ is what makes $ch_C(E)$ and $ch_{\sim C}(E)$ exist and gives them their values. Unfortunately many other aspects of causation need to be settled before we can say what makes statements like (4) and (4~) true, and then we shall see that (5) and (5~) are not quite right [14.3]. But they will do for the time being: their deficiencies will not affect any of the ensuing arguments.

In particular, they will not affect the deduction from (5) and (5~) of the fact, noted above, that E's chance $ch(E)$ is $ch_C(E)$ when 'C' is true and $ch_{\sim C}(E)$ when '~C' is true. The deduction goes as follows. According to (5), $ch_C(E)$ is what $ch(E)$ is in the closest world to ours where 'C' is true. But if 'C' is true, that world is our world, so $ch_C(E)$ is what $ch(E)$ is in our world, i.e. what it actually is. So (5) entails, as it should, that when 'C' is true, $ch(E)=ch_C(E)$. Similarly of course with (5~), which entails that when '~C' is true, $ch(E)=ch_{\sim C}(E)$. QED.

## 4  Chance, sufficiency and necessity

So far so good for (5) and (5~). We can now use these equations to answer the question left over from chapter 1: what makes a cause C sufficient and necessary for an effect E?

We have seen why 'C⇒E' cannot express C's sufficiency for E [1.7]: its being entailed by 'C&E' would make every fact sufficient for every other fact. We must therefore find a stronger condition that will (a) pick out the causes we think are sufficient for their effects, (b) show what makes them so, i.e. give a clear and credible sense in which they 'necessitate' their effects, and (c) generate a corresponding condition for C to be necessary for E that shows how ~C would necessitate ~E in the very same sense.

I said in §1 that, with the right reading of chance, we can do all this as follows: C is sufficient for E iff it gives E a zero chance of not existing; and C is necessary for E iff ~C would give E a zero chance of existing. We can now state these conditions properly, recalling that all I mean by 'the fact E exists' is that 'E' is true [1.4]. Similarly, all I mean by 'E does not exist' is that 'E' is false. So when I say that a cause C gives E a zero chance of not existing what I mean is that it gives 'E' a zero chance of being false. Given the equation (3), $ch(\sim P)=1-ch(P)$, this is equivalent to saying that C gives 'E' a chance 1 of being true, i.e. that $ch_C(E)=1$.

From this, (5) gives us the following condition for any cause C to be sufficient for any effect E:

(6)   C is sufficient for E iff $C \Rightarrow ch(E)=1$.

Similarly (5~) gives us the following condition for any cause C to be necessary for any effect E:

(6~)   C is necessary for E iff $\sim C \Rightarrow ch(E)=0$.

If (6) and (6~) are right, then conditionals can after all express the sufficiency and necessity of a deterministic cause C for its effect E: namely, the closest-world conditionals '$C \Rightarrow ch(E)=1$' and '$\sim C \Rightarrow ch(E)=0$'. But these are not what I have been calling 'causal conditionals' [1.5]: because, since their consequents are not 'E' and '~E' but '$ch(E)=1$' and '$ch(E)=0$', they are not in any reasonable sense readings of 'if C then E' and 'if ~C then ~E'.

Thus in my original common sense of 'causal conditional', there are no causal conditionals. No reading of 'if C then E' will express a deterministic cause C's sufficiency for E, and no reading of 'if ~C then ~E' will express its without-which-not necessity for E. But this being so, we may as well hijack the otherwise useless term 'causal conditional', which I hereby do, to mean an instance of (4), '$C \Rightarrow ch(E)=p$', or (4~), '$\sim C \Rightarrow ch(E)=p'$'.

This of course assumes that (6) and (6~) are right, or at least as right as (5) and (5~). But are they? Well, (6) at least evades the original objection to '$C \Rightarrow E$' [1.7]: it does not make all facts sufficient for all other facts. The reason is of course that 'C&E', although it entails '$C \Rightarrow E$', does not entail '$C \Rightarrow ch(E)=1$', because 'E' does not entail '$ch(E)=1$'.

Take for example the tossing, $Tj$, of our coin $j$. In the circumstances, $Tj$ gives $j$ a fifty-fifty chance of landing heads: $ch_{Tj}(Hj)=0.5$. Since $j$ is tossed, i.e. '$Tj$' is true, $j$ actually has this chance, less than 1, of landing heads: $ch(Hj)=ch_{Tj}(Hj)=0.5$. Now suppose that $j$ does in fact land heads, so that '$Tj\&Hj$' and hence '$Tj \Rightarrow Hj$' are true. But since '$ch(Hj)=1$' is false, so is '$Tj \Rightarrow ch(Hj)=1$'. $Tj$ cannot then necessitate $j$'s landing heads, even if $j$ does land heads, since it gives $j$ a non-zero chance of failing to do so.

Next, suppose for the sake of argument that $j$ lands heads *because* it is tossed, since its chance of doing so had it not been tossed would have been zero: $\sim Tj \Rightarrow ch(Hj)=0$. Suppose in other words that $Tj$, since it satisfies (6~), is a *necessary* cause of $Hj$. But it is obviously not a sufficient one, even though '$Tj \Rightarrow Hj$' is true, because it fails (6), since '$Tj \Rightarrow ch(Hj)=1$' is false. Whereas if $j$ had been double-headed and '$Tj \Rightarrow ch(Hj)=1$' true, $Tj$ obviously would have been a sufficient cause of $Hj$.

This and other cases show that (6) does satisfy our desiderata (a), (b) and (c). It (a) picks out the very causes we take to be sufficient for their effects and (b) shows, given the right reading of chance, what makes them sufficient. And finally, (c), (6) generates (6~), which if satisfied makes ~C necessitate ~E in the same sense in which satisfying (6) makes C necessitate E: namely, by giving what it necessitates a zero chance of not existing.

The importance of the third desideratum (c) lies in the fact that the case for (6~) depends on the case for (6). For the only real argument for (6~) is that it takes (6~) to make (6) satisfy (c). There is no independent case for (6~), because '$\sim C \Rightarrow \sim E$', unlike '$C \Rightarrow E$', is not entailed by '$C \& E$'. The '$\sim C \Rightarrow \sim E$' test for C's without-which-not necessity for E therefore lacks the absurd implication that all facts are necessary for all other facts. This is why it is less obvious that the '$\sim C \Rightarrow \sim E$' test fails to satisfy the analogue of (a) than that the '$C \Rightarrow E$' test fails (a) itself: the '$\sim C \Rightarrow \sim E$' test does arguably pick out all and only those causes which we take to be necessary for their effects. Hence the widespread acceptance of the idea that what makes a cause C necessary for an effect E is that '$\sim C \Rightarrow \sim E$' is true.

But just as satisfying (a) is not enough to justify a test for sufficiency, so satisfying (a)'s analogue is not enough to justify a test for necessity. The '$\sim C \Rightarrow \sim E$' test must also satisfy the analogues of (b) and (c). That is, it must give a sense of not-possibly-not necessity, in which ~C necessitates ~E, that is (b) clear and credible and (c) the same as that in which its counterpart makes a sufficient C necessitate E. This is where the '$\sim C \Rightarrow \sim E$' test fails, on both counts. For (b) it gives no sense to ~C necessitating ~E, and (c) its counterpart test for sufficiency, '$C \Rightarrow E$', does not even satisfy (a).

In other words, '$\sim C \Rightarrow \sim E$' can express C's necessity for E no better than '$C \Rightarrow E$' can express C's sufficiency for E. So since we must strengthen the latter to '$C \Rightarrow ch(E)=1$' to satisfy (a), (b) and (c), we must also strengthen the former to '$\sim C \Rightarrow ch(E)=0$'. This is why, pending later corrections [14.3], I shall from now on take (6) and (6~) to say what it is that makes a deterministic cause C sufficient and necessary for its effects. But they will only do this given the right reading of the chances which they say C's effects have in the circumstances with and without C. Our next task is to see what that right reading of chance is.

# 3  *Interpretations of probability*

## 1  Probability and necessity

We need a reading of chance, i.e. an interpretation of the probability calculus, which will allow '$ch_C(E)=1$' to express the kind of not-possibly-not necessity that a sufficient cause C gives its effect E. What interpretation will allow this?

The kind of necessity which '$ch_C(E)=1$' must express is usually if not always contingent: it can exist in our world without existing in all other possible worlds and so cannot be metaphysical necessity [1.6]. Don's falling must be able to necessitate his dying in our world without doing so in all worlds, or even in all worlds where he falls in circumstances which are relevantly similar (except that the laws of nature may differ). Not even total causes must need to necessitate their effects in all possible worlds in order to necessitate them in ours.

But even if the necessity that '$ch_C(E)=1$' expresses is weaker than meta-physical necessity, it must still entail existence. Nothing which does not exist can be necessary in any not-possibly-not sense, and certainly not in the sense we need: the whole point of saying that a sufficient cause C *necessitates* E is that C somehow ensures or guarantees E's existence. If Don falls but does not die, his falling cannot in any sense have necessitated, ensured or guaranteed that he dies.

So for $ch_C(E)=1$ to make C necessitate E, $C\&chs_C(E)=1$ must entail E: Don's falling and having a chance 1 of dying if he falls must entail that he dies. But when 'C' is true, $ch_C(E)=ch(E)$ [2.3]: when Don falls, his chance of dying if he falls is just his chance of dying. So for $C\&ch_C(E)=1$ to entail E, $ch(E)=1$ must entail E: Don cannot have a chance 1 of dying and not die.

Thus for '$ch_C(E)=1$' to express C's sufficiency for E, chances must meet what I shall call the *Necessity condition*, that for all P,

(7)    $ch(P)=1$ entails P.

Similarly, for '$ch_{-C}(E)=0$' to express C's without-which-not necessity for E, $\sim C\&ch_{-C}(E)=0$ and hence $ch(E)=0$ must entail $\sim$E. But this follows from the Necessity condition, since by (3), $ch(\sim P)=1-ch(P)$ for all P. So $ch(P)=0$ entails $ch(\sim P)=1$ which, by (7), entails $\sim P$.

Thus, in order to give a reading of chance that will serve our turn, we need an interpretation of probability which meets the Necessity condition. It is not however clear that we can have it, since there is a serious objection to this condition which I must now rebut. To see the objection, imagine a spinning pointer with an equal chance of stopping in any equiangular sector of the circle it marks out. Its chance $ch(\alpha)$ of stopping in any sector of angle $\alpha°$ is $\alpha/360$, which for $\alpha=0$ is 0. In other words, the pointer has a zero chance of stopping at any given point on the circle: yet it must stop somewhere. How then can $ch(P)=0$ entail $\sim P$?

The answer lies in the fact that, as I (1971 ch. 6; 1991 ch. 9 §4) and others have argued, nothing can have a point value of a continuous quantity. It is for example absurd to credit me with a height of precisely 162.0000...cm, excluding any other value, however close. Values of quantities – lengths, volumes, temperatures, etc. – should really be represented by intervals of numbers, like 162.0±0.5. In other words, to say that my height is 162 cm is really to say that 162 lies in some explicit or implicit interval of numbers which represents my height in centimetres.

Similarly with our pointer. It is absurd to credit it with stopping at 25.0000...° West of North, meaning that it stops at no other angle, however close: no pointer could possibly do that. To say that it stops at 25° is really to say that 25 lies in an interval of numbers, say 25.0±0.5, which represents its stopping angle in degrees. But then the pointer's chance of stopping at any given angle is not zero but $1/360\approx0.0028$. So the fact that a pointer must stop somewhere does not refute our condition (7).

Chances could therefore meet the Necessity condition which is required for '$ch_C(E)=1$' and '$ch_{\sim C}(E)=0$' to express respectively C's sufficiency and necessity for E. Let us now see which interpretations of probability, if any, will in fact let them do so.

## 2 Credence

The subjective interpretation of the probability calculus uses it to measure the strength of our beliefs. It is obvious that my belief that P (i.e. that P is a fact), say that a particular horse will win the Derby, can come by degrees which will, for example, affect the odds at which I will bet on P. On this basis Ramsey (1990 ch. 4) and others have defined a probability measure of my degree of belief that P, which is called P's *subjective probability*, or my *credence* in P, and which I shall write '$cr(P)$'.

The concept of credence is by no means uncontentious. In particular, to many philosophers it seems absurd to credit me with a precise credence

$cr(Hj)=0.4000...$ in a tossed coin $j$'s landing heads $(Hj)$; and so it is. But no more absurd, as we have just seen, than crediting me with a precise height, temperature or blood pressure. Credences, like other quantities, should really be represented by intervals of numbers: to say that my $cr(Hj)=0.4$ is really to say that 0.4 lies in an interval of numbers between 0 and 1, say $0.40\pm0.05$, which represents my degree of belief that $j$ will land heads.

Credences are contentious in other ways too, which need not concern us, since all that matters here is whether chances are credences. If they were, I should need to defend credences more thoroughly, as I have done elsewhere (1971 ch. 3; 1991 ch. 3 pt II). But I need not do so here, because chances cannot be credences. The subjective interpretation of probability cannot give us the reading of chance we need, for one simple reason. Credences cannot meet the Necessity condition, since for few if any effects E can $cr(E)=1$ entail E or $cr(E)=0$ entail ~E.

That credences cannot meet this condition is obvious, because what any utterance of '$cr(E)=1$' says is that the speaker is sure that E is a fact, e.g. sure that Don dies. But however sure I am about this, I can still be wrong. No degree of belief in Don's dying can entail that he dies, and similarly for almost all other effects. Only in a few freak cases, like Descartes's 'Cogito ergo sum', where 'E' is 'I exist', can $cr(E)=1$ entail E. But for the chances of effects to be credences, this entailment would have to hold for every E which might have a chance of 1, and obviously it does not. Chances cannot be credences.

I labour this point because many accounts of causation tacitly treat chances as credences, which makes it important to see why that is a mistake. It is also worth seeing how the mistake can arise. One possible cause is an ambiguity in saying that chances are not credences. This may mean what I mean, that chances and credences are never *identical*, i.e., using '≡' to mean 'is identical to', that '$ch(E)\equiv cr(E)$' is always false. It may also mean that $ch(E)$ and $cr(E)$ are never *equal in value*, that '$ch(E)=cr(E)$' is always false. But in this sense of course '$ch(E)=cr(E)$' is often true.

Indeed a fairly uncontentious principle entails that this equation often *should* be true. The principle, which I shall call the *Evidence condition*, is this. For any state of affairs P, if all the evidence I have about P is that $ch(P)=p$, my $cr(P)$ should also be $p$. Thus if my evidence about whether Don will die is that his chance of doing so is $p$, $p$ is also the credence I should have in his dying. So if $ch(P)$ is my evidence about P, '$cr(P)=ch(P)$' should be true.

The Evidence condition is undeniable. But it provides no excuse for identifying chances with credences. On the contrary, to say that my $cr(P)$ should have the same value as a $ch(P)$ that is my evidence about P presupposes that these are values of two different things. This is so even if the condition is used, as it has been by me (1971 ch. 3), first to define chances by the fact that knowledge of them justifies credences, and then to make the credence which a chance justifies measure that chance. This definition does in a way apply the subjective interpretation of probability to chances, because it uses the fact that credences satisfy the probability calculus to make chances do so too. This means that we need no independent reason to use the probability calculus to measure chances: the fact that credences are probabilities is reason enough. But this does not make chances credences, any more, for example, than using the visual sensations which red light gives us to define its colour – red – makes the colour of light a kind of sensation. (For more discussion of this analogy see my 1991 ch. 14.)

The ambiguity in 'chances are credences' is however too obvious to be the main cause of confusion between the two. The confusion mostly occurs when accounts of causation invoke probabilities without saying what interpretation of the calculus is meant, and then use arguments that apply only to credences to justify assumptions that need to be true of chances.

The most serious example of this is the widespread equation of $ch_C(E)$ with the so-called *conditional probability* of E given C. This probability, which I shall write '$p(E/C)$' in order to avoid begging questions of interpretation, is defined, for $p(C)>0$, by

(8)    $p(C\&E) = p(E/C) \times p(C)$, i.e.
         $p(E/C) = p(C\&E)/p(C)$.

Interpreted subjectively, as *conditional credence*, this concept is often if contentiously used to say how we should adjust our credences to new data, as follows. Suppose I see Don falling and this raises $cr(C)$, my credence that he falls, to 1. Then, by (8), my conditional credence in his dying given that he falls, $cr(E/C)$, must now equal my credence in his falling and dying, $cr(C\&E)$; and this, since my credence in his falling, $cr(C)$, is now 1, must equal my credence, $cr(E)$, in his dying.

So provided my coming to see that Don falls does not change the old value of my $cr(E/C)$, my new $cr(E)$ will come to equal that value. Seeing Don fall will then make my new unconditional credence in his dying equal my old conditional credence in his dying given that he falls. This way of changing my $cr(E)$ if my $cr(C)$ is raised to 1 is called *conditionalisation* and is recommended by so-called *Bayesians* like Jeffrey (1983 ch. 11) on grounds we need not go into.

For as we shall now see, no rationale for conditionalising *credences* gives any reason to identify $ch_C(E)$ with the conditional *chance* $ch(E/C)$. To see this, we must first recall that every chance $ch(P)$ of any fact P is a property of some fact before P [2.1]. In particular, any chance $ch(E)$ of any effect E is a property of an earlier fact C&S, where C is a cause of E and S is the conjunction of facts about the circumstances, simultaneous with C, of which $ch_C(E)$ and $ch_{-C}(E)$ are properties [2.2]. Thus Don's chances of dying if he falls and if he does not fall are properties of the circumstances, before he dies, in which he falls.

And this has an obvious and obviously true consequence: namely, that $ch_C(E)$, Don's chance of dying if he falls, is logically independent of any chance, $ch(C)$, which Don has of falling. For every such chance must by the same token be a property of a fact *before* Don falls – e.g. that he is climbing without a rope – which therefore cannot be the simultaneous fact S of which $ch_C(E)$ is a property. Yet any *conditional* chance, $ch(E/C)$, of Don's dying given that he falls does by definition depend logically on a corresponding $ch(C)$, since by (8),

(9)   $ch(E/C) = ch(C\&E)/ch(C)$.

This being so, $ch_C(E)$ cannot be *identical* to any $ch(E/C)$, the two being logically independent properties of quite different facts located at quite different times.

Moreover $ch_C(E)$, Don's chance of dying if he falls, may not even *equal* $ch(E/C)$. Suppose that, as Don climbs, his chance of dying if he does not fall is almost zero. Suppose also that he has a chance of falling, $ch(C)=0.1$, made up of a chance that he falls head up (H), $ch(C\&H)=0.04$, and a chance that he falls otherwise (~H), $ch(C\&\sim H)=0.06$. Finally, suppose his chance of dying will be 0.4 if he falls head up and otherwise 0.9. In other words, $ch_C(E)$ will be 0.4 if the circumstances S in which Don falls contains H, and 0.9 if S contains ~H.

Yet $ch(E/C)$, Don's conditional chance of dying given that he falls, will as he climbs be neither 0.4 nor 0.9. For now the relevant

$$ch(C\&E) = 0.04 \times 0.4 + 0.06 \times 0.9 = 0.06;$$

so that, by (9),

$$ch(E/C) = ch(C\&E)/ch(C) = 0.06/0.1 = 0.6.$$

So whatever happens the relevant $ch(E/C)$ will not equal $ch_C(E)$.

In short, the widespread equation of $ch_C(E)$ with $ch(E/C)$ not only fails to follow from whatever case there may be for conditionalising credences, it is often false. Taking this case for conditionalisation to justify equating $ch_C(E)$ with $ch(E/C)$, thus tacitly treating chances as credences, is not only invalid, it can cause serious mistakes about the values of the chances which causes give their effects.

And even when this assumption does not cause such mistakes, there is still no excuse for it. For suppose that as I see Don fall, my credence in his dying, $cr(E)$, does equal his chance of dying, $ch(E)=p$ – ideally because my evidence about E is that $ch(E)=p$. Now my credence $cr(E)=p$ is of course a property of me. $ch(E)=p$, on the other hand, is a property of local facts about how Don falls [2.1]. So for this $ch(E)$ and my $cr(E)$ to be not just equal in value but the very same thing, my $cr(E)$ must *be* that property: the degree $p$ to which I believe that Don will die must be what gives him his chance of dying! But not even I credit my credences with such powers. God's credences may entail corresponding chances, but no one else's do.

It is in short sheer nonsense to treat chances as credences. But that still leaves one tenable reason for replacing chance with credence in an account of causation. This is that one disbelieves in chance and hence in causation – or thinks at least that we cannot know what chances exist nor therefore what really causes what. Yet in everyday life we all think we know such things, and talk and act accordingly, as my examples show. A sceptic must therefore take many of these beliefs, statements and actions of ours to be, if not downright false, at least unwarranted. But then, to make sense of them, the sceptic must provide subjective surrogates for their apparent content and rationale. And this is where credence comes in. For even if chances cannot be credences, our apparent beliefs in chances might still really be credences in something else. Thus my apparent belief in the chance $ch_C(E)$ that a cause C gives its effect E might really be a conditional credence, $cr(E/C)$, in E given C: a state which, as (8) shows, requires me only to have credences in C and in C&E, not in any chance.

But why should we buy this reconstruction of our beliefs about chances? To do so we need some reason to think that chances cannot exist or that we cannot know what their values are. Now whether there is such a reason will depend on what chances are and how we get to know them. But saying what chances are is the business of this chapter and the next; and once we know what they are we shall see no reason either to deny their existence or to suppose that we cannot know their values.

On the contrary, our very senses need chances in order to tell us facts about the world, since they do this by making those facts give us a high chance of having true beliefs about them [6.3]. Thus for me to know that the desk I am now looking at is brown, my eyes must make the fact that it is brown give me a high chance of believing that it is. Without this and the many other high chances of getting true beliefs that my senses give me, I should have no reason to trust the evidence of my senses at all. And with such chances, my senses can give me as trustworthy evidence about chances as about anything else: because chances can also give me high chances of getting true beliefs about them [6.3]. This is reason enough to take our apparent knowledge of chances at face value, and to resist its replacement by credences in other things.

## 3  Evidential probability

If chance is not credence, perhaps it is an *evidential probability*? By this I mean a probability measure of how far some evidence Q supports the hypothesis that some state of affairs P is a fact, a measure which I shall write '*P*(P,Q)'. To cover both true and false hypotheses, and possible as well as actual evidence, I shall follow the custom of treating *P*(P,Q) as a relation between states of affairs or propositions rather than facts [1.2]. I shall also identify *P*(P,Q) with the credence *cr*(P) we should have if Q is our evidence about P. This assumption, although contentious, begs no present question: it just ensures that *P*(P,Q), like *cr*(P), is indeed a probability, i.e. has a measure which satisfies the probability calculus.

Are chances in general, and the chances of effects in particular, evidential probabilities so understood? Is Don's chance of dying if he falls the credence I ought to have in his dying if my evidence is that he falls? Note that this does not follow from the Evidence condition of §2, that if my evidence about P is that $ch(P)=p$, my credence in P should be $p$. For all this says, symbolised as an evidential probability, is that

(10)  $ch(P)=p$ entails $P(P,ch(P)=p)=p$.

In other words, the relation of evidential probability which $ch(P)=p$ entails holds between P and itself, not between P and anything else. The Evidence condition makes the fact that $ch(P)=p$ evidence about P in its own right.

However the chance $ch(E)$ of an effect E may still *be* an evidential probability. For just as my credence in E, $cr(E)$, may be taken to relate the proposition 'E' to me, so $ch(E)$ may be taken to relate 'E' to the fact of which $ch(E)$ is a property: namely, the conjunction C&S of E's cause C with the relevant circumstances S. Since moreover this conjunction always includes C, we can also take $ch_C(E)$ to relate 'E' to the fact C and hence, to cover possible as well as actual causes of E, to the proposition 'C'.

The problem is that the conjunction C&S also includes S, the circumstances in which C causes E. So if $ch_C(E)$ is an evidential relation between 'C' and 'E', it is contingent on S, since $ch_C(E)$ would obviously differ if S differed. If for example Don were to fall less far, or onto something soft, his chance of dying if he fell would be less than it actually is. Thus since the relevant S can always differ in these and other ways, so too can $ch_C(E)$. So if $ch_C(E)$ *is* an evidential relation between 'C' and 'E', it must be a contingent one, because it is contingent on S and S is contingent. And this is so even when C is what I have called a total cause of E. For even then, S will still contain the relevant instances of the laws that fix $ch_C(E)$ [2.2], laws which are rarely if ever metaphysically necessary [1.6].

This contingency in the chances which causes give their effects is what really stops the concept of evidential probability giving us the reading of chance we need. For while calling $ch_C(E)$ a 'credence' does at least say – wrongly – what it is, namely a degree of belief, calling it 'evidential' does not even do that. It only says what, by meeting the Evidence condition, $ch_C(E)=p$ *does*: namely, justify my having $cr(E)=p$ if my evidence about E is that $C\&ch_C(E)=p$ and hence that $ch(E)=p$. But this is not enough, even if it does make $ch_C(E)$ an evidential probability. For then we still need to know *why* the fact that $ch_C(E)=p$ makes my evidence C justify my credence $cr(E)=p$. And what $ch_C(E)$'s contingency on S shows is that the explanation of this must invoke something more than the identities of the propositions 'C' and 'E'.

This means in particular that $ch_C(E)$ cannot be a *logical probability* in the sense of Keynes (1921) and Carnap (1962). That is, it cannot be a probability measure of a relation of *partial entailment* between 'C' and 'E', a measure whose value is derivable *a priori* in an inductive logic. Such a relation, like entailment proper, would indeed depend only on 'C' and 'E', and if $ch_C(E)$ measured such a relation it would certainly be an evidential probability. Unfortunately $ch_C(E)$ cannot measure any such relation, and not only because it is usually contingent: for even if it were metaphysically necessary, we could still not deduce it *a priori* from the identities of 'C' and 'E', any more than we can deduce 'E' from 'C' [1.6].

I doubt if any evidential probability $P(P,Q)$ is deducible *a priori* when 'P' and 'Q' are consistent, neither entails the other and 'Q' neither is nor entails a chance that 'P' is true. The real objection to taking chance to be a logical probability is 'the obvious one that there really do not seem to be any such things as the probability relations [Keynes] describes' (Ramsey 1990, p. 57). And even among those who think there are such things, most, like Carnap (1955), agree that they do not include chances. For as Ramsey says, 'anyone who tries to decide by Mr Keynes' methods what are the proper alternatives to regard as equally probable in molecular mechanics … will soon be convinced that it is a matter of physics rather than pure logic' (1990 p. 85).

## 4  Frequency

If chances cannot be logical probabilities, perhaps they can be *frequencies*? Perhaps for example the chance that our coin *j* [2.1] will land heads, *Hj*, when tossed, *Tj*, is a frequency $f(H)$ of heads in a class – the so-called *reference class* – of many suitably similar actual or hypothetical coin tosses. If the reference class is finite, $f(H)$ is the fraction of the tosses in it that land heads; if infinite, as it may well be if the tosses are hypothetical, this fraction is not defined and we need another definition of $f(H)$.

We can define $f(H)$ for an infinite reference class of coin tosses as follows. First, suppose the tosses in the class form a sequence S. Next, let $f_n(H)$ be the fraction of heads in the first $n$ tosses, as in the sequence below:

| S: | H | T | H | H | H | T | ... |
|---|---|---|---|---|---|---|---|
| $n$: | 1 | 2 | 3 | 4 | 5 | 6 | ... |
| $f_n(H)$: | 1 | 1/2 | 2/3 | 3/4 | 4/5 | 2/3 | ... |

Then as $n$ increases without limit, $f_n(H)$ may tend to a limit, $f_\infty(H)$. If it does, we can identify this so-called *limiting frequency* $f_\infty(H)$ with $f(H)$, the frequency of heads, by definition – provided another condition is met.

This condition is needed to exclude sequences like $H\,T\,H\,T\,H\,T\,H\,T$ ... with limiting frequencies (1/2 in this case) which clearly do not manifest chances. The condition requires all sub-sequences of S selected *at random* (e.g. not all heads) to have the same $f_\infty(H)$ – which of course raises the question of how to define 'at random' without invoking chance. This question, however, I shall waive, assuming for the sake of argument that a good and non-question-begging definition of frequency can be given for all infinite cases. Any class of actual or hypothetical instances of some kind that satisfies the definition is called a *collective* (von Mises 1957).

Thus assuming that the class of people like Bill who smoke as he does would, if infinite, be a collective, then Bill's chance of getting cancer could be the frequency in that class of those who get cancer. Don's chance of dying could likewise be the frequency of deaths in a finite or infinite class of equally heavy and brittle-boned people who fall as far as he does onto equally hard ground. And similarly in other cases.

These cases show that frequency readings of chance need resemblance relations to define both the reference class and the feature whose frequency in that class the chance is to be identified with. Sometimes the relation is obvious, as with the relevant feature of our coin tosses (how they land), which they share iff they land the same way up. What is less obvious is how tosses must resemble the toss of our coin $j$ in order to be in its reference class, i.e. for their frequency of heads to fix $j$'s chance $ch(Hj)$ of landing heads. Similarly in other cases: how must people resemble Bill in metabolism and smoking habits for the incidence of cancer among them to be what fixes his chance of getting it?

It is not obvious that the resemblances which the frequency reading of chance needs always exist, but again I shall assume that they do. This means that something about any state of affairs P with a chance $ch(P)$ of being a fact, and any fact Q of which that $ch(P)$ is a property, must define *kinds* of states of affairs P* and Q* (like landing heads, $H$, and being fairly tossed, $F$) whose instances can yield a frequency $f(P*)$ with which $ch(P)$ could be identified. But even then, it does not follow that $ch(P)$ *is* $f(P*)$. Even when chances correspond to well-defined frequencies, the question still remains: *are* they those frequencies?

There is a case for saying that they are. Frequency readings of chance are certainly better than subjective or logical ones. They make chances objective and contingent, which the chances of effects must be. They also give a clear sense to chance measuring a quantitative kind of possibility. For suppose the chance of $j$ landing heads is greater than 0 and less than 1: $0<ch(Hj)<1$. We want this to mean that in some sense $j$ *can* land heads, and *can* also land tails, so that each outcome is possible and neither is necessary. Now imagine many such tosses. Since any of them can but need not land heads, we should expect them to land heads sometimes but not always, i.e. we should expect $0<f(H)<1$. In other words, we take $f(H)>0$ to show that $Hj$ is possible, and $f(H)<1 - f(\sim H)>0$ – to show that $\sim Hj$ is possible. $f(H)$ is moreover a natural measure of *how* possible $Hj$ is: the more possible it is that this toss of $j$ will land heads, the more frequently we should expect to see $j$ land heads in many such tosses.

So far so good for frequency readings of chance. But not good enough, since chances must meet the Necessity condition of §1: $ch(P)=1$ must entail P. Yet our definition of $f(P)$ stops $f(P*)=1$ entailing P if the reference class can be infinite. Finite classes are all right: if any of a finite number of coin tosses fail to land heads, $f(H)$ cannot be 1, so that for all finite $n$, however large, $f_n(H)=1$ entails $Hj$. But with infinitely many tosses the entailment fails. For then, since $f(H)$ is $f_\infty(H)$, which is simply the limit of $f_n(H)$ as $n\to\infty$, all $f(H)=1$ entails is that, as $n\to\infty, f_n(H)\to1$: which is consistent with many – indeed infinitely many – of this infinite number of tosses landing tails, and hence with $\sim Hj$.

The obvious solution to this problem is to keep $n$ finite. But as there is no limit to the number of merely hypothetical cases, this means limiting the members of reference classes to actual cases. But this will not work if the number of actual cases throughout the past, present and future of our world is infinite, which it may well be. And even if it is not, that only poses other and worse problems. The most obvious one is that finite reference classes can only yield a finite number of frequencies, in the extreme case only 1 and 0. For if $j$ is the only coin ever tossed, then $f(H)$ – $f_1(H)$ – can only be 1, if $j$ lands heads, or 0, if it does not. But the fact that $j$ is the only coin tossed can hardly make $Hj$ entail that $ch(Hj)=1$ and $\sim Hj$

entail that $ch(Hj)=0$. Similarly in other cases: Don's *possible* chances of dying if he falls can hardly depend on how many similar people actually fall in a similar way.

There is another reason also why an *actual frequency* reading of chance will not do. This is that it makes Don's *actual* chance $ch(E)$ of dying as he falls depend logically on whether other people die, which is equally absurd. Thus suppose that in the whole history of the world 1000 people like Don fall as he does and 572 of them die, so that $f(E^*)=f_{1000}(E^*)=0.572$. If just one of these people, maybe living in a distant galaxy a million years hence, survived, as he or she well might with a roughly fifty-fifty chance of doing so, $f(E^*)$ would by definition be different: 0.571. But we cannot take Don's chance $ch(E)$ of dying here and now to depend *logically*, as $f(E^*)$ does, on what happens to anyone so remote – or indeed to anyone else at all.

Chances generally cannot then be actual frequencies. And the chances of effects in particular cannot be actual frequencies for another reason too. This is that they could not then be properties of facts earlier than those effects [2.1]. For example, since people like Don may fall at any time, the frequency with which these people die is a property of the whole history of the world, past, present and future, not of anything that can be, as it must be, earlier than Don's death. This is why actual frequencies can at best be general surrogates for singular chances and hence for singular causation [1.1].

In short, the actual frequency interpretation of probability, like the subjective interpretation, can really only be used as a surrogate for chance by those who do not really believe in it. And as we have just seen, it can rarely even be that: since without the right number of actual members of the relevant reference class, the right actual frequency will not exist.

The only $f(P^*)$ that could possibly correspond to an apparent $ch(P)=p$ for all $p$ is the *limiting* frequency $f_\infty(P^*)=p$ in a hypothetical collective. This too, since $f_\infty(P^*)=1$ does not meet the Necessity condition, can only be a surrogate for $ch(P)=p$; but at least it could always exist. But will it? What ensures that an infinite class of hypothetical coin tosses will be a collective with a limiting frequency $f_\infty(H)=p$? Something is needed to ensure this, since by hypothesis the tosses need only be possible, and *any* frequency of heads, from 0 to 1 inclusive, is *possible* in any sequence of tosses, however long. What then ensures the existence and fixes the value $p$ of the unique $f_\infty(H)=p$ that is to be the frequency theorist's surrogate for $ch(Hj)=p$? It cannot be the frequency of heads in other actual coin tosses, which by hypothesis need not exist and will anyway be far outnumbered by the merely possible members of our hypothetical collective. So what in the world does the truth of '$f_\infty(H)=p$' depend on?

It depends on each of the hypothetical tosses having a probability $p$ of landing heads, a probability which as in §2 I shall write '$p(H)$' in order to avoid begging questions of interpretation. This probability must meet certain conditions, not entailed by the probability calculus, to satisfy the so-called *laws of large numbers* which for all $p$ make $p(H)=p$ entail $f_\infty(H)=p$ (Kingman and Taylor 1966 p. 347). These conditions, which we need not go into, are certainly met by chances; but not only by chances, so invoking a $p(H)$ that meets them does not beg the present question. They can for example be met by credences (de Finetti 1937 ch. 3), thus making $cr(Hj)=p$ entail the belief that $f_\infty(H)=p$, i.e. $cr(f_\infty(H)=p)=1$. This does not of course mean that a $p(H)$ which entails $f_\infty(H)=p$ can itself be a credence: for since actual frequencies no more depend on our credences than chances do, $p(H)$ must at least be objective. $p(H)$ is simply an objective probability which, by satisfying the laws of large numbers, entails the existence and value of a hypothetical $f_\infty(H)$.

But what then is this objective probability: what in the world makes '$p(H)=p$' true? It must be something actual that makes $p(H)=p$ for all the hypothetical members of the collective of which $f_\infty(H)=p$ is a property. But this can only be a property of facts about the actual toss of the coin $j$ which (a) fixes the kind of toss that can be a member of $j$'s reference class and (b) makes that class, if infinite, a collective. But this is just what $ch(Hj)=p$ does [2.1]. This chance is a property of facts about $j$'s toss which, by satisfying the laws of large numbers, entails the existence of a hypothetical $f_\infty(H)=p$. Hence, far from being a surrogate for $ch(Hj)=p$, $f_\infty(H)=p$ depends on a property $p(H)=p$ which is just like it.

But what then stops $p(H)=p$ *being* the chance $ch(Hj)=p$? Nothing, and certainly not the fact that $ch(Hj)=1$ entails $Hj$ and $f_\infty(H)=1$ does not. For $p(H)=p$ need only entail $f_\infty(H)=p$: it need not be entailed by it. So $p(H)=p$ can easily have entailments that $f_\infty(H)=p$ lacks. And since the same $f_\infty(H)$ can hardly be fixed by two different properties of the very same toss, I conclude that the property $p(H)$ is indeed the chance $ch(Hj)$.

Where does this leave frequency readings of chance? It is true that all chances, *via* the laws of large numbers, entail hypothetical limiting frequencies. That is, for every $ch(P)$, a kind Q* of possible facts, including the fact Q of which that $ch(P)$ is a property, yields a collective such that

(11)   $ch(P)=p$ entails $f_\infty(P^*)=p$,

for a kind P* of states of affairs that includes P. This is what I shall call the *Frequency condition* on chance.

Note that the Frequency condition gives chance a frequency measure, just as the Evidence condition of §2 gives it a subjective measure. This means that because frequencies, including limiting frequencies, automatically satisfy the probability calculus, the Frequency condition makes chances satisfy it. And this is the other reason why we need no independent rationale for using the probability calculus to measure chance: the fact that chances entail limiting frequencies is rationale enough. But this fact no more turns chances into limiting frequencies than the Evidence condition turns them into credences. Just as no $ch(P)$ is ever the same thing as the $cr(P)$ which it justifies, despite having the same value, so it is never the same thing as the $f_\infty(P^*)$ it entails, despite having the same value.

To see just how different chances and limiting frequencies are, consider again Don's chance of dying, $ch(E)$. This is a property of a conjunction of his falling, C, with the circumstances S he falls in. The $f_\infty(E^*)$ which it entails, the limiting frequency of deaths in a collective of falls like Don's, is clearly no such thing. Even if the collective were actual, and an infinite number of people like Don actually fell as he does, they could not all fall when and where he does: no actual $f_\infty(E^*)$ could possibly have $ch(E)$'s location. And of course $f_\infty(E^*)$ is not actual. It is merely hypothetical, like the credence $cr(E)=p$ of a merely hypothetical person whose evidence about E is that $ch(E)=p$. And merely hypothetical quantities like this $f_\infty(E^*)$ and this $cr(E)$ can only get actual values from an actual quantity, in this case from $ch(E)$, Don's actual chance of dying. So in the only sense that matters here, the frequency reading is wrong. Chances in general, and the chances of effects in particular, are not frequencies. What then are they?

# 4 Chance

## 1 The conditions on chance

I have said that every chance, $ch(P)$, that a state of affairs P is actual, i.e. is a fact, is a property of a (usually conjunctive) fact Q preceding P. More precisely, since P has no location in time if it is not a fact [1.2], every $ch(P)$ is a property of some Q preceding what, if P *is* actual, will be the fact that P. Thus Don's chance of dying is a property of a conjunction of facts about how he falls, before he dies, if he does die. $j$'s chance of landing heads is a property of how $j$ is tossed, before it lands heads, if it lands heads. And so on.

What kind of property of a fact Q is a chance $ch(P)$? We have seen that it cannot be the credence, $cr(P)$, which $ch(P)$ justifies [3.2]. Nor can it be the limiting frequency, $f_\infty(P^*)$, with which $ch(P)$ entails that a collective of facts of kind $Q^*$ would yield facts of kind $P^*$, such as tosses of coins like $j$ landing heads or people who fall like Don dying [3.4]. But we can still use these credences and frequencies to define chances, as follows.

Chances are properties that meet the Necessity, Evidence and Frequency conditions. That is, every $ch(P)=p$ that is a property of a fact Q entails that:

(i) if $p=1$, P is a fact;
(ii) if $ch(P)=p$ is my evidence about P, then $cr(P)$, my credence that P is a fact, should be $p$;
(iii) any collective of facts of a kind $Q^*$ with the property $ch(P^*)=p$ will have the limiting frequency $f_\infty(P^*)=p$.

This I maintain is all there need be to chance. For chances to exist is for properties of facts to exist that meet these conditions. For any P to have a chance is for some fact that precedes P to have such a property.

But why must a single property meet these three conditions? One reason for (i) we have seen already: it lets '$ch(P)=1$' express the necessity that a sufficient cause must give its effects [3.1]. More generally, it lets $ch(P)$ 'measure a contingent and quantitative … possibility' [2.1], namely a possibility that P is a fact. For, obviously, the lower limit of this possibility is that P is *im*possible. But just as nothing that is necessary can fail to exist

44

[3.1], so nothing can exist that is impossible. Thus for $ch(P)=0$, $ch(P)$'s lowest value, to make P impossible, it must entail ~P. Similarly, for $ch(P)=1$ to entail the upper limit of P's possibility, i.e. make P *necessary*, it must entail P. That is obvious, as it is why $ch(P)$ must also satisfy (iii), so that frequencies of P*s can be measures of this possibility of P [3.4].

What is much less obvious is why (ii) and (iii), the Evidence and Frequency conditions, should go together. Why should the evidence that some fact has a property which entails a hypothetical $f_\infty(P^*)=p$ justify the credence $cr(P)=p$? This is the hard question we now need to answer.

## 2 Frequencies and credences

The answer to this question starts from the fact that we want our beliefs to be true in order to make the actions they combine with our desires to cause succeed, i.e. achieve the object of those desires. Take Don's sister Sue, who believes that her local pub, the Bull, has gin, a belief which makes her visit the Bull when she wants some gin. Let 'B' be the proposition that the Bull has gin. Then if Sue's belief that B is a fact is true, she will get the gin she wants – her action will succeed – and if it is false she will not – her action will fail.

Now suppose Sue knows that the Bull always restocks its gin before it sells out. This is a property of the Bull which entails that *any* pub with the property would have gin if Sue visited it. That is, it entails both B and $f_\infty(B^*)=1$: it meets the Necessity condition and the Frequency condition for $p=1$. And Sue's knowing that the Bull has this property obviously justifies her complete conviction that B, $cr(B)=1$. So in this case the property that meets the Frequency and Necessity conditions for $p=1$ also meets the Evidence condition: it gives the Bull a chance 1 of having gin. Similarly of course for $p=0$.

That is the easy part of the answer to our question. The hard part is to show what links the Frequency and Evidence conditions when $p$ is less than 1 and more than 0. Let us start by supposing that Sue *only* visits the Bull to get gin: otherwise she stays at home. She may also want her gin more or less: her desire for it comes by degrees, as does her desire to avoid the Bull. Suppose that these desires are measurable, say by the most Sue is willing to pay for her gin and by the least free cash she would visit the Bull to be given. These measures are Sue's so-called 'subjective utilities', which for reasons to be given later I prefer to call her *valuations*, reserving the term 'utility' for something more objective [7].

Now call Sue's getting her gin 'G' and her visiting the Bull 'V' and let $b$ (for benefit) be Sue's valuation $v(G)$ of G and $c$ (for cost) her valuation $v(\sim V)$ of ~V. Then if Sue believes the Bull always has gin, she will visit it if $b>c$, i.e. if she values getting her gin more than she values avoiding the Bull. Conversely, if $b<c$ Sue will not visit the Bull. If $b=c$ she may visit it or not, but since she must do one or the other, we can simplify matters by assuming she does not – in short, that she will visit the Bull iff she values G more than ~V.

So far I have assumed that Sue not only believes but *knows* that the Bull always has gin, i.e. that this belief of hers is both true and warranted, never mind how. Let us now also assume that her desires are warranted, in the following minimal sense: that $b$ measures not only how much Sue wants her gin before she gets it but how much she will actually like it if she does get it; and similarly that $c$ measures how much Sue will actually dislike the Bull if she goes there. Finally, let us assume that nothing else of any consequence turns on whether Sue visits the Bull or on whether she gets her gin. Given all this, Sue's valuations measure objective utilities, so that not only *will* she visit the Bull iff $b>c$, there is an obvious sense in which she *should* visit it iff $b>c$.

But what should Sue do in these circumstances if she knows, not that the Bull always has gin, but that it runs out half the time, and not regularly, e.g. every other day, but at random, so that $f_\infty(B^*)=0.5$? Now she knows that her visits are gambles, which in the long run she must expect to lose as often as she wins. So for it to be worth running the risk of losing – getting no gin – winning must matter twice as much as when she knows that $f_\infty(B^*)=1$: so she should now visit the Bull iff $b>c/0.5$.

Similarly for any value $p$ of $f_\infty(B^*)$: Sue should visit the Bull iff $b>c/p$. And similarly in general. Suppose a stake $c$ will win me a benefit $b$ iff some state of affairs P is a fact, and my evidence about P is $f_\infty(P^*)$ for some $P^*$ of which P is an instance: then I should stake $c$ for this chance of winning $b$ iff $c/b<f_\infty(P^*)$. In short, for any person $x$,

(12)   on evidence $f_\infty(P^*)$, to get $b$ iff P, $x$ should pay $c$ iff $c/b<f_\infty(P^*)$.

Yet whatever Sue *should* do, in fact she *will* not visit the Bull without some credence $cr(B)$ in its having gin. And obviously the less her credence in this, the more she must want her gin before she will go, i.e. the more $b$ must exceed $c$. So there is a $cr(B)$ that *will* make Sue go iff $c/b<f_\infty(B^*)$, and this is the $cr(B)$ she *should* have if her evidence is $f_\infty(B^*)$. The problem is to show that this $cr(B)=f_\infty(B^*)$, and to solve that problem we need some subjective decision theory.

First, consider Sue's valuations of the following states of affairs: she visits the Bull and gets her gin (V&G), she visits and gets no gin (V&~G), she gets gin without visiting (~V&G), and she neither visits nor gets gin (~V&~G). Now we can simplify what follows without begging any relevant questions by setting Sue's valuation of the status quo, ~V&~G, to zero. This lets $b$ and $c$ fix her other valuations as follows: $v(V\&G)=b-c$, $v(V\&\sim G)=-c$ and $v(\sim V\&G)=b$, as shown in the *valuation matrix* below (Figure 3).

| Valuations | G | ~G |
|:---:|:---:|:---:|
| V | $b$-$c$ | $-c$ |
| ~V | $b$ | $0$ |

Figure 3: Valuation matrix

Next, suppose that Sue knows in advance how strongly she will believe that she will get her gin, i.e. what her credence $cr(G)$ will be, (i) if she visits the Bull (V), and (ii) if she does not (~V). These credences, by analogy with $ch_C(E)$ and $ch_{\sim C}(E)$, I shall write '$cr_V(G)$' and '$cr_{\sim V}(G)$'. Sue's corresponding degrees of belief that she will not get her gin are of course 1 minus these: $cr_V(\sim G)=1-cr_V(G)$ and $cr_{\sim V}(\sim G)=1-cr_{\sim V}(G)$.

What are the values of these four credences? Well, since Sue knows that she has no gin at home, $cr_{\sim V}(G)=0$ and $cr_{\sim V}(\sim G)=1$. Moreover on obvious assumptions – e.g. that she can afford the gin and the Bull will sell it to her – $cr_V(G)$ equals $cr(B)$, Sue's credence that the Bull has gin to sell. All this is shown in the *credence matrix* below (Figure 4).

| Credence in | G | ~G |
|:---:|:---:|:---:|
| if V | $cr(B)$ | $1$-$cr(B)$ |
| if ~V | $0$ | $1$ |

Figure 4: Credence matrix

We can now define what are usually called 'subjective expected utilities' but which I shall call *expected valuations* or, for short, *e-valuations*. Sue's e-valuation of visiting the Bull, which I shall write '$ev(V)$', is an average of her valuations of V&G and V&~G, weighted respectively by $cr_V(G)$ and $cr_V(\sim G)$, i.e. by how strongly she will believe, if she visits the Bull, that she will and that she won't get her gin. Similarly for $ev(\sim V)$. In symbols:

(13)  $ev(V) = cr_V(G)\times v(V\&G) + cr_V(\sim G)\times v(V\&\sim G)$;
(13~) $ev(\sim V) = cr_{\sim V}(G)\times v(\sim V\&G) + cr_{\sim V}(\sim G)\times v(\sim V\&\sim G)$.

Finally, we need a principle of subjective decision theory, usually called the principle of 'maximising subjective expected utility' but which I shall call the *expected valuation principle*. This says that if Sue is sensible she will do whichever of V or ~V she e-valuates more highly. So it says that she will visit the Bull if $ev(V)>ev(\sim V)$ and stay at home if $ev(\sim V)>ev(V)$. If $ev(\sim V)=ev(V)$ it says nothing, thus letting us assume, as before, that she stays home, i.e. that she visits the Bull iff $ev(V)>ev(\sim V)$.

The expected valuation principle is indeed contentious, but no more so than credences, which we can take for granted [3.2], and especially here. For chances can hardly be required to meet the Evidence condition by justifying credences unless credences exist. And if they do exist, then their values must satisfy the expected valuation principle. For this principle is what defines our measures of the beliefs and desires which it relates to the actions they cause; just as our measures of Newtonian force $F$ and mass $M$ are defined by the law, that $F=MA$, which relates them to the accelerations $A$ they cause. This is why our measures $F$, $M$ and $A$ of any specific force, mass and consequent acceleration must always satisfy the equation $F=MA$. (I use small capitals '$F$', '$M$' and '$A$' to represent (measures of) specific forces, masses and accelerations, as opposed to the generic properties $F$, $M$ and $A$ of being a force, a mass or an acceleration [14.4; 16.4].)

The fact that this principle and this law define measures of the properties that occur in them does not of course make decision theory or Newtonian mechanics true of us by definition. It is still contingent that our actions are caused by beliefs and desires which conform to the expected valuation principle and so are measurable by it, just as it is contingent that accelerations are caused by forces and masses which conform to the law that $F=MA$ and so are measurable by that. But then just as masses which do conform to this law must have the measure that it defines, so credences which conform to the expected valuation principle must have the measure that it defines. (For more discussion of this parallel, see Mellor 1991 ch. 3 pt II).

This being so, (13) and (13~) can be taken as much for granted here as $F=MA$ can be in Newtonian mechanics. And then, applying (13) and (13~) to the data in Figures 3 and 4, the expected valuation principle tells us that Sue will visit the Bull iff

$$cr(B)\times(b\text{-}c) + (1\text{-}cr(B))\times(\text{-}c) > 0\times b + 1\times 0;$$

which, simplifying and generalising to any state of affairs P and any person $x$, means that

(14)   to get $b$ iff P, $x$ *will* pay $c$ iff $c/b<cr(P)$.

This is the result we need. For (12) tells us that, on evidence $f_\infty(P^*)$, to get $b$ iff P, $x$ *should* pay $c$ iff $c/b<f_\infty(P^*)$. So the $cr(P)$ that the evidence $f_\infty(P^*)$ *should* give $x$ is the $cr(P)$ that *will* make $x$ pay $c$ iff $c/b<f_\infty(P^*)$. And this credence, (14) tells us, is $cr(P)=f_\infty(P^*)$. In other words, the property

that meets the Frequency condition also meets the Evidence condition. This is what ensures that the three conditions which we require chance to meet can all be met by a single property.

## 3  What chance is

So far so good. But it may still seem to leave unanswered the question of what chance is. For what, we may still ask, *is* the property $ch(\mathrm{P})=p$ which (i) if $p=1$ entails P, (ii) if it is my evidence about P justifies my having $cr(\mathrm{P})=p$ and (iii) entails $f_\infty(\mathrm{P}^*)=p$? Showing that a single property can meet these three conditions does not seem to tell us what that property, if it exists, is. And if it does not tell us this, then the fact that chances meet these conditions by definition, and hence necessarily, will not tell us either. The question will still remain: what is the property that satisfies this definition?

I maintain however that this question needs no answer. Provided some property does satisfy our conditions, then identifying chance with it does tell us what chance is. This way of defining a property is neither inadequate nor unusual. Take the property of mass. This occurs in many laws besides the law that $F=MA$: it occurs for example in the law of gravity, $F=GMM'/R^2$, that any two things of the same or different masses $M$ and $M'$ at any distance $R$ attract each other with a force $F=GMM'/R^2$, where G is a constant. Now imagine that we know not just some but all of the laws that mass occurs in. We could still ask what this property, mass, which occurs in all these laws, is. But if we did, then obviously no further answer could be given. We could only say that mass just *is* the property which occurs in the laws of motion, gravity, etc.; just as chance is the property which meets the conditions (i), (ii) and (iii). That is all there is to mass. And if that answer is good enough for mass, it is good enough for chance. If we knew not only (i)–(iii) but all the laws that chances occur in, we should know all that could be known about what chances are.

Indeed, even our present knowledge arguably tells us more about what chance is than it tells us about what mass is. For my definition of chance differs in one important respect from the definition of mass. It makes the Necessity, Evidence and Frequency conditions hold necessarily, whereas our definition of mass does not make the laws that mass occurs in hold necessarily. The reason for this is partly that the laws of motion and gravity are mutually independent, which our conditions on chance are not: i.e. neither $F=MA$ nor $F=GMM'/R^2$ entails the other, whereas (iii) entails (ii) [§2]. There may therefore be possible worlds where some of the laws in which mass occurs hold and others fail. If so, then the property of mass which our definition picks out might still exist in some of these worlds, namely those where only a few of the laws in which mass occurs in our world fail. Thus mass might well survive the loss of any one, if not of many, of the laws it occurs in, just as I might survive the loss of any one, if not of many, of my vital organs. In this way our definition of mass can allow each of the laws that mass occurs in to be contingent, unlike the conditions (i)–(iii).

But then (i)–(iii) should if anything give a better answer to the question of what chance is than Newton's laws give to the question of what mass is. For what (i)–(iii) say about chance is true in all worlds, whereas what Newton says about mass is not. Yet this does not really make us better off than Newton in this respect. For if we can still ask what the property *M* is that conforms contingently to the law that *F*=*MA*, we can also ask what the property *ch*(P) is that conforms necessarily to (i)–(iii). And the right reply in both cases is the same: namely, that if this question has an answer at all, the question already contains it.

For if '*F*=*MA*' and (i)–(iii) do not suffice to tell us what mass and chance are, nothing will. No further statement about these properties could, after all, do other than add more conditions for them to meet, either contingently or necessarily. Thus either we shall never know what mass and chance are, or we know already what they are: they are the properties which meet the conditions already given. So to accept that the Necessity, Evidence and Frequency conditions apply, whether to the coin *j*'s being tossed, to Don's falling, to Bill's smoking or to Sue's visiting her pub, just *is* to accept that the chances which these conditions define exist; just as to accept that the laws of motion and of gravity apply to terrestrial and celestial things is to accept that those things have the property, mass, which these laws define.

## 4  Chances and propensities

More of course needs saying about properties like masses and chances, and especially about how they embody causation, which they both do. Thus my mass *M* is what makes a net force *F* cause me to accelerate at *F/M*, just as Don's chance of dying if he falls is part of what makes his falling cause him to die. We cannot however discuss these matters properly until we have learned more about causation and about how it depends on chances, and hence on laws of nature. But before turning to that, and in particular to the prospects for indeterministic causation, we should note one more similarity between chances and other causal properties like mass.

For the time being we are taking $ch_C(E)$, the chance of an effect E with its cause C, to be given by

(5)    $ch_C(E) = (\imath p)(C \Rightarrow ch(E)=p)$

[2.3], where '...⇒...' symbolises a closest-world conditional [1.7]. (5) makes the facts of causation include facts of the form $C \Rightarrow ch(E)=p$, C's so-called *propensity* to yield E (Popper 1990). In this sense of 'propensity', my mass $M$ embodies an infinity of propensities, namely those of all possible net forces $F$ to accelerate me at $A=F/M$. For my having this mass makes '$F \Rightarrow ch(A=F/M)=1$' true of me for all $F$.

Chances also embody propensities in this sense, namely the propensities of actual finite reference classes to yield actual frequencies. Suppose for example that our tossed coin $j$'s chance $ch(Hj)$ of landing heads is 1/2. For two similar tosses this entails the following chances: of two heads, 1/4; of two tails, 1/4; of one each, 1/2. This means that $ch(Hj)$'s being 1/2 makes all the following closest-world conditionals true:

'$n=2 \Rightarrow ch(f(H)=0)=1/4$';
'$n=2 \Rightarrow ch(f(H)=1/2)=1/2$';
'$n=2 \Rightarrow ch(f(H)=1)=1/4$';

where '$n=2$' means there are two tosses and $f(H)$ is the frequency of heads. Similarly for any value of $ch(Hj)$ and any number of tosses. And similarly for all chances. Every chance $ch(P)$ embodies an infinity of propensities of different finite reference classes to yield various $f(P^*)$s, just as every thing with any mass $M$ embodies the infinity of propensities which different forces $F$ have to make that thing accelerate at $F/M$.

Suppose now we let the $p$ in a true '$C \Rightarrow ch(E)=p$' measure the strength of C's propensity to yield E: the greater $p$, the stronger the propensity. Then as the figures above show, $ch(Hj)=1/2$ gives even two tosses a propensity (1/2) to yield the closest $f(H)$ – 1/2 – to $ch(Hj)$ which is stronger than their propensities (1/4) to yield the other $f(H)$s, 0 and 1. And the more tosses there are, the stronger their propensities are to yield $f(H)$s that are close to $ch(H)$. This is what the laws of large numbers [3.4] show, and is why observing an actual frequency in a large reference class is usually the best way to detect the value of a chance.

This propensity of any chance to yield frequencies close to itself means indeed that, for example, tossing many coins with the same chance $ch(H)=p$ of landing heads can *cause* the actual frequency $f(H)$ of heads to be close to $p$ – thus making the inference from $f(H) \approx p$ to $ch(H) \approx p$ merely a special case of inferring a cause from its effect [6.3]. That however is another story, and assumes something I have not yet shown, namely that a cause need be neither sufficient nor necessary for its effects. But now we have seen what chances are, we can go on to see why and how this can be so, i.e. why and to what extent a cause can fail to determine its effects.

# 5 Indeterministic causation

## 1 Radioactivity

We have seen how, and in what sense, the existence of sufficient causes and the non-existence of necessary ones necessitate the existence and non-existence respectively of their effects, by giving them chances of 1 and 0. Now we know what this causal kind of necessitation is, we can see whether causation really needs it. Must causes be in this sense sufficient and necessary for their effects: is what I shall call *causal determinism* true?

Modern physics suggests that it is not. Take the decay of atoms of radio-elements [2.1]. These are radioactive isotopes of chemical elements like radium and uranium whose atoms decay when subatomic particles, such as $\alpha$ or $\beta$ particles, 'tunnel' out of their nuclei, thereby turning them into atoms of other elements. This process of decay is not deterministic [2.1]: its laws do not make any atom of a radioelement $E$ certain to decay ($D$) in any given interval of time. Instead they give each such atom $x$ in its normal state a certain chance of decaying within any subsequent time interval of length $t$ units (seconds, hours, etc.). This chance, $ch(D(x,t))$, is given by

(15)   $ch(D(x,t)) = 1-e^{-\lambda t}$,

where $e^y$ is the sum to infinity of $1 + y/1 + y^2/1 \times 2 + \ldots y^n/n! + \ldots$ for any real number $y$, and '$D(x,t)$' means that $x$ decays within $t$ units of time. $\lambda$ is a constant, $E$'s so-called *decay constant*, often re-expressed as its half life, the value of $t$ for which $ch(D(x,t))=1/2$ [2.1]. And since $e^y \approx 1+y$ when $y$ is very small, $ch(D(x,t)) \approx \lambda t$ when $t$ is very small, so that $\lambda$ is itself a chance, namely the chance, which I shall write '$ch(Dx)$', of any normal $E$ atom $x$ decaying in any sufficiently small unit time.

(15) entails that any normal $E$ atom has a finite chance of decaying, and also of not decaying, within any finite time interval. Take a sufficiently small unit interval, from $t_0$ to $t_0+1$. Then it is a fact about the nuclear structure of every $E$ atom $x$ at $t_0$ that $ch(Dx)=\lambda$, where $0<\lambda<1$ [2.1]. So one $E$ atom $h$ may decay, $Dh$, in the interval from $t_0$ to $t_0+1$ while another, $i$, does not, $\sim Di$. Since (15) gives neither $Dh$ nor $\sim Di$ a chance of 1, this

seem to entail that the causes of these facts are insufficient and thus indeterministic.

In fact this does not follow: we could simply deny that $Dh$ and $\sim Di$ have causes. For since to say that all causation is deterministic is not to say that all contingent facts have causes, we can easily reconcile causal determinism with natural radioactive decay by denying that it has any causes at all. But determinism is not so easily reconciled with what I shall call *forced* decay. Suppose that at $t_0$ we bombard the nucleus of our $E$ atom $h$ ($Bh$) with a subatomic particle. If $h$ were in its normal state its chance of decaying by $t_0+1$, $ch(Dh)$, would be $\lambda$, which we may take to be minute: say $10^{-10}$. But bombarding $h$ makes it almost certain to decay by $t_0+1$, i.e. raises $ch(Dh)$ to a value, $\lambda'$, very close to 1: say to $1\text{-}10^{-10}$. Suppose now that $h$ does decay by $t_0+1$. In these circumstances did it not do so *because* it was bombarded: is not '$Dh$ because $Bh$' true?

If so, we have a cause that is neither sufficient nor necessary for its effect. For $Bh$ to be sufficient for $Dh$, $ch_{Bh}(Dh)$, $h$'s chance of decaying if bombarded, must be 1, which it is not: it is $1\text{-}10^{-10}$. For $Bh$ to be necessary for $Dh$, $ch_{\sim Bh}(Dh)$, $h$'s chance of decaying if not bombarded must be 0, which it is not: it is $10^{-10}$. The effect has a finite chance of existing without this apparent cause and a finite chance of not existing with it.

Causal determinists must therefore deny that bombarding $h$ causes it to decay. But then they must also deny that we cause atomic bombs to explode by forcing together two masses of fissile material, such as uranium–235 ($^{235}U$). For this apparent causation also relies on indeterministic facts like those I have just cited. Take a particular thing $d$ made of $^{235}U$. When $d$'s atoms split, releasing energy, they usually emit between one and three neutrons, and we can simplify matters without begging any questions by supposing that they always emit two. These neutrons may then hit the nuclei of other $^{235}U$ atoms before leaving $d$, the mean chance of their doing so increasing of course as $d$'s mass gets larger. If they do hit other nuclei, they raise the chance that those nuclei will split, emitting more energy and two more neutrons, almost to 1. So once $d$'s mass is large enough for an emitted neutron's mean chance of hitting another nucleus to exceed $1/2$, $d$ becomes *supercritical*: the chance of a rapidly accelerating chain reaction, splitting $^{235}U$ atoms and releasing energy so fast that $d$ explodes, rises almost to 1.

This then is how atomic explosions are produced: high explosive is used to force two *subcritical* masses of fissile material together into a super-critical mass, which then explodes. But this process is not deterministic. As with the forced decay of single $E$ atoms, the chance that a supercritical mass will explode is still less than 1, and the chance that a subcritical mass will explode is greater than 0. So if causes must be sufficient and necessary for their effects, an atomic explosion cannot be caused by turning a subcritical mass of fissile material into a supercritical one. Yet that *is* how atomic explosions are caused.

## 2  Hidden variables

Determinists could however take atomic explosions, and the forced decay of $E$ atoms, to be caused by *hidden variables*: unknown differences between $E$ atoms like $h$ and $i$ that provide deterministic causes of $Dh$ and $\sim Di$. Perhaps at $t_0$ the atom $h$ has and $i$ lacks some property $C$ such that, for any $E$ atom $x$, $ch_{Cx}(Dx)=1$ and $ch_{\sim Cx}(Dx)=0$.

But is such a hidden variable consistent with (15), which says that at all times it is a fact about every $E$ atom $x$, including $h$ and $i$, that $ch(Dx)=\lambda$, where $0<\lambda<1$? How can $Dh$ have two different chances, 1 and $\lambda$, at the very same time $t_0$? Facts like $Dh$ can indeed have different chances at different times, just as people like Kim can have different temperatures at different times [2.1]. But it no more follows that $Dh$ can have two chances at $t_0$ than that Kim can have two temperatures at $t_0$, and obviously she cannot. (More precisely, even though Kim's temperature at $t_0$, say 38.2±0.05°C, can include both 38.19°C and 38.21°C [3.1], it cannot also be, say, 38.5±0.05°C or even 38.25±0.05°C.)

Yet although it does not follow, $Dh$ can in fact have two different chances at once: because chances, unlike temperatures, are not properties of the entities we apparently ascribe them to [2.1]. Kim's temperature is a property of Kim, which she can only have if and while she exists. This is why she cannot have two temperatures at once: temperatures are mutually incompatible properties of the people and things we ascribe them to. But the chance $ch(Hj)$ of a tossed coin $j$ landing heads, $Hj$, is a property not of $Hj$ but of some earlier fact about $j$. So because there are many such facts, there can be many $ch(Hj)$s, despite the mutual incompatibility that stops more than one of them being a property of the same fact. But if different $ch(Hj)$s can be properties of different facts about $j$ at different times, why can they not be properties of different facts about $j$ at the same time?

If they can, then our $E$ atom $h$ may indeed have two different $ch(Dh)$s at $t_0$. $ch(Dh)=\lambda$ will be a property of a conjunction of facts about $h$'s nuclear structure at $t_0$ which it shares with $i$: call this conjunctive fact '$Eh$'. $ch(Dh)=1$ will be a property of a larger conjunction, including the fact that, at $t_0$, $h$ has the property $C$ which $i$ lacks. Although this larger fact need not include every conjunct of $Eh$ it will be simpler and beg no relevant questions to suppose that it does, i.e. that $ch(Dh)=1$ is a property of $Eh\&Ch$. Then since $Eh$ and $Eh\&Ch$ are different facts, they may well give $Dh$ different chances at $t_0$, so making the hidden variable $C$ compatible with (15).

However, to show that these chances really are compatible, we must check that they can both meet the Necessity, Evidence and Frequency conditions imposed on chance in chapter 4. These make $ch(Dh)=p$ entail: (i) if $p=1$, $Dh$; (ii) the evidential probability $P(Dh,ch(Dh)=p)=p$; (iii) the limiting frequency $f_\infty(D)=p$ in a collective of hypothetical $E$ atoms $x$ such that $ch(Dx)=p$. Let us take these entailments in turn.

(i) The Necessity condition obviously presents no problem: $ch(Dh)=1$ can obviously entail $Dh$ without $ch(Dh)=\lambda$ doing so, just as $Eh\&Ch$ can entail $Ch$ without $Eh$ doing so.

(ii) It is less obvious that the Evidence condition presents no problem, because the concept of evidence is less clear than that of entailment. In particular, it is hard to say what it takes to make a fact Q 'my evidence' about a hypothesis P [3.3]. That issue we can however continue to evade, since we shall only need two innocuous assumptions about it. The first is that if my evidence Q about P entails P, it justifies $cr(P)=1$. This in turn entails that adding more evidence R to Q cannot justify any other $cr(P)$, since if Q entails P, so must Q&R. The second assumption is that with this exception (and its counterpart when Q entails ~P), extra evidence may always justify a new $cr(P)$. In short, the evidential probability $P(P,Q\&R)$ need not equal $P(P,Q)$ unless Q entails P, ~P or R.

Let us now apply these assumptions to the present case. Since the evidence $ch(Dh)=1$ entails $Dh$ and so justifies $cr(Dh)=1$, no extra evidence can justify any other $cr(Dh)$. In particular, the evidence that $ch(Dh)=\lambda$ cannot do so. But this just means that if my evidence includes both of these chances then my $cr(Dh)$ should be 1, as it obviously should. The evidence $ch(Dh)=\lambda$ on its own can still justify $cr(Dh)=\lambda$, as the Evidence condition requires.

(iii) The Frequency condition makes $ch(Dh)=1$ and $ch(Dh)=\lambda$ define collectives of hypothetical $E$ atoms with limiting frequencies $f_\infty(D)=1$ and $f_\infty(D)=\lambda$ respectively. Can they do so? Obviously not if these collectives are the same: no one collective can have two different $f_\infty(D)$s. But they are not the same. All the atoms in the first collective must be $C$, since only $C$ atoms have the property $ch(Dh)=1$ that entails $f_\infty(D)=1$. The second also contains $\sim C$ atoms, since they too share the property $ch(Dh)=\lambda$ that entails $f_\infty(D)=\lambda$. Indeed, since all and only $\sim C$ atoms fail to decay, the second collective must also have a limiting frequency $f_\infty(C)=\lambda$ of $C$ atoms.

This raises a question, because it seems to require all $E$ atoms at $t_0$ to have a chance $\lambda$ of being $C$ at $t_0$. Yet I have said that for all P, a $ch(P)$ is always a property of a fact that precedes P. This indeed, although I have not yet shown it, is entailed by what makes causes precede their effects [17]. It cannot therefore be a property of facts about $h$ at $t_0$ that $h$ has a chance $\lambda$ of being $C$ at $t_0$. How then can we reconcile $h$'s two chances of decaying between $t_0$ and $t_0+1$?

The answer to this question starts from the fact that time is *dense*, i.e. that between any two times there is a third. There is thus no first instant of time after $t_0$ and no last instant before $t_0+1$. Nevertheless, we can still distinguish the so-called *closed* interval $[t_0,t_0+1]$ that includes both $t_0$ and $t_0+1$ from the so-called *open* interval $(t_0,t_0+1)$ that includes neither. More to the present point, we can distinguish two *half open* intervals: $[t_0,t_0+1)$, which includes $t_0$ but not $t_0+1$, and $(t_0,t_0+1]$, which includes $t_0+1$ but not $t_0$. And even though both these intervals are defined by the same times, $t_0$ and $t_0+1$, and both have the same temporal measure – 1 unit (hour, second, etc.) – $[t_0,t_0+1)$ is obviously earlier than $(t_0,t_0+1]$.

Next we must note that our atom $h$'s chance $\lambda$ of decaying between $t_0$ and $t_0+1$ is a property of its being $E$ not just at $t_0$ but for as much of this interval as it *is* $E$. But this makes the fact $Dh$ whose chance is $\lambda$ seem simultaneous with the fact $Eh$ of which $\lambda$ is a property: both span the same interval from $t_0$ to when $h$ decays (or to $t_0+1$ if that is earlier). So to make $Eh$ precede $Dh$ we must distinguish our two half open intervals and say that $h$'s being $E$ for as much of $[t_0,t_0+1)$ as $h$ *is* $E$ is what gives $h$ its chance $\lambda$ of decaying in the later $(t_0,t_0+1]$. Then it will also be what gives $h$ its chance $\lambda$ of being $C$ – and hence $E\&C$ – for as much of $(t_0,t_0+1]$ as $h$ is $E$.

So far so good: the facts $Dh$ and $Ch$ that have these chances $\lambda$ are later than the fact $Eh$ that these chances are properties of. But we are not home yet. For $h$ must get its chance 1 of decaying in $(t_0,t_0+1]$ not from $h$'s being $E\&C$ in $(t_0,t_0+1]$ but in the earlier $[t_0,t_0+1)$. We must show therefore that $h$'s chances of being $C$ in these two intervals are the same. And so they are, because they differ only in which of the instants $t_0$ and $t_0+1$ they contain. But $h$'s chance of decaying precisely at $t_0$ or at $t_0+1$ is zero: for since (15) makes $ch(D(x,t))=0$ when $t=0$, no $E$ atom can decay precisely at any instant [3.1]. The atom $h$'s chances of decaying in $[t_0,t_0+1)$ and $(t_0,t_0+1]$ are therefore always the same, and so therefore are $h$'s chances of being $C$ for as much of these intervals as it is $E$. So fixing either chance automatically fixes the other. This is how $h$'s being $E$ for any interval $[t_0,t_0+1)$ can give $h$ the simultaneous chance $\lambda$ of being $C$ that we need, by giving it a chance $\lambda$ of being $C$ for the later $(t_0,t_0+1]$.

## 3  The irrelevance of hidden variables

So the conditions we require chances to meet do let a radioactive atom have two simultaneous chances of decaying in a given time. A hidden variable could therefore, consistently with (15), provide deterministic causes of radioactive decay. However, unfortunately for causal determinists, no such variable has been shown to exist and many physicists think none does exist.

Determinists might then conclude that even the forced decays of radioactive atoms, and hence atomic explosions, have no causes at all. This conclusion is incredible enough to make a strong case for letting causation be indeterministic. But an even stronger case can be made, namely that many effects which do have deterministic causes also have indeterministic ones. For no deterministic cause of an effect E can explain E's apparent causation by a C which does *not* determine it. Thus a hidden cause *Ch* of a bombarded atom *h*'s decay will not make *bombarding h* cause it to decay. Yet this is what it needs to do. For what our examples suggest is not just that a fact E has *some* cause, but that E's causes include the fact C that we bring about in order to make E a fact. But if C does not already determine E, no other deterministic causes of E can make C determine it.

The existence of hidden variables is, in short, irrelevant: apparent cases of indeterministic causation are as persuasive with them as without them. Take Bill's smoking causing him to get cancer. So far, for the sake of argument, I have taken this cause to determine this effect, which of course it does not. Bill's chance of getting cancer is greater if he smokes than if he does not, but it is still less than 1; and it would still be greater than 0 if he did not smoke. Must we then deny that Bill gets cancer because he smokes? Surely not. Yet with or without hidden variables his smoking can only cause him to get cancer if causes need not determine their effects.

To see this, suppose there *are* hidden variables here: suppose there are always relevant metabolic differences between smokers who get cancer and smokers who do not; and similarly for non-smokers. Let us grant then that, unlike an atomic explosion, Bill's getting cancer in an interval $(t_0,t_1]$ has a deterministic cause: namely, his having during $[t_0,t_1)$ a metabolic property C such that, if he smokes during $[t_0,t_1)$, his chance of getting cancer in $(t_0,t_1]$ is 1 if he is C during $[t_0,t_1)$ and 0 if he is not.

But some indeterministic causation is still needed here, as we can see by asking what causes Bill to be C. First, if causation must be deterministic, it cannot be the fact that he smokes. For as with radioactivity, if Bill's being C is a deterministic cause of his getting cancer, then his chances of being C during $[t_0,t_1)$ and of getting cancer in $(t_0,t_1]$ must be the same. So if the latter is less than 1 if he smokes and greater than 0 if he does not, so also must the former be. Indeterminism in the causation of his cancer by his smoking reappears as indeterminism in the causation of its deterministic cause, or of the deterministic cause of that cause, or … and so on.

However, although Bill's smoking may cause him indeterministically to get cancer by causing the deterministic causes of his getting it, it need not. For smoking *could* correlate with cancer not by causing it *via* causing $C$ but by being a side effect of $C$. But this hypothesis, while attractive to tobacco firms, is useless to a causal determinist, since it too demands some indeterministic causation. For if Bill's being $C$ caused him to smoke and to get cancer deterministically, then his chances of getting cancer would have to be 1 if he smoked and 0 if he did not, which by hypothesis they are not.

In short, causal determinists can no more explain the appearance of causal indeterminism here than they can in the case of atomic explosions. Causation can only link Bill's smoking directly or indirectly to his getting cancer if some of the causation involved is indeterministic. So if causation must be deterministic, much apparent causation, with or without hidden variables, must be illusory. Is it?

## 4  The connotations of causation

It takes more than plausible cases to show that causation can be indeterministic. For as intuitions about cases can be as contentious as the theses they are used to support, determined determinists may simply deny that these really are cases of indeterministic causation. They may insist in the nuclear case that there *must* be hidden variables because, like Einstein, they cannot believe that God plays dice. Or they may insist that without such variables there can be no causation, since it is part of our concept of causation that causes determine their effects.

Neither side can rest here. Determinists must say what they think we mean by our talk of causing atomic explosions, or of smoking causing cancer, when we think these causes do not determine their effects. Their opponents must say why, if causation does not entail determinism, it seems to – and what it does entail instead. One way or the other these apparent cases of indeterministic causation must be explained or explained away. But which is it to be? To answer that question we need to ask why we apply our concept of causation as we do. To reverse an old and overrated adage, we must ask not just for the use of terms like 'cause' and 'effect' but for the point of their use, i.e. for what we mean by them. What, in other words, do we take to follow from saying or denying that one fact or particular causes another: what are the connotations of causation?

Putting the question like this does not commit me to what Strawson (1959) has called *descriptive* metaphysics. I am not, as he puts it (p. 9), 'content to describe the actual structure of our thought about the world'. It is not safe to constrain our metaphysics by the structure of 'our thought', as enshrined in everyday speech, since much of that is demonstrably false.

The metaphysics of time yields several examples of this, one of which I gave in the Introduction. Another is the assumption that whether a celestial event is happening *now* is always a matter of fact, an assumption which the special theory of relativity shows to be false (Reichenbach 1928 §§19–20). It may matter to semantics that much of our thought still presupposes a spatially unrestricted concept of simultaneity. It does not matter to metaphysics. What matters there is that this is a mistake which can be and has been corrected. And the question whose answer does not matter at all is whether the concept with which the special theory of relativity has replaced classical simultaneity is similar enough to deserve the same name.

So it is with causation. Much of our thought may well presuppose that causes determine their effects. Yet, given the evidence, we also think that smoking causes cancer and that we cause atomic explosions. But as we have seen, given what we now know about the relevant metabolic and subatomic processes, these thoughts cannot all be true. Something must give: no metaphysics of causation can rescue all our thought about it.

What then should we say? If our indeterministic cases lacked most of causation's other connotations (as we shall see shortly that 'C causes C' does) we should of course say that these are not cases of causation. But in fact we should say no such thing, since nearly all causation's connotations survive in these cases [§5–7; 7]. Only determinism goes, and even then it remains as an ideal special case [8]. The concept we need to replace deterministic causation with is thus obviously similar enough to it to deserve the name 'causation', which is why I shall call it that. But even if it were not, that would not matter. All that matters is seeing how, and how far, the other connotations of causation can survive the loss of determinism.

To see this we need not examine all causation's connotations, since many of them stay too close to home to tell us much. Anscombe (1971), for example, says that 'causality consists in the derivativeness of an effect from its causes' (p. 67), which she says does not entail determinism. Maybe not: but to show how and when effects can 'derive' from causes that do not determine them we need an independent account of 'derivativeness', which we lack. Salmon (1984) similarly defines causation in terms of 'the two basic concepts of *propagation* and *production*' (p. 139). But in his examples (e.g. 'the electrical discharge produces a fire') 'produces' is just a synonym for 'causes', to which 'propagates' merely adds the truism that effects can be caused by causing their causes, i.e. that causation is not intransitive. This tells us nothing, because no constraint on indeterministic causation needs to make it intransitive in the first place.

It has been said (e.g. by Taylor 1966 p. 39) that causation's connotations are all too close to home for it to be analysed in non-causal terms.

Fortunately this is not true. Causation has several obvious connotations that will serve our turn. Here are four.

Temporal: causes generally *precede* their effects.
Contiguity: causes are *contiguous* to their immediate effects.
Evidential: causes and effects are *evidence* for each other.
Explanatory: causes *explain* their effects.

All these connotations link causation to very different concepts, and they all need accounting for. The first two require our theories of causation, time and space to say between them why causes precede and are contiguous to their immediate effects. (An immediate effect of a cause C is an E such that C causes E but not by causing any D that causes E.) Similarly for causation's other connotations. Our theory of causation must combine with our theories of evidence and explanation to say what makes causes and effects evidence for each other and how causes explain their effects.

These connotations do therefore constrain causation: for example, by ruling out self-causation [1.6]. The reason nothing can cause itself is that nothing can precede, be evidence for or explain itself. Nor can anything be the means to itself that, as we shall see later, causes must be to their effects [7]. What makes 'C causes C' false for all C is the fact that 'C causes E' loses almost all its connotations when E=C.

Causation's connotations also constrain time, evidence and explanation. But those constraints I shall not discuss, apart from those on time [17]. Causation is my business here, not evidence or explanation. About them I need only assume enough to show why their links with causation do not require causes to determine their effects. That is the task of this chapter. In the next, we shall see what causation's connotations do require the chances of effects to be.

It is obvious that none of causation's connotations entails determinism. No one will deny that a cause can precede and be contiguous to effects for which it is neither sufficient nor necessary; nor will anyone deny that it can be evidence for them and they for it. None of the many conflicting theories of evidence requires it to be either conclusive (sufficient) or exclusive (necessary), let alone both. No one for example thinks that statistical evidence must be the only evidence that a drug is safe, nor that such evidence must leave no chance of error. Similarly, statistical explanations of the roughly equal numbers of male and female births can obviously fail to be either sufficient or necessary for what they explain.

If it is easy to see *that* our connotations let causation be indeterministic, it is less easy to say *why* they do so. But we must see why if we are to see how causation's connotations do constrain the chances of effects. For this is not at all obvious. It is not for example obvious that causation's temporal and contiguity connotations depend on effects having chances. Yet they do, as we shall see [17.4–5], which is why I have listed them here. But I cannot invoke them here, since they too are contentious. Just as the cases in §1 persuade me that a cause need not determine its effects, so other cases persuade others that it need not always precede nor – when they are immediate effects – be contiguous to them.

In fact every cause must do both these things, but only because its effects must have chances with and without it. So to derive our constraint on causation from the assumption that causes precede or are contiguous to their immediate effects would beg the question. We must go the other way round, deriving causation's temporal and contiguity connotations from constraints derived from other, less contentious, connotations. But first we must see why these do not entail determinism. Let us take them in turn.

## 5 Evidence

That causes and effects are evidence for each other is a long-standing and uncontentious connotation of causation. Hume (1748) thought that

> all reasonings concerning matter of fact seem to be founded on the relation of *Cause and Effect*. By means of that relation alone we can go beyond the evidence of our memory and senses (§22).

This may be too strong: some evidence for matters of fact may not be founded on causation. But obviously most of it is. And certainly causes generally do provide at least some evidence for their effects. For example, if Don dies because he falls, his falling as he does must give some reason to fear that he will die. Effects likewise generally provide evidence for their causes: Bill's getting cancer is some evidence that he is a smoker. And effects of common causes provide evidence for each other: thus 'heat and light are collateral effects of fire, and the one effect may justly be inferred from the other' (Hume 1748 §22).

That causation generates evidence in these three ways is obvious enough. It is also fairly obvious that the strength of this evidence could be measured by the probabilities which causes and effects give each other. These are the evidential probabilities $P(P,Q)$ that are measured by the credence $cr(P)$ which I ought to have in P if Q is my evidence about P [3.3]. They raise many questions [§2], but again we only need two innocuous assumptions about them.

The first is the Evidence condition [3.3], that for all P and $p$,

(10)   $ch(P)=p$ entails $P(P,ch(P)=p)=p$.

Take the chances of radioactive decay [§1]. The half life of radium's most stable form, $^{226}$Ra, is 1622 years: i.e. the chance of any normal $^{226}$Ra atom $x$ decaying in that time is 1/2. So on this evidence the evidential probability that $x$ *will* decay in the next 1622 years is also 1/2.

This if anything is what makes a cause C evidence for an effect E: the chance $ch_C(E)=p$ which C gives E entails that $P(E,C\&ch_C(E)=p)=p$. Of course more needs saying about how this entailment can make C itself evidence for E [3.3]. But the Evidence condition at least makes $P(E,C)$'s dependence on $ch_C(E)$ fairly obvious and straightforward.

It is however far less obvious how chances can make E evidence for C, or two effects E and E′ of a common cause C evidence for each other. The problem here is that E and E′ do not give C, or each other, whatever chances they may have. Don's dying is not what gave his falling whatever chance it has, and the light of a fire is not what gives the fire its chance of giving off heat. Yet it is as obvious that the evidential probabilities $P(C,E)$, $P(E,E')$ and $P(E',E)$ exist as it is that $P(E,C)$ does, and indeed the evidence of our senses depends on them [6.3].

But this is no excuse for postulating chances to correspond *via* (10) to all these evidential probabilities. The distinction between chance and evidential probability is fundamental, and failure to draw it only generates nonsense, such as the so-called *anthropic principle* (Leslie 1989). This principle exploits our knowledge that the laws and initial conditions of our world have led to us, i.e. that, given us, the evidential probability of their not doing so is 0. But from this tautology anthropicists infer that our world's laws and initial conditions had a zero *chance* of not leading to us, thus making our existence probable in a sense that calls for teleological explanation. This is absurd: it is like inferring, from seeing clearly that a coin lands on edge (evidential probability 1), that it had no chance of doing otherwise (chance 1)!

In short, even if $P(C,E)$ and $P(E,E')$ always depend on chances, as I believe they do, they must do so in a far less obvious and straightforward way than $P(E,C)$ does. Just how they do so is however a question we can leave until later [6.3], since the connection which (10) entails between the chance and the evidential probability that C gives E is enough to show how causation can be indeterministic, as follows.

First we must note that the truth of 'E because C' cannot make C and E evidence for each other just by entailing 'C&E'. When I see Don fall and infer that he will die, I am not making the trivial inference from 'Don dies because he falls' to 'Don dies': I am inferring 'Don dies' from 'Don falls'. How can the fact that Don dies because he falls make this what Hume would have called a 'just' inference?

The short answer is that it cannot, since the inference would be equally just if Don did not die. His falling is evidence that he will die even if he lives: we often have evidence for the truth of predictions that turn out to be false. But if Don does not die, he cannot die because he falls: so that cannot be what makes his falling evidence for his dying. What makes it evidence must be something which does not entail that he dies. What can it be?

It cannot be the fact that *if* Don falls he dies, since the material conditional 'Don falls ⊃ Don dies', the strict 'Don falls ⊰ Don dies' and the closest-world 'Don falls ⇒ Don dies' all satisfy *modus ponens* [1.7]: they all conjoin with 'Don falls' to entail 'Don dies'. So if Don falls but does not die, all these conditionals are false. And if 'Don falls ⇒ Don dies' is false then so, by the Necessity condition, is 'Don falls ⇒ $ch$(Don dies)=1': since $ch$(E)=1 must entail E if 'C⇒$ch$(E)=1' is to express C's sufficiency for E [3.1]. In short, Don's falling cannot be sufficient for his dying if he falls and lives. But it can still be evidence for it. So a cause need not be sufficient for its effects to be evidence for them.

Causation's evidential connotation thus cannot entail causal determinism. But the chance that C gives E may still be what makes C evidence for E, since conditionals like 'Don falls ⇒ $ch$(Don dies)=$p$' can be true even if Don falls and lives, provided $p<1$. Yet it may still be that not any $p<1$ will do: that causation's evidential connotation limits the chances that causes can give their effects. And so it does, as we shall see. But first we must see why causation's explanatory connotation also fails to entail determinism.

## 6  Explanation

It is an obvious connotation of causation that causes explain their effects – but not *vice versa*. To see what this implies, we must choose between two ways of putting it. Hempel's classic (1965) account treats an explanation as a statement giving 'an answer to a why-question' (p. 334). Put this way, it is not causes that explain their effects but rather statements of causes that explain statements of their effects. A true 'E because C' gives a causal explanation not of E but of what Hempel calls the *explanandum* statement 'E', the explanation being not C but the *explanans* statement 'C'.

I put the matter in terms not of statements but of facts, which comes to the same thing provided *explananda* and *explanantia* must be true. And so they must, since the relevant why-question is 'why did Don die?', not 'why "Don dies"?' It is the fact that Don dies, not the statement 'Don dies', that needs explaining. No one who thinks that 'Don dies' is false will think that what this statement says, as opposed to the fact that someone says it, either requires or admits of explanation.

As for *explananda*, so for *explanantia*. No one who thinks that the statement 'Don falls' is false, i.e. that Don does not fall, will take this statement to explain anything. It is not 'Don falls' but the fact that Don falls which explains the fact that he dies. The mere content of a statement, as opposed to the fact that it is true, explains nothing.

Thus to satisfy its explanatory connotation, 'E because C' must entail 'C' and 'E', as it does [1.3]: no one denies this. Nor does anyone really deny that, put in terms of facts, causes do explain their effects. The explanatory connotation only seems to be denied by those who, like Davidson (1980 Essay 7), take causes and effects to be particulars, i.e. entities that correspond not to truths like 'Don falls' and 'Don dies' but to referring terms like 'Don's fall' and 'Don's death'. And here I agree. It takes more than a referring term to be an *explanans* or an *explanandum*: it takes a true sentence. This indeed implies that particular events like Don's fall and Don's death, while they may be causes and effects, can neither be nor have explanations. But facts about them can, including the facts that these particulars exist [1.2]. We can still say therefore that Don's fall explains Don's death, meaning by this that his death exists because his fall does.

Read like this, no one denies causation's explanatory connotation. Even Davidson takes the causal 'because' to be 'best expressed by the words "causally explains"' (1980 Essay 7 p. 162). We can all agree that the causing of one fact by another satisfies the explanatory connotation.

We can also all agree that indeterministic causation can satisfy this connotation. No account of explanation and its link with causation requires causal explanations to be deterministic. Only one, the so-called 'deductive-nomological' or 'DN' account of Hempel (1965 §2), even comes close to doing so. Since it is also the best known and best articulated account, this is the one I will discuss. Showing how even Hempel can admit indeterministic causal explanations should suffice to make my case.

Hempel takes singular causes and effects to be particulars, not facts. On the other hand, he does constrain causal links between facts by requiring causally linked particulars to instantiate deterministic laws, as follows:

> The law tacitly implied by the assertion that *b* [Don's death], as an event of kind *B* [a death], was caused by *a* [Don's fall] as an event of kind *A* [a fall] is a general statement of causal connection to the effect that, under suitable circumstances, an instance of *A* is invariably accompanied by an instance of *B* (p. 349).

Thus for Don's fall to cause Don's death, the circumstances S – his being brittle-boned, fifteen metres above rocks, etc. – must be 'suitable', i.e. be of a kind S* such that it is a law that falls in S* circumstances are invariably accompanied by deaths.

The trouble here lies in the phrase 'invariably accompanied'. For only a chance 1 of $B$ events accompanying $A$ events will make them accompany $A$ events invariably. The phrase thus implies that for $a$ to cause $b$, the law N which they instantiate must be deterministic. That is, N must make the existence of an $A$ event in any S* circumstances sufficient for there to be a $B$ event, i.e. it must make 'there is an $A$ event $\Rightarrow$ $ch$(there is a $B$ event)=1' true.

And as for the existence of particular events, so for causes and effects generally. Hempel's account of causal explanation makes 'E because C' require causes to be sufficient for their effects. But not necessary in the without-which-not sense: his account says nothing about E's chances *without* C. However, if Hempel's idea of causation is weaker in this respect than our deterministic one [2.4], his idea of explanation is stronger. For a DN explanation is, as its full name implies, deductive: it entails what it explains. But causes rarely if ever entail their effects [1.6]. In particular, if the relevant law N is contingent, the effect, Don's dying, will not be entailed even by its total cause – Don's falling fifteen metres onto rocks, with brittle bones, etc. – let alone by his simply falling. So his falling cannot by itself provide a DN explanation of his dying: what does that is the combination of the total cause of his dying with the law N that makes it the total cause.

Hempel's deductive condition seems then to stop most if not all causes satisfying causation's explanatory connotation. But this is not so. For by making 'Don dies because he falls' entail the existence of a deterministic law linking this cause and effect, Hempel makes it entail that some such explanation, including Don's falling, exists. And this provides a clear and far more credible derivative sense of 'explain' in which Don's falling does explain his dying: by making 'Don dies because he falls' entail that there is a law which makes his falling sufficient for his dying.

Hempel's account can thus accommodate a non-deductive sense in which sufficient causes do explain their effects. And so it should, since no one thinks that all explanations are deductive. Even Hempel (1965 §3) admits what he calls 'inductive–statistical' explanations, with indeterministic laws, which explain facts they do not entail by giving them chances less than 1. And even if Hempel himself will not let *causes* give their effects chances less than 1, we can do so; and if we do, we can then let those causes explain their effects in some such probabilistic way.

To say all this is not to endorse Hempel's own account of probabilistic explanation, which is highly contentious. What is not now contentious is that explanation can be probabilistic, i.e. that it can give what it explains a probability less than 1. So no one now thinks that causation's explanatory connotation requires causes even to be sufficient for their effects, let alone necessary.

## 7  Conclusion

We have seen that four at least of causation's major connotations can survive causal indeterminism. A cause which does not determine its effects can still be evidence for them, and they for it and for each other. It can also precede, be contiguous to and explain them. Nothing about time, space, evidence or explanation need deprive indeterministic causation of any of its temporal, contiguity, evidential and explanatory connotations. Our apparent cases of indeterministic causation may indeed be as causal as they seem to be.

So far so good; but not good enough. Causation's connotations may survive some indeterminism; but they may still constrain the chances that causes can give their effects; and they do. In the next chapter we shall see how and why causation's evidential and explanatory connotations require them to do so. But that will not be the end of it. For on the one hand the constraint which these connotations impose is contentious, as are some of the assumptions I must make about evidence and explanation to derive it. Yet on the other hand the same constraint is entailed by an even more basic connotation, namely that, when effects are ends, their causes are means to them. I have left this connotation until last because it needs a chapter to itself [7], where I shall clinch my case by showing that it constrains effects' chances just as causation's evidential and explanatory connotations do. But first we must see what that constraint is: what the chances of effects must be, and why, if their causes are to be evidence for, and to explain, them.

# 6   *Raising the chances of effects*

## 1   The limits of indeterminism

I shall argue in this chapter and the next that causation's connotations require every cause to raise the chances of its effects. But what does this mean? It must not mean that causes must *cause* their effects' chances to be higher than they would otherwise be. Whether my account of causation makes causes do this I shall leave readers to find out for themselves; but even if it does, that will just be another case of causation, which can hardly tell us what it takes for one fact or particular to cause another.

What I mean by a cause C raising the chance of an effect E is this: E's chance in the relevant circumstances S with C, $ch_C(E)$, is greater than its chance without C, $ch_{\sim C}(E)$. In symbols,

(16)   $ch_C(E) > ch_{\sim C}(E)$,

where for the time being we may equate $ch_C(E)$ with $(\imath p)(C \Rightarrow ch(E)=p)$ and $ch_{\sim C}(E)$ with $(\imath p')(\sim C \Rightarrow ch(E)=p')$ [2.3].

Our question therefore now becomes: why do causation's connotations require it to entail (16)? But before tackling this question, I must deal with some apparent counter-examples to (16): that is, apparent cases of causes which fail to raise the chances of their effects (Salmon 1984 pp. 192–202). Suppose for example that Sue, leaving the Bull to play golf, pulls her first drive to the left, thus making her ball bounce off a tree and, by a fluke, into the hole, giving her a hole in one. So her pulled drive causes her to hole out in one, even though she would have had a greater chance of doing so had she not pulled her drive. Does this not show that causes need not raise the chances of their effects?

No: and we can see why not by recalling the distinction between particular and factual causes [1.2]. Just as we distinguish the particular event, Don's fall, from the fact that he falls, so we must distinguish the particular event, Sue's drive *d*, from the fact D that she drives the ball. Then it is indeed true that Sue holes out, H, because she drives the ball, D. But this is not a counter-example to (16), because D does raise H's chance, since if Sue had not driven the ball at all, her chance of holing out, $ch(H)$, would have been zero. And from the fact that D causes H it follows, as we shall see [11.3], that Sue's drive *d* causes the particular event *h* that is her holing out. What does not follow, and I say is false, is that she holes out because she *pulls* her drive, P. I say she holes out despite that fact, not because of it: although 'H because D' is true, 'H because P' is false, because P lowers H's chance.

Other apparent counter-examples to (16) can all be disposed of in much the same way. But does it not beg the question to invoke (16), as I have just done, in order to reject an apparent counter-example to it? Not necessarily. (16) does after all admit the two obvious causal facts in this case: that Sue holes out because she drives the ball, and also that she holes out because the ball hits the tree, without which her chance of holing out would again have been zero. All (16) denies is that Sue holes out because she pulls her drive, a claim which, when distinguished from these others, is by no means obviously true.

To this opponents of (16) may retort that the claim *is* obviously true, or is at least not obviously false. If so, then at the level of intuitions about cases, we shall reach a stand-off, no doubt because our intuitions are affected by the theories we use them to support. Intuitions about cases can therefore no more settle this question than they could settle the question of whether causation can be indeterministic [5.4]. What settled that is the fact that none of causation's major connotations entails determinism [5]; and what will settle this is the fact that, as we shall see in this chapter and the next, three of them do entail (16). This is what really shows that Sue's pulling her drive does not cause her to hole out, and hence that any intuition that it does is wrong.

## 2  Causes as evidence

Let us start with causation's evidential connotation, that a cause is evidence for its effects, as they are for it and for each other [5.5]. The first and simplest of these three requirements, that causes must be evidence for their effects, is enough to show, as follows, that they must raise their effects' chances.

We saw in the last chapter that a cause C need not determine an effect E in order to be evidence for it. E's chances in the circumstances may be less than 1 with C and more than 0 without C. The question now is this: how much can $ch_C(E)$ and $ch_{\sim C}(E)$ differ from 1 and 0 respectively before C ceases to be evidence for E?

There is an obvious answer to this question, which conflicts with (16): namely, that causes must make their effects probable. There is moreover an obvious argument for this answer, which suggests that, for C to be evidence for E, $ch_C(E)$ must be greater than 1/2. The argument runs as follows. First, C will be evidence *for* E rather than *against* it iff C is better evidence for E than for ~E. Next, since $ch_C(E)$ measures the evidential probability of E given C, then the greater $ch_C(E)$ is, the greater that probability is, and hence the better evidence C is for E. Similarly, the greater $ch_C(\sim E)$ is, the better evidence C is for ~E. So C will be better evidence for E than for ~E, and thus evidence *for* E, iff $ch_C(E) > ch_C(\sim E)$, i.e. iff $ch_C(E) > 1/2$. To satisfy causation's evidential connotation, causes must make their effects more probable than not.

This argument may be obvious; it is also quite wrong. To see why, we must recall that $ch_C(E)$ is contingent on the relevant circumstances S in which C causes E. Don's chance of dying if he falls depends for example on how he falls, being much greater than it would have been had he fallen one metre instead of fifteen. Bill's chance of getting cancer if he smokes would be much less if he did not inhale. And so on.

Next, we must note that these circumstances S on which $ch_C(E)$ depends will generally if not always include other causes of E. If Don's falling causes him to die, so – since he falls – does the brittleness of his bones. If Bill's smoking causes him to get cancer, so – since he smokes – does his inhaling. In fact most if not all effects E have several simultaneous causes, each of which is a conjunct in the conjunctive circumstances on which the efficacy of E's other causes depends. This is what prevents $ch_C(E)$ alone determining whether C is evidence for E.

It may be easier to see this in a more clear-cut case. Take the sparks that make a car's petrol engine run by causing the mixture of air and inflammable gas in its cylinders to explode in turn, thereby forcing back their pistons and thus rotating its crankshaft. Consider one cycle of one such cylinder. In the circumstances – with gas (G) and oxygen (O) – there is an explosion (E) because there is a spark (C): 'E because C' is true. But so in the circumstances – with a spark and oxygen – is 'E because G'; and so is 'E because O'. E has at least three simultaneous causes: C, G and O.

Now consider $ch_C(E)$, $ch_G(E)$ and $ch_O(E)$, the chances that E has in the relevant circumstances with C, G and O respectively. Their values, given by equation (5) [2.3], are $(\imath p)(C \Rightarrow ch(E) = p)$, $(\imath p)(G \Rightarrow ch(E) = p)$ and $(\imath p)(O \Rightarrow ch(E) = p)$. But since there *is* a spark, and gas, and oxygen, 'C', 'G' and 'O' are all true, i.e. true in our world. So the closest world to ours in which they are true is *our* world. Thus all these chances must equal E's actual chance in these circumstances [2.3], so that

$$ch_C(E) = ch_G(E) = ch_O(E) = ch(E).$$

What this shows is that $ch_C(E)$ does not in fact measure the spark's contribution to the chance of an explosion. It does indeed measure the chance of an explosion in the cylinder in the circumstances if there is a spark. But 'in the circumstances' here means 'with all the other relevant facts', including E's other simultaneous causes: the fact that the cylinder also contains gas and oxygen. So what $ch_C(E)$ really measures is the chance of an explosion with all these facts. What it measures thus has no more to do with there being a spark than with any of these other causes of the same effect. And the same goes for $ch_G(E)$ and $ch_O(E)$, which is why all three chances have the same value as the simple $ch(E)$.

What does measure how much there being a spark contributes to the chance of an explosion is the *difference* this makes to that chance, i.e. the difference between $ch_C(E)$ and $ch_{\sim C}(E)$. For if these chances were equal, the chance of an explosion would be the same whether there was a spark or not. In that case there being a spark would be evidence neither for nor against there being an explosion. While if $ch_C(E)$ were less than $ch_{\sim C}(E)$, there being a spark would lessen the chance of an explosion: C would be evidence against E. To be evidence *for* E, C must in the circumstances raise the chance of an explosion: $ch_C(E)$ must be greater than $ch_{\sim C}(E)$.

Causation's evidential connotation does therefore require a cause to raise the chances of its effects. A cause need not determine its effects by raising their chances from 0 to 1, but it must raise their chances somewhat: it must satisfy (16). No cause C that fails to do this can be evidence for an effect E, and every cause C that does do it will be some evidence for E: weak evidence perhaps, if $ch_C(E)$ is not much greater than $ch_{\sim C}(E)$, but some evidence nonetheless.

## 3 The evidence of our senses

The fact that any cause C must raise its effect E's chance to be evidence for it is enough to show that causation's evidential connotation entails (16), $ch_C(E)>ch_{\sim C}(E)$. To make this point we need not therefore analyse the more complex links between (16) and the fact that E must also be evidence for C and for C's other effects [5.5]. But there is one special case, where E is the evidence that our senses give us for C, whose connection with (16) we need to consider.

In typical cases of true perception our senses give us knowledge by making a fact C cause us to believe that C, i.e. that C is a fact: as when my eyes make snow cause me to believe it is snow, my skin makes a hot fire cause me to believe it is hot, my tongue makes beer cause me to believe it is beer, and so on. Here the effect E is that I believe C, i.e. that my credence $cr(C)\approx 1$ [3.2], which I shall write '$B(C)$'. And we may assume for simplicity that if I do *not* believe C then I believe ~C, $B(\sim C)$, i.e. that in the perceptual circumstances S my senses leave me in no doubt, one way or the other, about C.

Suppose now, again for simplicity, that in S the fact C has the same propensity $p$ to yield $B(C)$ that ~C has to yield $B(\sim C)$, as shown below in Figure 5. Thus if in S my eyes make snow give me a 0.99 chance of believing there is snow, they make whatever I would see if there were no snow give me a 0.99 chance of believing there is no snow.

| Chance in S that | $B(C)$ | $B(\sim C)$ |
|------------------|--------|-------------|
| if C | $p$ | $1-p$ |
| if ~C | $1-p$ | $p$ |

Figure 5: The chances of perception

Now let us ask how reliable my senses are in S, i.e. what chance they give me of getting a *true* belief. Obviously my belief will be true iff either C is a fact and I believe C, or ~C is a fact and I believe ~C. So my chances in S of getting a true belief about C are those of my believing C if C, and of my believing ~C if ~C, which on our assumptions are both $p$, as shown in Figure 6. So either way my chance of getting a true belief, which we may take to measure the reliability of the perceptual circumstances S, is the same: $p$.

| Chance in S that | $B$ is true | $B$ is false |
|------------------|-------------|--------------|
| if C | $p$ | $1-p$ |
| if ~C | $p$ | $1-p$ |

Figure 6: The reliability of perception

But I have assumed that, in these cases of true perception, C *causes* me to believe C, so that $B(C)$ is an effect E of C. And this, given (16), $ch_C(E) > ch_{\sim C}(E)$, requires my chance $p$ of believing C if C is a fact to be greater than my chance $1-p$ of believing C if ~C is a fact: i.e. it requires $p$ to exceed 1/2. In short, my senses can only let a fact C cause me to believe in C by giving me a greater chance of getting a true belief about C than a false one. But then the fact that the belief which my senses give me *is* $B(C)$ rather than $B(\sim C)$ is evidence that C *is* a fact, i.e. that my belief is true.

This is how the causal mechanism of my senses makes the fact that they give me a particular belief evidence that this belief is true – *if* causes must raise the chances of their effects. And the more these chances are raised, i.e. the lower the chance of my senses giving me a false belief, the more reliable my senses are and the stronger the evidence of my senses is. In the extreme case, where $p=1$ and my chance of getting a false belief is 0, my believing C rather than ~C is conclusive evidence for C; but even when $p<1$ and the evidence is not conclusive, it is still evidence, since $p>1/2$.

As for this kind of direct perception, so for what I shall call *indirect perception*, where what I see causes me to believe in a cause of what I see. Thus suppose I weigh myself on my bathroom scales. In the circumstances S (the earth's gravitational field, fairly accurate scales), the fact, B, that my mass is 73 kg – i.e. 73±0.5 kg [3.1] – causes my scales to read '73'. Call this effect 'C'. Then among C's effects is my direct perception of C: my eyes make C cause me to believe that my scales read '73'. Then the fact that I believe this, D, in turn causes me to believe that my mass is 73 kg, E. So here we have a chain of causation: B causes E – the fact that I believe B – because B causes C, C causes D and D causes E.

Indirect perception is very common not only in measurement but whenever we cannot or will not use direct perception: as when I see that it is cold outside by seeing the snow which the cold has caused instead of going outside and feeling the cold directly. The extra causal links involved in such indirect perception may of course make it more fallible than direct perception; and indeed the causation here is not transitive: the facts that B causes C, C causes D and D causes E do not *entail* that B causes E. But the causal links between them usually do make B cause E, especially if the links are nearly deterministic. And if they do make B cause E, then the fact that B must raise E's chance will again make E evidence for B. If my scales and eyes are good enough to make the fact that my mass is 73 kg cause me to believe that it is, my having this belief can be as good evidence for its own truth as if I had perceived my mass directly.

Indirect perception matters here mainly because it is how we measure chances, by directly perceiving the facts about frequencies which chances cause. We saw in chapter 4.4 how a coin $j$'s chance of landing heads, $ch(Hj)=p$, entails a propensity, to yield a fraction $f_n(H)$ of heads close to $p$ in $n$ such tosses, a propensity that strengthens rapidly with $n$. Suppose then that B is the fact that $j$ is slightly biased toward heads, say that $ch(Hj)=0.54$, i.e. 0.540±0.005. Suppose next that I toss $j$ 1000 times and see that $f_{1000}(H)$ is 0.539 and so 0.54: call this latter fact 'C'. Now suppose C causes me deterministically to believe C (D), and D in turn causes me to believe that $ch(Hj)=0.54$ (E). Then the strong propensity of any $ch(Hj)$ to yield a $f_{1000}(H)$ close to itself makes $ch(C)$, and hence $ch(D)$ and $ch(E)$, far greater if $ch(Hj)$ really *is* 0.54 (B) than if it is not – i.e. if my belief that B is a fact is true.

This makes the fact that my belief that $ch(Hj)=0.54$ is caused by my seeing that $f_{1000}(H)=0.54$ strong evidence that this belief is true, just as the fact that my belief that my mass is 73 kg is caused by my seeing my scales read '73' is strong evidence for the truth of that belief. The two cases are exactly alike: evidentially, perceptually and – if both perceptions *are* true – causally. For then, just as the fact that my mass is 73 kg causes my scales to tell me truly that my mass is 73 kg, so the fact that each of my 1000 tosses of $j$ has a 0.54 chance of landing heads causes $f_{1000}(H)$ to be 0.54, a fact which in the circumstances tells me truly that $ch(Hj)=0.54$.

## 4 Explanation and inference

So far so good. What about causation's explanatory connotation? We have seen that a cause need no more determine its effects to explain them than to be evidence for them. But the explanatory connotation, like the evidential one, may still limit the chances of effects. But how and why – and even whether – it does so are controversial questions. Some, including Hempel (1965), think an explanation must make the fact which it explains probable. Others, such as Jeffrey (1969), think an explanation can give what it explains any probability, high or low. I think they are both wrong, and for reasons that have nothing to do with causation. All explanations, whether causal or not, must raise the probabilities of what they explain; which is why, if a cause is to explain its effects as well as being evidence for them, it must raise their chances.

Why must an explanation raise the probability of what it explains? Perhaps because it must constrain that probability in whatever way evidence constrains the probability of what it is evidence for. Hempel in particular (1965) thinks it must do this, because he takes explanations to be arguments, in which the *explanandum* statement is inferred from the *explanans* statement. This is why he thinks explanations must make probable what they explain. For since the aim of inference is to deliver true conclusions, then the more probable the truth of an inference's premises makes the truth of its conclusion, the better the inference is. And this probability is obviously evidential: it measures how strongly an inference's premises, read as evidence for its conclusion, support that conclusion [3.3].

But from this equation of explanation with argument, Hempel's claim that explanations must make probable what they explain does not follow [§2]. Don's chance of dying if he falls, $ch_C(E)=p$, may be an evidential probability of E given C, and thus the probability which the premise C of the corresponding inference would give to its conclusion E. But $ch_C(E)$ is also contingent on S: Don's chance $p$ of dying if he falls depends on his being brittle-boned, falling fifteen metres onto rocks, and so on. This is why *p* does not tell us how much the truth of the premise that Don falls, as opposed to these other facts, contributes to the credibility of the inference that he will die.

Nor does it help to add these other facts to the inference as extra premises, like 'Don's bones are brittle'. This only makes it clearer that *p* depends on all these premises, and not just on the original premise that Don falls. What measures how *p* depends on that premise is how much *p* differs from the value *p'* got by replacing 'Don falls' with its negation while keeping all the other premises the same. For only if *p>p'* does the premise 'Don falls' improve the inference to 'Don dies'. But *p'* here is just Don's chance of dying in the same circumstances S if he does not fall: $ch_{\sim C}(E)$. And as in this case, so in general: where $ch_C(E)$ and $ch_{\sim C}(E)$ exist, the premise 'C' will improve the inference to 'E' iff $ch_C(E)>ch_{\sim C}(E)$.

In short, *if* explanation is inference, then a cause will explain its effects only if it raises their chances. And this, *pace* Hempel, does not require a cause to make its effects' chances high. Bill's smoking can explain his getting cancer, provided it raises his chance of getting it, even if it does not raise that chance to 1/2, let alone to 1. That is, Bill's smoking can explain his getting cancer even if it leaves him more likely than not to die of something else first. And as in this case, so in general. For a cause to explain its effects, as well as to be evidence for them, it need not make their chances high; but it does need to raise them.

But not for Hempel's reason: not because explanations are inferences. For as Jeffrey (1969), Salmon (1984 ch. 4) and others have observed, explanations are *not* inferences. An *explanandum* is not a hypothesis whose truth needs inferring from better known premises. On the contrary, its truth is normally taken for granted: since what needs explaining is not the statement itself but the fact that it is true [5.6]. Thus the more likely it is that a statement is true, the more likely it is to need explaining; but, by the same token, the less need there is to infer it from something better known.

It is true that explanation and inference are linked in ways that may tempt one to confound them. There is the principle of *inference to the best explanation*, which invites us to infer what would if true best explain the known facts. The principle is contentious, and has obvious limitations, but also many applications (Lipton 1991). For example, most hypotheses about prehistory are assessed by it, i.e. by how well they would if true explain the archaeological record. Indeed this is what makes archaeological data worth collecting in the first place, since few remains are of enough intrinsic – e.g. aesthetic – interest to be worth explaining for their own sake. That is why explanations of archaeological remains are usually proposed as hypotheses, about the people whose remains they are, to be assessed by how well the hypotheses would if true explain those remains. But this does not make archaeological explanations inferences: on the contrary. The theories about prehistory which explain archaeological data are conclusions, not premises. They are inferred from the data they explain, not the other way round.

In short, even the principle and practice of inference to the best explanation, far from implying that explanations are inferences, implies – quite rightly – that they are not. But if explanations are not inferences, then the fact that an inference's premise should always raise its conclusion's probability will not tell us why explanations need to raise the probability of the facts they explain. Yet our examples all suggest that they do. Why?

## 5 Explanation and necessity

I think we require explanations to raise the probability of what they explain because we want to know why a state of affairs is a fact when, for all we know, it might not have been. In other words, a principal object of explanation is to close, or at least to reduce, the gap between what we know to be so and what we know to be necessarily so in some not-possibly-not sense. And to have no chance of being otherwise is to be necessary in just such a sense: hence the Necessity condition on chance, that $ch(P)=1$ must entail P [3.1].

This is why, as we have seen, chances must be more than evidential probabilities. The latter only measure the force of evidence: how likely it is, given some evidence Q, that some hypothesis 'P' is true, i.e. that P is a fact. Chances do more than this. They measure possibilities – of Don's dying, Bill's getting cancer, a radium atom's decaying – that are properties of facts about the world, and not merely of facts about our knowledge of the world. This is the kind of possibility that explanation needs to reduce, which is why it takes chances, and not merely evidential probabilities, to measure it. And this in turn explains why, although a cause's effects can be evidence for it, as it is for them, they cannot explain it: for since a cause's chance never depends on its effects, the only probabilities they can give it are evidential ones [5.5].

The present hypothesis, that we want explanations to show the not-possibly-not necessity of the facts they explain, is itself supported by an inference to a best explanation. This is the explanation which the hypothesis provides of why explanation figures far less in logic and mathematics than it does in science and history. For to know a fact in logic and mathematics is usually to have proved it and thus also to know that it is necessary. So in these subjects our knowledge of what is necessary includes most of our knowledge of the facts: the gap between the two that calls for explanation is rare. Where it occurs, as with the conjecture that every even number is the sum of two primes, believed only because no counter-example is known, we do want a proof partly in order to explain something we already think we know. But this situation is unusual, which is why explanation is no big deal in logic and mathematics, since it is mostly supplied automatically by the very evidence that establishes the facts to be explained.

In science and history, by contrast, explanation is a very big deal. The reason is that what we observe is never explained by our observing it, precisely because a perception of a fact is only an effect of it, and so can only give it an evidential probability, not a chance. This is why our observations continually reopen the explanatory gap between what we know and what we know to be necessary. Seeing a radioactive atom decay in a certain time interval [5.1] does not tell us what, if anything, made its decaying then necessary: so why, we ask, did it decay then? Seeing the Berlin wall fall did not tell us what, if anything, made its fall necessary: so why, we ask, did it fall? These questions are not requests for evidence for, inferences to or proofs of these physical or political facts. We know the facts, because we have perceived them. But although perception can tell us *that* they are facts, by giving them high evidential probabilities, it cannot tell us *why* they are facts, because it cannot give them high chances.

This demand on explanation, that it make what it explains necessary, is obviously satisfied by deterministic causal explanation. For by definition, if C is sufficient for E, then $ch_C(E)=1$, a fact which, with C, makes E necessary: C in the circumstances gives E zero chance of not existing. Thus a cause that is sufficient for its effects thereby makes them necessary – provided of course they would not be necessary anyway, i.e. provided $ch_{-C}(E)$ is less than 1 and hence less than $ch_C(E)$. Finding a cause of a known fact E that raises its chance to 1 does therefore explain why E is a fact, by revealing something that makes E necessary.

Sometimes however no such explanation is to be had. There may be no sufficient cause of the fact to be explained, as (probably) with the decaying radium atom in chapter 5. Or, as with Bill's getting cancer, the sufficient causes, if any, do not include those that concern us, such as Bill's smoking. In all these cases, since the relevant cause C does not make E necessary, knowing that C causes E does not close the gap that calls for explanation.

But it may still narrow it – provided C raises E's chance. For this means lowering the chance of ~E, i.e. of E not being a fact. And the less chance the fact E has of not existing, the less its existence needs explaining. Now to this it may be objected that the necessity expressed by '$ch(E)=1$' does not come by degrees, and nor does it. But the possibilities which this necessity rules out do come by degrees, measured by the different possible values of $ch(\sim E)$. The less possible $\sim E$ is, i.e. the less $ch(\sim E)$ is and hence the greater $ch(E)$ is, the closer the fact E is to being necessary. This is the sense in which a cause C may explain E better or worse, depending on how close it comes to making E necessary, i.e. on how much it raises $ch(E)$.

This comparative hypothesis, that (other things being equal) the more C raises E's chance the better it explains it, is further supported by two other considerations. First, the principle of inference to the best explanation invoked above presupposes that some explanations are better than others, and this is one obvious way in which they can be better. Second, as Harman (1973 p. 137) and others have noted, this principle is itself closely related to another one, the so-called *maximum likelihood* principle (Fisher 1959 pp. 68–75). This tells us to infer the hypothesis that makes the known facts most probable, as for example we tacitly do in the indirect perception of masses and chances discussed in §3. And as our hypothesis, that the more probable an explanation makes what it explains the better it is, both explains and makes most probable this link between these two principles, it is itself supported by both of them.

So far so good. But our hypothesis is still ambiguous. Do we rate C's explanation of E by how close E's chance with C is to 1, or by how far C raises E's chance: i.e. do we rate it by $ch_C(E)$ or by $ch_C(E)-ch_{\sim C}(E)$? The same question arose about causation's evidential connotation [§2], and the answer to it is basically the same. At first sight what seems to matter is how far a causal explanation reduces the gap that called for explanation in the first place. If so, what matters is how close $ch_C(E)$ is to 1: the closer it is, i.e. the greater $ch_C(E)$, the better in this respect the explanation is.

The objection to this is, as before, that $ch_C(E)$ has nothing especially to do with C [§2]. As in the car engine example, so in general: because $ch_C(E)$ is just $ch(E)$, E's chance in all the relevant circumstances S as well as C, it tells us nothing about C's contribution to reducing the chance of $\sim E$. C may have contributed nothing to this, however high $ch(E)$ and hence $ch_C(E)$ are: for $ch(E)$ might have been just as high had 'C' been false. Indeed it might have been higher, in which case the fact C widens rather than narrows the gap between $ch(E)$ and 1 that makes E need explaining. And then no one would say that C explains E, however close $ch(E)$ is to 1. Thus however high Bill's chance of getting cancer may be, no one would take his smoking to explain his getting cancer if they thought that chance would have been higher still had he not smoked. What makes us take Bill's smoking to explain his getting cancer, even when his chance of getting it if he smokes is less than 1/2, is that we think his chance of getting it if he did not smoke would be even less.

In short, C can explain E even if $ch_C(E)$ is low, provided only that it exceeds $ch_{\sim C}(E)$. Like causation's evidential connotation, if for different reasons, its explanatory connotation requires causes to raise the chances of their effects. This is essential if every cause C is to give some explanation of an effect E: a poor explanation no doubt if $ch_C(E)$ is low and thus not much greater than $ch_{\sim C}(E)$, but some explanation nonetheless.

# 7    Causes as means

## 1  The means–end connotation

A cause can explain and be evidence for effects that it does not determine, so long as it raises their chances [6]. Indeterministic causation could therefore, provided it meets this condition, keep causation's evidential and explanatory connotations. But this is not enough to show that causation can be indeterministic, since causes must do more than explain and be evidence for their effects: causation has other connotations, which causal indeterminism might violate. There are its (admittedly contentious) temporal and contiguity connotations, that causes must precede and be contiguous to their immediate effects [5.4]. These too depend on effects having chances with and without their causes [17.4–5]. But they do not require causes to determine their effects. Causes need be neither sufficient nor necessary for their immediate effects in order to have to precede and to be contiguous to them.

So far so good. But causation has yet another connotation, the most important of all, which I shall call its *means–end connotation*:

Means–end: causes are *means* of bringing about their effects.

By this I mean that whenever an effect is an end, its causes automatically supply means of achieving it. In other words, bringing about a cause is always a way of bringing about its effects. Or more accurately, to allow for the fact that a fallible means may fail to achieve its end, a cause is always a means to what will be its effects if they exist. Thus if Don's falling will cause him to die if he does die, it follows that his falling would be a means to that sad end. If Sue's visiting the Bull will be a cause of her getting her gin there if they have it, then her visiting the Bull is a way for her to get her gin. And so on.

The means–end connotation of causation is as obvious and undeniable as its evidential and explanatory connotations. And it is not news. It has long been noted, e.g. by Dummett (1964 p. 333); and Gasking (1955) based his account of causation on it. I think he was right. Causation's means–end connotation is even more basic than its evidential and explanatory connotations, being to my mind the very core of the concept: causation is essentially the feature of the world that gives ends means. But essential or not, the fact is undeniable: causation is in fact what gives ends means.

This may not however tell us much about causation. For to bring about a means in order to bring about an end is just to cause the means in order to cause the end. This makes it look as if we need to invoke causation to say what it is to be a means to an end. If we did, the means–end connotation would be as useless as the connotations of chapter 5.4, that effects are 'produced by' or 'derived from' their causes, expressions whose meaning here obviously derives from that of 'caused by'. If the means–end connotation were like that, it would tell us nothing about causation; in particular, it could not constrain the chances that causes can give their effects. On the contrary, the chances that means give their ends would have to take whatever values causation's other connotations require causes to give the chances of their effects.

In fact the means–end connotation is not as useless as the connotations of chapter 5.4. It can constrain the chances of effects, because we can say what a means is without invoking causation. We can do this by invoking an objective variant of the so-called *non-causal decision theory* of Jeffrey (1983) and others which I have already put to a quite different use in chapter 4.2. This is what I shall now do; but first I must make clear how my present use of decision theory differs from my previous use of it.

## 2  Valuations and utilities

In chapter 4.2 I used subjective decision theory to show how Sue's belief that the Bull stocks gin (B) affects her decision about whether to visit it (V) to get her gin (G). More precisely, I showed how this decision depends on her credence $cr(B)$ in B, and on how much her desire for G outweighs her desire not to visit the Bull ($\sim$V): desires measured by Sue's *valuations*, $v(G)$ and $v(\sim V)$, of G and of $\sim$V. These then fix her *expected valuations (e-valuations)* of V and of $\sim$V, $ev(V)$ and $ev(\sim V)$, as follows:

(13)   $ev(V) = cr_V(G) \times v(V\&G) + cr_V(\sim G) \times v(V\&\sim G)$;
(13$\sim$) $ev(\sim V) = cr_{\sim V}(G) \times v(\sim V\&G) + cr_{\sim V}(\sim G) \times v(\sim V\&\sim G)$;

where $cr_V(G)$ is the credence Sue will have in G if she visits the Bull, which obviously equals $cr(B)$, and similarly for her other credences. Then the *expected valuation principle* says that Sue will 'do V', i.e. make V a fact by visiting the Bull, iff $ev(V) > ev(\sim V)$, i.e. iff she e-valuates visiting the Bull more highly than not visiting it [4.2].

Three points now need making about this use of the expected valuation principle to give a causal explanation of what Sue does. First, the principle is *subjective*, in this sense: it explains Sue's action by her credence in B and her valuations of G and of ~V, not by the objective chance that B is a fact or the objective utilities, if any, of G and of ~V. Second, although most decision theorists defend the expected valuation principle as a prescription, i.e. as saying what Sue *should* do given her credences and valuations, I do not. For reasons given in my (1991 ch. 16), I follow Ramsey (1990 ch. 4 p. 69) in taking the principle to be *descriptive*, i.e. to say what Sue's credences and valuations *will* make her do. To me, as to Ramsey, the theory that (in his words) 'we act in the way we think most likely to realise the objects of our desires, so that a person's actions are completely determined by his desires and opinions ... seems ... a useful approximation to the truth'. And this is my third point: the principle is *deterministic*. It says that Sue's e-valuating V more highly than ~V will in the circumstances (e.g. she is physically able to reach the Bull) be a sufficient and necessary cause of her doing V. This stops the principle begging the question either for or against the possibility of indeterministic causation.

The second of these three points is the contentious one. Here however we can waive it and suppose for the sake of argument that, whether or not Sue actually does what the expected valuation principle says, she should do so. For we can still add that it will be best for her to do so with credences and valuations that match the corresponding chances and objective utilities if they exist. Thus whatever the descriptive or prescriptive merits of the expected valuation principle, the best thing for Sue to do will be given by an objective counterpart of it, which we may derive as follows.

First we replace Sue's subjective valuations $v(V\&G)$, $v(V\&\sim G)$, ... in (13) and (13~) with objective utilities $u(V\&G)$, $u(V\&\sim G)$, ... of the same possible facts. Next, we replace her credences $cr_V(G)$, $cr_V(\sim G)$, ... with the corresponding objective chances $ch_V(G)$, $ch_V(\sim G)$, ... of her getting and of her not getting her gin if she does and if she doesn't visit the Bull. These objectified versions of (13) and (13~) then define what I shall call the *mean utilities* $mu(V)$ and $mu(\sim V)$ of Sue's visiting and not visiting the Bull (their usual name, 'objective expected utilities', falsely suggests a dependence on what someone expects):

$$mu(V) = ch_V(G) \times u(V\&G) + ch_V(\sim G) \times u(V\&\sim G);$$
$$mu(\sim V) = ch_{\sim V}(G) \times u(\sim V\&G) + ch_{\sim V}(\sim G) \times u(\sim V\&\sim G).$$

This makes the mean utility of Sue's visiting the Bull the average of the utilities of her visiting and getting gin and of her visiting and not getting gin, weighted by the chances of her getting and of her not getting gin if she visits. Similarly for the mean utility of Sue's not visiting the Bull.

To these equations we then apply what I shall call the *mean utility principle* (usually called 'the principle of maximising objective expected utility') or, for short, *mean utility*. This tells Sue to visit the Bull if the mean utility of her doing so exceeds that of her not doing so, and *vice versa*. That is, it prescribes doing V if $mu(V)>mu(\sim V)$, and doing $\sim V$ if $mu(V)<mu(\sim V)$. If $mu(V)=mu(\sim V)$, the principle says nothing: it puts V and $\sim V$ on a par.

Mean utility is the principle which I shall use to say what it takes to be a means to an end, e.g. for visiting the Bull to be a means for Sue to get her gin. But first I must defend the principle against two widespread objections to the objective utilities it relies on. The first is that the objective values which they purport to measure do not exist: all values are subjective. The second is that, even if objective values do exist, they have no common measure. Thus the objective values of Sue's getting her gin, G, and of her not visiting the Bull, $\sim V$, either reduce to her subjective desires for G and for $\sim V$ or, if they do not, they cannot be compared.

Both these objections are mistaken. The answer to the first one is this. The value of G and of $\sim V$ may indeed depend on how much Sue likes gin and dislikes visiting the Bull. But this does not make those values subjective, not even if they depend on nothing else (like how good or bad in other medical and psychological ways G and V are for Sue and others). For even then we must distinguish the objective utilities $u(G)$ and $u(\sim V)$ from Sue's valuations, $v(G)$ and $v(\sim V)$, since the latter do not automatically measure how much Sue will actually like her gin if she gets it and dislike the Bull if she actually goes there [4.2]. All her valuations measure directly is how much, in advance, Sue *wants* to get her gin, and *wants* not to visit the Bull, which is quite a different matter. In short, Sue's valuations $v(G)$ and $v(\sim V)$ are at best predictions of the objective utilities, $u(G)$ and $u(\sim V)$, predictions that may be completely wrong.

Suppose for example that if Sue gets her gin she will hate it (realising that her lust for it was a mere expense of spirit in a waste of shame...). Then however much she wants her gin in advance, she will obviously be better off without it; and similarly if she is wrong about how much she will actually dislike the Bull if she goes there. This is why Sue will always do best by acting on valuations $v(G)$ and $v(\sim V)$ which are, or are based on, accurate predictions of how much she will in fact like G and $\sim V$, i.e. on predictions of $u(G)$ and $u(\sim V)$.

And as for Sue, so for everyone. Even if the value of a fact P depends only on how P strikes me later, it will still not reduce to my previous desire for P. So we need not discuss whether, when and how the values of facts depend on more than our reactions to them, even though it is obvious that they usually do. But I need not press that point here. All I need, in order to distinguish objective utilities from subjective valuations, is the undeniable fact that, whatever we want and however much we want it, we may not like it if we get it.

So much for the first objection to objective utilities. What about the second? What gives objective values a common utility measure satisfying the mean utility principle? To see the answer to this question, recall the Evidence condition on chance [3.2], which says that if my evidence about some state of affairs P is that it has a chance $ch(P)$ of being actual, my credence $cr(P)$ should equal that chance. This condition looks as if it requires chances to have an intrinsic probability measure to match that of credences. In fact all it requires is a one–one correspondence between chances and the credences they justify, which lets us impose the latter's probability measure on the former [3.2]. This is what lets the chance $ch_V(G)$, that Sue will get her gin if she visits the Bull, have the same measure as the corresponding credence, $cr_V(G)$, which she will have in G if she is right.

Similarly, we can measure the utility $u(G)$ of Sue's getting her gin by the valuation $v(G)$ that she would have if she knew in advance what $u(G)$ would be. Suppose for example that her prediction about how much she will like her gin if she gets it is right, so that if she gets it she will be neither pleasantly nor unpleasantly surprised by how much she likes it. Then in the simple case assumed above, where the value of her getting it depends only on how much she likes it, her valuation $v(G)$ will in fact measure the objective utility $u(G)$.

But then, if we use Sue's correct credences and valuations to measure the chances and utilities that make them correct, the function of the former (e-valuation) which says what Sue *will* do will also (as a function of the latter) tell us what she *should* do [4.2]. Hence the prescriptive force of the mean utility principle.

## 3  Means and ends

Much more needs saying about mean utility, especially about how we come to know the utilities it depends on. But important as these questions are, they are questions we can waive. For all I need mean utility to do here is to enable me to say, without appeal to causation, what makes something a means to an end. And for this purpose any problems we may have in assessing the values of ends are immaterial. For even if means–end links did depend on how valuable ends are, those problems would only make it hard to say whether something really is a means to an end, not to say what it is to be one. And in fact, as we shall see, means–end links do not depend on the values of the ends: in my account of these links, the utilities involved will all cancel out. We can know therefore what means a given end has without knowing the objective value of that end: all our ignorance of its value does is stop us knowing whether that end would in fact justify using that means.

In what follows therefore we can take the utilities I shall invoke for granted, regardless of what they depend on or of how we know what they are. All that matters here is how, given that the relevant utilities and chances exist, we can use the mean utility principle to define the means–end link. To see how we can do this, let us vary the example and consider not Sue but Kim, taking some medicine, M, in order to recover, R, from a painful illness.

The first point to be made about ends is that, for a state of affairs R to be an end, R's being a fact must in the circumstances be more valuable than ~R's being a fact. The values that matter here are comparative: for Kim's recovering to be an end, it must be more valuable for her to recover than not. Indeed, since differences between utilities are all that matter here, we may set an arbitrary zero – e.g. for the utility of necessary facts like R∨~R (i.e. R or not-R) – in order to give good facts like R positive utilities and bad ones like ~R negative utilities (Jeffrey 1983 ch. 6.2).

The next point to consider is why we need the concept of a means to an end at all. The reason is that we cannot make all our ends actual at will. Kim, for example, cannot at will recover from her illness: in the idiom of the last section, she can neither 'do R' nor 'do ~R'. So she must look for a means of recovering, such as taking her medicine, 'doing M', which she can make actual at will. But which then of the things that she *can* do at will *should* she do as a means to that end? Decision theory, taken prescriptively, is meant to tell us what fixes the right answer to that question.

Bill, by contrast, given cigarettes, a lighter, and the ability to use them, can smoke at will. Unlike Kim, he need not look for a means to make that end actual, and needs no decision theory to tell him what to do as a means to it. But this is not to say that Bill uses no means to his end: he does. To make an end actual at will is still to cause it, and its causes include more than an act of will. There is a long chain of intermediate causes and effects between Bill's deciding to smoke a cigarette and his actually smoking it: he puts the cigarette in his mouth, strikes a light, applies it to the cigarette, draws on it, and so on. All the actions in this sequence are means to their successors and hence to the final end of Bill's smoking. So whether Bill needs it or not, decision theory, if it is to tell us what means are, must apply as much to Bill's means of smoking as to Kim's means of recovering. And so, fortunately, it does, as we shall see.

Finally, before starting to define the means–end link, I must make explicit a point that I left implicit in chapter 4.2. This is the irrelevance here of the distinction between action and inaction. The only distinction that matters here is between acts, like Kim's taking her medicine or Bill's striking a match, and their possible outcomes, like Kim's recovering or Bill's match igniting. And by 'act' here, following Jeffrey (1983 ch. 5.8), I mean intentionally making a state of affairs actual, i.e. making a proposition like 'Kim takes her medicine' true. This broadens the usual sense of 'act' to include intentional *in*action, like Kim's deliberately *not* taking her medicine, i.e. doing ~M. We need the broader sense because we need to cover all intentional actualising of states of affairs, whether by action in the narrow sense or by inaction. The distinction between action and inaction may well matter for other purposes – e.g. for moral assessment [§6] – but not here. Here, Kim's doing M and her doing ~M are on a par.

## 4 Means and mean utilities

We can now see what it takes to make Kim's taking her medicine, M, a means to her recovering, R. Each of her alternative acts, doing M and doing ~M, has two relevant possible outcomes: either she recovers, R, or she does not, ~R. So again, as in chapter 4.2, we have four states of affairs to consider: Kim takes the medicine and recovers, M&R; she recovers without taking the medicine, ~M&R; she takes the medicine but does not recover, M&~R; she neither takes the medicine nor recovers, ~M&~R.

Suppose that in the circumstances each of these alternatives would, if it were actual, have the following utilities on some suitable scale: $u(M\&R)=7$, $u(M\&\sim R)=-3$, $u(\sim M\&R)=8$ and $u(\sim M\&\sim R)=-2$. These are represented in the objective analogue of the valuation matrix of chapter 4.2, the *utility matrix* shown below as Figure 7.

| Utilities | R | ~R |
|-----------|---|-----|
| M | 7 | -3 |
| ~M | 8 | -2 |

Figure 7: Utility matrix I

The fact that R is the end, and so is more valuable than ~R, is represented in Figure 7 by the utility in each row being greater in the R column than in the ~R column. Kim's doing M, on the other hand, has no such value: M is not worth doing for its own sake. On the contrary, her taking her medicine has *dis*value, let us say because the medicine is expensive and unpleasant to take. So ~M is the act that would be worth doing for its own sake. This fact is represented in Figure 7 by the utility in each column being less in the M row than in the ~M row.

However, despite the disvalue of Kim's medicine, it may still be worth her taking it in order to recover. Whether it is worth taking will depend of course on Kim's chances of recovering if she takes it and if she does not, i.e. on $ch_M(R)$ and $ch_{\sim M}(R)$. To see how these chances affect what Kim should do, suppose that $ch(R)$ will be 0.4 if Kim does M and 0.1 if she does ~M, so that $ch_M(R)$, $ch_M(\sim R)$, $ch_{\sim M}(R)$ and $ch_{\sim M}(\sim R)$ are respectively 0.4, 0.6, 0.1 and 0.9. This is represented in the *chance matrix* shown below as Figure 8.

| Chances of | R | ~R |
|:---:|:---:|:---:|
| if M | 0.4 | 0.6 |
| if ~M | 0.1 | 0.9 |

Figure 8: Chance matrix I

We can now use the equations of §2, adapted to this example, to calculate the mean utilities of Kim's taking her medicine, $mu(M)$, and of her not taking it, $mu(\sim M)$, as follows:

(17)  $mu(M) = ch_M(R) \times u(M\&R) + ch_M(\sim R) \times u(M\&\sim R);$
(17~) $mu(\sim M) = ch_{\sim M}(R) \times u(\sim M\&R) + ch_{\sim M}(\sim R) \times u(\sim M\&\sim R).$

(17) and (17~), with the values given in Figures 7 and 8, yield

$mu(M) = 1$ and $mu(\sim M) = -1$, so that
$mu(M) > mu(\sim M)$.

In these circumstances the mean utility principle says that taking her medicine is the right thing for Kim to do, basically because her increased chance of recovering if she does so outweighs its cost. This is what makes mean utility say that, even though the cost of Kim's medicine makes it not worth taking for its own sake, it is worth taking in order to recover.

But these facts, which make the mean utility principle prescribe doing M, look like the very facts that make M a means to the end R. More importantly for us, they include no facts about causation: they are merely the facts about utilities and chances displayed in Figures 7 and 8. The mean utility principle should therefore tell us, without invoking causation, what it takes to make M a means to R and, specifically, what chance any means must give any end to which it is a means.

The principle cannot however tell us this immediately, because there is more to being a means than being prescribed by mean utility. For given Figure 7, Kim's taking her medicine, M, is not *purely* a means to her recovering, R. M's cost, although obviously irrelevant to whether it is a means to R, does affect the relative values of *mu*(M) and *mu*(~M).

Specifically, by making the utilities in the M row of Figure 7 less than those in the ~M row, M's cost may affect whether the mean utility principle prescribes M. In Figure 7 the principle does let the end R justify the means M; but it need not, and if M cost much more it would not. To see this, suppose the utilities in the M row of Figure 7 are reduced to those shown below in Figure 9.

| Utilities | R | ~R |
|-----------|---|-----|
| M | 4 | -6 |
| ~M | 8 | -2 |

Figure 9: Utility matrix II

Inserting these utilities in (17) and (17~) makes

$mu$(M) = -2 and $mu$(~M) = -1, so that now
$mu$(M) < $mu$(~M).

The mean utility principle now no longer prescribes M, despite M's obviously still being a means to R. The reason of course is that this means is now too costly for the value of the end R to justify using it.

In short, M's being prescribed by mean utility only shows it to be a means to R if it is *purely* a means, i.e. if M has no value or disvalue of its own. So if mean utility is to tell us what a means is, we need to state this condition without invoking the concept of a means. And so, fortunately, we can. For obviously M will lack intrinsic value or disvalue iff, whether or not R is actual, doing M will make the situation neither better nor worse. In other words, M will be, if a means at all, purely a means iff the M and ~M rows of our utility matrix are identical.

This is the situation shown below in Figure 10, where the utilities in the R and ~R columns are $u$ and $u'$ respectively in both rows, and where – because by hypothesis R is the end and hence more valuable than ~R – $u$ is greater than $u'$:

| Utilities | R | ~R |
|-----------|---|-----|
| M | $u$ | $u'$ |
| ~M | $u$ | $u'$ |

Figure 10: Utility matrix of a pure means

If the utilities are as shown in Figure 10, then if Kim's taking her medicine *is* a means of recovering, it is a pure means. And then it *will* be a means iff the mean utility principle prescribes it. Let us suppose therefore that Kim's chances of recovering if she does take her medicine, $ch_M(R)$, and if she does not take it, $ch_{\sim M}(R)$, are $p$ and $p'$ respectively, as shown in Figure 11:

| Chances of | R | ~R |
|:----------:|:---:|:----:|
| if M | $p$ | $1-p$ |
| if ~M | $p'$ | $1-p'$ |

Figure 11: General chance matrix

The mean utilities of M and ~M are now:

$$mu(M) = pu + (1\text{-}p)u';$$
$$mu(\sim M) = p'u + (1\text{-}p')u'.$$

From this it follows that $mu(M)>mu(\sim M)$ iff

$$(p\text{-}p')(u\text{-}u') > 0$$

and hence, since $u>u'$, iff $p>p'$, i.e. iff

$$ch_M(R) > ch_{\sim M}(R).$$

And as in this example, so in general. Something that is a pure means if it is a means at all will *be* a means, i.e. the mean utility principle will prescribe it, iff it raises the chance of its end.

## 5  Causes as means to ends

From this it follows in particular that any cause C of any effect E will be a means to E iff in the circumstances it raises E's chance, i.e. iff it meets the condition

(16)  $ch_C(E) > ch_{\sim C}(E)$

[6.1]. So causation's means–end connotation imposes the same constraint on the chances of effects as its evidential and explanatory connotations do.

This seems to me to clinch the case for (16). Any apparent cause that failed to raise its effects' chances would not only neither be evidence for them nor explain them, it would not be a means to them if they were ends. And nothing that satisfied none of these three connotations could be a cause: the whole point of calling it a cause would be lost. In particular, to call something a cause that provides no way of bringing about its effects seems to me an obvious contradiction in terms.

One might however grant all this, and still question the wisdom of using as contentious a principle as mean utility to say what it takes to be a means to an end. I must therefore make clear how innocuous my use of this principle is.

The first point to emphasise is that causation's means–end connotation does not imply that any effect actually is an end. Nor does it imply that any cause can actually be brought about by us – or by any other agents – or that a cause is only worth bringing about for the sake of its effects.

These disclaimers matter because these apparent implications obviously often fail. Let us take them in turn. First, many effects, like Bill's getting cancer, are not ends: no one who knows what cancer is wants to get it. Then there are all the unknown effects that are not ends because no one even thinks of them. And if our world contained no agents with ends it would contain no ends at all. But it could obviously still contain effects.

Similarly with causes. Many causes are unusable as means because no one can bring them about. None of us, for example, can affect the weather by changing the earth's orbit. And many causes that people do bring about, like Bill's smoking, are brought about more for their own sake than for the sake of their effects.

My account of causation's means–end connotation must be consistent with all this; and so of course it is. It does not require effects to be ends, nor does it require causes to be realisable, or to lack any value or disvalue of their own. It simply requires causation to entail that *if* any effect E were an end while being an effect of a cause C, that cause would be a means to it. In other words, *if* in those circumstances C had no value or disvalue of its own, and could be brought about directly when E could not, *then* the mean utility principle would prescribe bringing it about. In short, the means–end connotation is conditional. This is why it does not rule out causation in worlds without values or agents and hence without ends or means. In such worlds, as in ours, causation can still exist as what, if only there were ends, would give them means.

This, in particular, is what stops the means–end connotation starting a vicious regress. The reason it may seem to do so is that to bring about a cause C as a means to an effect E is to cause C [§1]. But being caused makes C an effect as well as a cause; and similarly for its cause, for its cause's cause, and so on. So we do have a regress here; but it need not be actual, and it is not vicious. For since the effect E need not actually be an end, its cause C need not actually be brought about as a means to that end. And even if C is brought about for this reason, all this entails is that the cause – B say – that is used to bring C about must also be such that if C were itself an end, B would be a means to it, i.e. such that in the circumstances $ch_B(C) > ch_{\sim B}(C)$. And so on.

## 6 The limitations of mean utility

So much for the means–end connotation itself. Now for my use of the mean utility principle to say what it takes to be a means. Here I need to emphasise that my use of this principle does not force me to endorse all its applications. For example, the principle does not distinguish between action and inaction [§3]: it makes no odds to the mean utility of a cause C whether or not it takes positive action to bring C about. Yet the answer to that question may well affect whether it is right to bring C about.

Suppose for example that Bill's cancer is incurable and so painful that he wishes to die. His doctor may arguably do right to let him die, by not giving him medicine to prolong his life, and yet not do right to kill him. Suppose this is so. That is, suppose Bill's dying, D, is an end to which in this case his *not* getting medicine, ~M, is a means, so that $ch_{\sim M}(D) > ch_M(D)$, and the relevant chances and utilities make mean utility prescribe ~M. Bill's doctor may still not be justified in acting positively to withdraw Bill's medicine; but this does not show that his doing so would not be a means to make Bill die. All it shows is that it takes more than the mean utility principle to justify using this means to this end. The principle may still be all we need to tell us what makes something a means.

Similarly, we can afford to let the mean utility principle yield to the so-called *maximin* principle (Luce and Raiffa 1957 p. 278) in certain cases. The maximin principle ignores both chances and credences, ranking alternative acts by the utilities or valuations of their worst outcomes and then prescribing the act with the best such outcome. Thus in the circumstances shown in Figure 7, maximin would tell Kim to do ~M, since the worst outcome of that act – not taking the medicine and not recovering – is less bad than the worst outcome of doing M – taking the medicine and not recovering.

In this case it is obvious that the mean utility principle should prevail: Kim's increased chance of recovering can justify her taking an unpleasant and costly medicine even at the risk of its not working and so of making matters worse. In other cases perhaps maximin should prevail: some possibilities may be too bad to be worth risking for any end, however valuable. Where, if anywhere, the line should be drawn is hard to say; but fortunately we need not draw it. For the maximin principle does not deny, given the chances in Figure 8, that taking her medicine is a means to Kim's recovery. All it denies, given the utilities in Figure 7, is that this end justifies that means.

Apparent conflicts between mean utility and the so-called *dominance* principle (Jeffrey 1983 ch. 1.5) are less easily set aside. Dominance, like maximin, also tells Kim not to take her medicine, because the cost of taking it makes the utilities in both columns of Figure 7 greater in the ~M row than in the M row. In other words, if Kim recovers, it will be better if she does so without taking her medicine; and if she does not recover, it will also be better if she does not take the medicine. So either way it will be better if she does ~M; and in this situation – in which ~M is said to 'dominate' M – the dominance principle prescribes ~M.

Like maximin, dominance contradicts mean utility here because it will not let R's value make it worth doing M, however much M raises R's chance and thus M's mean utility. But the argument for dominance, unlike that for maximin, seems to imply that doing M is not merely unjustified by R but is not even a means to it. So to see what makes M a means to R, we must see what enables mean utility to outrank dominance when these two principles conflict.

To do this we need to compare the mean utility principle with the expected valuation principle [§2]. Both these principles apply to what are commonly called 'expected utilities', the former to 'objective' ones, the latter to 'subjective' ones. The subjective expected utilities that I call expected valuations are functions, given by equations like (13), of credences (subjective probabilities) and valuations (subjective utilities). The objective expected utilities that I call mean utilities are the same functions, given by equations like (17), of the corresponding chances (objective probabilities) and (objective) utilities.

The expected utility which the mean utility principle says it is best to maximise is thus an objective one. In Kim's case it depends only on the actual chances of R if she does and does not do M, and on the actual value of R and disvalue of M. The expected utility which the expected valuation principle says Kim will or should maximise, on the other hand, is a subjective one: it depends only on Kim's credences in R if she does or does not do M, and on her valuations of R and M.

Now it is only the expected valuation principle, not the mean utility principle, whose outranking of the dominance principle is contentious. And whereas I read the expected valuation principle descriptively, as saying that, generally and roughly, people *do* maximise their expected valuations, most decision theorists read it prescriptively [§2]. In other words, they take it to say that, whatever Sue and Kim actually do, they *should* do V and M respectively iff they e-valuate V and M more highly than ~V and ~M. If Sue and Kim know the relevant chances and utilities and conform their credences and valuations to them, thus making the expected valuation and mean utility prescriptions coincide, well and good; but even if they do not, the expected valuation principle tells them to maximise their expected valuations anyway.

In this situation, of 'decision making under uncertainty' (Luce and Raiffa 1957 p. 13), I deny that the expected valuation principle outranks dominance. I deny for example that Kim should take an unpleasant and costly medicine just because she *thinks* it will make her more likely to recover, i.e. raise her credence in R, unless it *will* make R more likely, i.e. raise R's chance. Of course Kim *will* take the medicine, if she does, because she thinks that her taking it will make her more likely to recover: read descriptively, the expected valuation principle is approximately true [§2]. But the prescriptive question is not what Kim *will* do but what she *should* do. And that question, I argue at length in my (1991 ch. 16), only the objective mean utilities of M and ~M can answer.

This is where I disagree with those decision theorists who think that maximising even the most ignorant or perverse expected valuations is rational enough to outrank dominance. But I need not argue against that view here. For no one thinks that the probabilities which means give their ends are mere credences: not even those who think that Kim's believing M to be a means to R justifies her doing M think that this belief of hers *makes* M a means to R. We can thus all agree that only the objective mean utilities of M and ~M, not anyone's subjective e-valuations of them, determine whether M really is a means to R. And when Kim knows what these mean utilities are, i.e. makes her decision not under uncertainty but under known *risk*, we can also all agree that the expected valuation principle does outrank the dominance principle (Luce and Raiffa p. 13). For then, when Kim's credences equal the corresponding chances and her valuations equal the corresponding objective utilities, the expected valuation principle says what the mean utility principle says: maximise the mean objective utility.

In short, whether or not the expected valuation principle outranks dominance, the mean utility principle certainly does so. This means that the case made in §4 for requiring every means to raise its end's chance needs no contentious assumptions about the prescriptive force and scope of the expected valuation principle. Nor therefore does our conclusion that, if causes are to satisfy causation's means–end connotation, they must raise the chances of their effects.

# 8  *Degrees of effectiveness*

## 1  Connotations that come by degrees

We have seen in the last two chapters how an indeterministic cause can be evidence for, explain and be a means to its effects, provided it raises their chances. Meeting this condition is what enables a cause to satisfy most of causation's major connotations. This however is still not enough to show that causation can be indeterministic, for until recently causal determinism was itself a widely accepted connotation of causation. Those who would retain that connotation must indeed explain away the many apparent cases of indeterministic causation, and meet the arguments, like those given in chapter 5, for accepting them as such. But equally those of us who would drop the connotation must explain its appeal and see what if anything we can put in its place. That is the business of this chapter, in which I shall show why and how, even though determinism is not essential to causation, it remains a desirable ideal. This I shall do by developing a sense in which causes can be more or less effective, and by showing why the causes that are most effective in this sense are those that determine their effects.

What lets causation be more or less effective is the fact that three of its major connotations entail links between cause and effect which come by degrees. The links are those of being evidence for something, of explaining it and of being a means to it. A cause C may be linked to an effect E in each of these ways to a greater or lesser extent: it may be stronger or weaker evidence for E, explain E more or less well and be a more or less useful means to E. These three links have moreover a common measure, which is thus a natural measure of how effectively C causes E.

And most importantly for my present purpose, the closer C comes to determining E, the stronger these three links between C and E are: the stronger the evidence is that C provides for E, the better C explains E and the more useful C is as a means to E. This is why deterministic causation is still the paradigm, because it alone makes these three links between cause and effect as strong as they can be. This is the sense in which deterministic causes are always more effective than indeterministic ones.

For the effectiveness of causation to vary in this way it is not of course necessary for all its connotations to come by degrees. This is just as well, since neither its temporal nor its contiguity connotations do so. Contiguity obviously does not, and nor does precedence, even though causes can be more or less earlier than their effects. An effect, such as the effect on my eyes of something I see, may indeed follow a cause after times ranging from microseconds, when I see an event nearby, to millions of years, when I see an event in a remote galaxy. But causation's temporal connotation does not say how *much* later effects will be than their causes. It says only that they will *be* later, and this fact does not come by degrees. The fact that the effects in our examples (people dying, getting cancer and recovering from illnesses) are always later than their causes (falling, smoking and taking medicine) is an all-or-nothing one. The proof that any cause C must precede any effect E does indeed require C and ~C to give E chances [17.4–5]. But it does not require C to raise E's chance; and even if it did, raising E's chance more cannot make it more true that C must precede E. This is why causation's temporal connotation does not come by degrees. But that does not stop its other connotations, and hence the effectiveness of causation itself, coming by degrees. Let us see how.

## 2  More or less evidence

How does causation's evidential connotation come by degrees? It is obvious enough that evidence does so, i.e. that we can have more or less evidence for or against something. But as causation's temporal connotation shows, this fact alone does not force its evidential connotation to come by degrees. It does not even show that a cause can provide more or less evidence for its effects. Still less does it show that, or how, the amount of evidence which a cause provides for its effects is fixed by how much it raises their chances.

There are in fact two ways in which evidence comes by degrees and only one of these varies with how much a cause C raises the chance of its effect E. The one that does not vary with this is how *much* evidence C provides for E. For whatever E's chances are in the circumstances with C and without it, i.e. whatever the values of $ch_C(E)$ and $ch_{\sim C}(E)$, the evidence for E is the same, namely C; and so therefore is the amount of evidence that C provides for E.

What can and does vary with $ch_C(E)$ and $ch_{\sim C}(E)$ is the degree to which this evidence C supports the hypothesis that E is a fact. But what is the right measure of this degree of support? Is it $ch_C(E)$, E's chance in the circumstances with C, or the extent to which in the circumstances C raises E's chance?

The answer is obvious enough. As we saw in chapter 6.2, what makes C evidence for E is not that it gives E a high chance but that it raises E's chance, i.e. that $ch_C(E)$ exceeds $ch_{\sim C}(E)$. The reason is that $ch_C(E)$ alone, which given C is just E's actual chance $ch(E)$, does not say what if anything C contributes to that chance. This is because, as the car engine example [6.2] shows, $ch(E)$ and hence $ch_C(E)$ are as contingent on E's other causes as they are on C. What makes C improve E's chance of being a fact, and so makes C evidence *for* E, is the fact that, in the circumstances, $ch(E)$ is greater with C than without it, i.e. that $ch_C(E)>ch_{\sim C}(E)$.

This makes it natural to use a measure of how much C raises $ch(E)$ to measure how strongly in the circumstances the evidence C supports the hypothesis that E is a fact. There are of course many such measures, the two simplest being $ch_C(E)/ch_{\sim C}(E)$ and $ch_C(E)-ch_{\sim C}(E)$. Of these the latter is the better, partly because when $ch_{\sim C}(E)$ is 0, i.e. when C is necessary for E, the former, $ch_C(E)/ch_{\sim C}(E)$, is not defined.

There is another reason to prefer $ch_C(E)-ch_{\sim C}(E)$ to $ch_C(E)/ch_{\sim C}(E)$, which is that the evidential significance of either measure derives from that of $ch(E)$. For despite what I have just said, what we most want to know is what $ch(E)$ tells us: namely, to what extent does our evidence support the hypothesis that E, as opposed to ~E, is a fact? The evidential virtue of C's raising $ch(E)$ derives in the end from the virtue of making $ch(E)$ high, or at least higher than $ch(\sim E)$. Hence the reluctance to call C 'strong' evidence for E unless it makes $ch(E)$ greater than $ch(\sim E)$, and thus greater than 1/2. And $ch_C(E)-ch_{\sim C}(E)$ brings out the evidential significance of $ch(E)$ better than $ch_C(E)/ch_{\sim C}(E)$ does: since what really matters is how far C moves $ch(E)$ toward 1 and hence $ch(\sim E)$ toward 0, not how many times greater it makes it than $ch_{\sim C}(E)$.

These reasons for preferring this measure of the strength of the evidence that C provides for E may not be conclusive. And when C is a very indeterministic cause of E, i.e. only raises $ch(E)$ a little, the two measures differ greatly in their dependence on $ch_{\sim C}(E)$. But for present purposes this does not matter. All that matters here is that, on either measure, a cause C which determines E will be stronger evidence for E than any cause of E which does not determine it. For in raising $ch(E)$ from 0 to 1, C raises E's chance of being a fact as much as it can be raised, and more than any indeterministic cause of E can raise it. So by either measure, a deterministic cause of any effect E provides as strong evidence for E as anything can, and stronger than any indeterministic cause of E can provide.

Causes which determine their effects thus satisfy causation's evidential connotation to its greatest possible extent. It is still true that any cause C which raises its effect E's chance at all will satisfy the connotation to some extent: it will provide some evidence for E. But the more C raises E's chance, and hence the closer it comes to being a sufficient and necessary cause of E, the stronger that evidence will be and the more fully the link between C and E will satisfy this connotation of causation.

## 3  Better and worse explanations

The same goes for causation's explanatory connotation, and for very similar reasons. Because 'a principal object of explanation is to close, or at least to reduce, the gap between what we know to be so and what we know to be necessarily so in a not-possibly-not sense ... a cause C may explain E better or worse, depending on how close it comes to making E necessary, i.e. on how much it raises $ch(E)$' [6.5].

Yet as with evidence, so with explanation, the question remains: how do we measure how well C explains E – by $ch(E)$ or by $ch_C(E)$-$ch_{-C}(E)$? And both the answer to this question and the reason for it are the same as they are for evidence. The answer is that what makes C explain E is not that C makes $ch(E)$ high but that it raises it, i.e. that $ch_C(E)$ exceeds $ch_{-C}(E)$. And the reason for this is that $ch_C(E)$ alone does not tell us what if anything C contributes toward making E necessary, i.e. to closing the gap between $ch(E)$ and 1 that called for explanation in the first place. What measures that is how much in the circumstances C reduces the chance of ~E by increasing $ch(E)$ – which is why $ch_C(E)$-$ch_{-C}(E)$ is the natural measure of how well C explains E, just as it is of how strong the evidence is for E that C provides.

This also explains why $ch_C(E)$-$ch_{-C}(E)$ provides a better measure than $ch_C(E)/ch_{-C}(E)$ of how well C explains E. For with explanation, as with evidence, what we most want to know is how close in the circumstances C gets to making E, as opposed to ~E, necessary. The explanatory virtue, like the evidential virtue, of raising $ch(E)$ derives from the virtue of making $ch(E)$ high – or at least higher than $ch(\sim E)$. Hence our reluctance to call C a 'good' explanation of E unless it makes $ch(E)$ greater than 1/2. This is why C's quality as an explanation of E is best measured by how far it moves $ch(E)$ toward 1 and hence $ch(\sim E)$ toward 0, not by how many times greater $ch_C(E)$ is than $ch_{-C}(E)$.

But again, as with evidence, it does not really matter to us whether $ch_C(E)$-$ch_{-C}(E)$ makes a better measure than $ch_C(E)/ch_{-C}(E)$ of how well causes explain their effects. For however differently these two measures rate poor explanations, they will agree that deterministic ones are the best: both will rate a cause C that determines its effect E more highly than any cause of E that does not. For in raising $ch(E)$ from 0 to 1, C raises it as far as it can go, and further than any cause can raise it which does not determine E. If E is in the circumstances necessary with C and impossible without it, C is in the circumstances the best possible explanation of why E and not ~E is a fact. This is why a deterministic cause of any effect E will explain it as well as anything can, and better than any indeterministic cause of E can do.

Causes that determine their effects thus satisfy causation's explanatory as well as its evidential connotation to its greatest possible extent. Any cause C that raises its effect E's chance will satisfy the connotation to some extent. But the more C raises E's chance, and hence the closer it is to being a sufficient and necessary cause of E, the better it explains E and so the more fully it satisfies this connotation too.

## 4 More or less useful means

How, finally, can causation's means–end connotation come by degrees? It is not immediately obvious that it can, since it is by no means obvious that the means–end link can come by degrees. But in fact it can, and does, because the usefulness of a means comes by degrees. By this I do not mean that a means may be more or less useful to us in the sense of being more or less feasible, i.e. more or less easy for us to bring about. That has nothing to do with the means–end link as such. But there is another sense in which different means which are all equally feasible can nevertheless differ in their usefulness, and this is the sense in which the means–end link itself can come by degrees.

Consider again Kim's taking her medicine, M, in order to recover, R, from an illness. What makes M a means to R is that M raises R's chance: $ch_M(R) > ch_{-M}(R)$ [7.4]. M is moreover a feasible means, since Kim can take her medicine at will. Yet despite this, the value of the end R may still fail in various ways to justify adopting this means to it [7.4].

In particular, given the values of $ch_M(R)$ and $ch_{-M}(R)$ in Figure 8, shown again here,

| Chances of | R | ~R |
|---|---|---|
| if M | 0.4 | 0.6 |
| if ~M | 0.1 | 0.9 |

Figure 8: Chance matrix I

Kim's medicine might be too costly or unpleasant to be worth taking – as we saw for example that it would be if the relevant utilities were as shown again below in Figure 9.

| Utilities | R | ~R |
|-----------|---|-----|
| M         | 4 | -6  |
| ~M        | 8 | -2  |

Figure 9: Utility matrix II

For since these chances and utilities make the mean utility of Kim's not taking the medicine, ~M (-1), exceed that of taking it, M (-2), the mean utility principle says that Kim should not take it. The mean utility of her recovering, R, does not justify using this means M to bring R about. In short, although M is a perfectly feasible means to R, it is not in these circumstances a useful one.

Now whether M is useful in this sense, of being prescribed by the mean utility principle, does not depend only on the relevant utilities, of M&R, M&~R, ~M&R and ~M&~R. It also depends on $ch_M(R)$ and $ch_{\sim M}(R)$, R's chances in the circumstances with and without M. In particular, the more $ch_M(R)$ exceeds $ch_{\sim M}(R)$, i.e. the more Kim's taking her medicine raises her chance of recovering, the more costly her medicine can be and still be worth taking as a means to that end. Or, putting it the other way round, the more $ch_M(R)$ exceeds $ch_{\sim M}(R)$, the less valuable R needs to be to justify, and hence to make useful, a means M with a given intrinsic disvalue. In other words, the less risk there is that a costly means will not produce the end, the more useful that means is: because the means needs to do less good if it does work in order to justify the risk of having incurred its cost without its working.

We can put this more generally and accurately in terms of objective costs and benefits. These are the objective counterparts of subjective costs and benefits, like those invoked in chapter 4.2: the subjective cost of Sue's visiting the Bull, V, and the subjective benefit of her getting her gin, G. What made those costs and benefits subjective is their being defined by how much the thought of V and G respectively repels and attracts Sue in advance: i.e. by the valuations of V and G that cause Sue to act as she does. But if we are to define V's actual rather than its supposed usefulness as a means to G, we must define the costs and benefits involved not by Sue's subjective valuations of V and G but by utilities that measure something objective, if only how much Sue will actually like her gin when she gets it and dislike visiting the Bull when she does so [7.2].

Suppose then, reverting to our symbols for Kim's recovering and taking her medicine, but now letting them stand for any end R and means M, R's chances in the circumstances with and without M are as shown in Figure 11 from chapter 7.4:

| Chances of | R | ~R |
|:---:|:---:|:---:|
| if M | $p$ | $1-p$ |
| if ~M | $p'$ | $1-p'$ |

Figure 11: General chance matrix

Now suppose that, on a suitable scale of utilities, the means M has a utility cost $c$ which is independent of whether M works. That is, in both the R and ~R columns of the utility matrix, the utility in the ~M row exceeds that in the M row by $c$. Suppose similarly that there is a utility benefit $b$ in getting the end R which is the same whether or not it is brought about by M. That is, in both the M and ~M rows of the utility matrix, the utility in the R column exceeds that in the ~R column by $b$. This, setting the utility of ~M&~R to zero, yields the objective cost-benefit matrix shown below in Figure 12.

| Utilities | R | ~R |
|:---:|:---:|:---:|
| M | $b-c$ | $-c$ |
| ~M | $b$ | 0 |

Figure 12: Cost-benefit matrix

Given these chances and utilities, the mean utilities of M and ~M are:

$mu(\text{M}) = p(b-c) + (1-p)(-c) = pb-c;$
$mu(\text{~M}) = p'b.$

So the means M is justified, i.e. $mu(\text{M}) > mu(\text{~M})$, iff $(pb-c) > p'b$; i.e. iff

(18)   $p-p' > c/b.$

Let us call $c/b$ the *cost-benefit ratio* of the means M to the end R, and the least value of this ratio for which M is not worth using M's *cost-effectiveness* as a means to R. Then what (18) shows is that M's cost-effectiveness is equal to the amount $p-p'$, i.e. $ch_\text{M}(\text{R})-ch_{\text{~M}}(\text{R})$, by which in the circumstances M raises R's chance. Thus the more M raises R's chance, the more cost-effective it is as a means to R, as shown below in Figure 13.

This then is how the means–end link between any means M and any end R comes by degrees: it comes by degrees of usefulness, measured by M's cost-effectiveness as a means to R. So therefore does causation's means–end connotation: when an effect is an end, its causes may be more or less useful means to it. And what Figure 13 shows is that the more a cause raises its effects' chances, the more useful it is as a means of bringing those effects about.

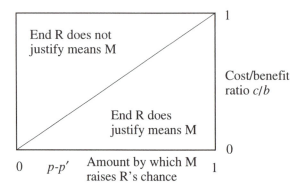

Figure 13: The cost-effectiveness of a means M to an end R

In particular, Figure 13 shows why a cause C which determines an effect E, i.e. which raises E's chance from 0 to 1, is the most useful means of bringing E about, since its cost-effectiveness is 1. For what this means is that when C is both sufficient and necessary for E it is worth incurring any cost $c$, less than the benefit $b$ of E, to bring about C in order to get E. Nothing could be more cost-effective than that.

This is what makes deterministic causes provide the most useful means of bringing about their effects, means that are more useful than any indeterministic causes of the same effects. The latter are not useless, as Figure 13 shows: provided they raise the chances of their effects, they will always be of some use as means to those ends. But the more they raise those chances, i.e. the closer they come to being sufficient and necessary, the more cost-effective they will be.

## 5  More or less effective causes

We have seen that and how causation's evidential, explanatory and means–end connotations all come by degrees, and that and why the more a cause raises its effects' chances the more it satisfies each one of them. All the connotations of causation that come by degrees at all therefore come more strongly as causation comes closer to being deterministic. This is what I mean by describing causes as more or less effective and by measuring their effectiveness by how much they raise the chances of their effects.

It is in this sense that deterministic causation is the most effective kind, since it satisfies all causation's connotations to the highest possible degree. By raising its effect E's chance from 0 to 1, a cause C that determines E provides at once the strongest possible evidence for E, the best possible explanation of E and the most useful means of bringing E about. This is why deterministic causes are still our paradigms of causation, and why many philosophers remain reluctant to admit that causes can fail to determine their effects. Their reluctance is understandable because indeterministic causation can never satisfy three of causation's most important connotations as well as deterministic causation does. The less a cause raises its effects' chances, the weaker is the evidence that it provides for them, the less well it explains them and the less useful it is as a means of bringing them about: in short, the less effective it is. But provided a cause does raise the chances of its effects, however little, it never becomes completely ineffective in any of these respects. Indeterministic causation is indeed always less than ideal, but it is not a contradiction in terms.

## 6 Overdetermination

This is my main argument for admitting causes which are less effective than deterministic ones. But the argument still requires every cause to have *some* efficacy, to raise its effects' chances to some extent. So before leaving the topic I must deal with some seeming counter-examples to this require-ment: two or more apparent causes of an effect E, each of which raises $ch(E)$ without the others but not with them. When $ch(E)=1$ these apparent causes are said to *overdetermine* E; and although the problem is the same when $ch(E)<1$, it will suffice to tackle it in the simplest case, where E has just two overdetermining causes C and C'.

Suppose for example that as Don falls (C) he is shot (C') and that in the (other) circumstances S his chances of dying (E) are as follows: 0 if he neither falls nor is shot, 1 if he falls whether or not he is shot, and 1 if he is shot whether or not he falls. Then if Don were not shot, i.e. in the circumstances S&~C', Don's falling would be a deterministic cause of his dying:

$$ch_C(E)=1 \text{ and } ch_{\sim C}(E)=0.$$

But since Don *is* shot, i.e. since the actual circumstances are S&C',

$$ch_C(E)=1 \text{ and } ch_{\sim C}(E)=1,$$

so that C does not raise E's chance at all.

It follows on my account that C does not cause E; and nor for the same reason does C′. Don's falling does not kill him, because his being shot would, and his being shot does not kill him, because his falling would. So he does not die because he falls, and he does not die because he is shot. But that seems absurd: what does cause Don to die, if not that he falls or that he is shot? The fact that his dying is overdetermined can hardly stop it being determined at all.

Nor does it. For in the circumstances S, if Don had neither fallen nor been shot, his chance of dying would have been zero. So between them C and C′ do provide one deterministic cause of E, namely C∨C′: Don dies because he falls *or* is shot. So on my account E is indeed determined – but not overdetermined, since neither of E's apparent causes, C and C′, causes E.

As a cause of E, C∨C′ may be an unattractive surrogate for C and C′. But it is better than nothing, and the best we can do if causes must raise the chances of their effects, as they must if causation is to keep its connotations. We have seen that no fact can be evidence for, explain or be a means to E unless it raises E's chance, which C and C′ here stop each other doing. But then, on pain of invalidating these three core inferences from 'C causes E', we must admit in this case that C and C′ stop each other causing E. What can we say to make this conclusion more palatable?

First, three facts help to explain our inclination to say that both C and C′ cause E. These are that in the circumstances S:

(a)    C and C′ are each sufficient for E;
(b)    C and C′ would each cause E without the other;
(c)    C and C′ each entail a cause of E, namely C∨C′.

This may well make it less misleading to say that C and C′ cause E than to deny it, since that might be taken to imply that (a), (b) or (c) is false.

Second, if we are not sure if C would determine E on its own, (b) may well make us act – and therefore speak – as if C′ causes E. For if, in the circumstances S&~C′, $ch_C(E)$ were even slightly less than 1, say 0.99, then C′ could raise it, say to 0.999, thus causing E. This can easily make C′, if not the most effective cause of E, cost-effective enough to be worth using as a means to E. The value of Don's dying to his assassin ('the Jackal'), for example, can certainly make it worth the Jackal's while to use a bullet to ensure that $ch(E)$ really is 0.999, especially if he cannot be sure that Don's chance of dying will be even as high as 0.99 if he falls without being shot.

Third, even when C and C′ would separately determine E, they may be less independent than I have so far tacitly supposed. They may for example have a common cause B: the Jackal may have frayed the rope whose snapping causes Don to fall. Suppose he has and, for simplicity, that B determines both C and C'. Then in the circumstances S&C the chance of C' and thus of E will be 1, while in the circumstances S&~C the chance of C' and thus of E will be 0. Similarly for the chances of C and E in the circumstances S&C' and S&~C'. Hence in the circumstances S:

$$ch_C(E)=1 \text{ and } ch_{\sim C}(E)=0;$$
$$ch_{C'}(E)=1 \text{ and } ch_{\sim C'}(E)=0.$$

So if C and C' have a zero chance in S of existing without each other, either because they have a common cause or because one causes the other, then each can raise the chance of E from 0 to 1. C and C' can then both cause E deterministically even in the presence of the other.

## 7 Overdetermination and mental causation

It is especially important to recognise this last possibility, because it shows in particular how a mental cause C and a distinct physical cause C' can both determine an effect E without overdetermining it. Suppose for example that Kim's being in pain causes her to take her medicine, M: let C be the mental fact that she is in pain and E the effect that she 'does M' [7.3]. Then let C' be the fact that Kim is in a physical state which also, in the other relevant circumstances S, causes her to do M. Physicalists such as Peacocke (1979 ch. III.3) and Papineau (1990) infer from this that C must either *be* C' or *supervene on* C', i.e. be entailed by C'&S, where S is also assumed to be physical: for otherwise, given C', C would overdetermine E. Similarly, they argue, in all other cases: any mental cause of any physical effect must either be identical with, or supervene on, one of its physical causes.

Although the invalidity of this inference should be obvious from §6, its popularity makes it worth exposing in some detail. First, let us grant for the sake of argument that every effect E of a mental cause C also has a physical cause C'. If so, it will in fact have many physical causes: namely, all the earlier physical facts that cause E by causing C or C', or by causing their causes, or the causes of those causes, or .... Here however we may ignore all these earlier physical causes of E, along with any earlier mental causes. All that matters here is the relation between C and a contemporary physical cause C' of E with which C could conceivably be identified.

Next we must recall that E, like most if not all effects, can have many simultaneous deterministic causes without being overdetermined at all. Take the spark, inflammable gas and oxygen in a car engine cylinder, each determining an explosion in the cylinder, which thus has three such causes [6.2]. These causes do not overdetermine the explosion, because each of them depends for its efficacy on the others: with any two of them, the chances of an explosion with and without the third are respectively 1 and 0. Cases like this present no problem for my account.

Nor therefore would the present case if C depended on C' for its efficacy – as indeed it obviously will depend on some other physical facts: Kim's pain will not for example cause her to take her medicine if she is paralysed. But that is irrelevant, for then E will also not be caused by any physical fact C' with which C might be identified or on which it might supervene. So for the above *reductio ad absurdum* argument to show that C must either be or supervene on C', it must assume that C *would* otherwise overdetermine E, just as we assumed that Don's being shot as he falls would overdetermine his dying.

And here lies the first flaw in the argument: its assumption that effects cannot be overdetermined in the sense of §6. But they can, and not only by mental causes, as Don's being shot as he falls shows: physical causes can and often do overdetermine their effects. This fact is indeed a problem for accounts of causation that require a cause to be necessary for its effects or, as mine does, to increase their chances. But however serious this problem, and whatever its solution, the fact remains: overdetermination in the sense of §6 exists. So the fact, if it is a fact, that a mental cause C which neither is nor supervenes on a physical cause C' of the same effect E would overdetermine E is no reason to deny that C is as effective a cause of E as C' is.

Moreover all the solutions canvassed in §6 to the problem that overdetermination poses for accounts of causation work here too. In particular, C and C' may in the circumstances have a zero chance of existing without the other, either because they have a common cause or because one of them causes the other. Some earlier fact, physical or mental, may cause Kim to be in pain, C, and in a certain brain state, C'. Or laws linking pains and brain states may make C cause C', or *vice versa*. In any of these cases C and C' can both, as in §6, be deterministic causes of E:

$$ch_C(E)=1 \text{ and } ch_{\sim C}(E)=0;$$
$$ch_{C'}(E)=1 \text{ and } ch_{\sim C'}(E)=0.$$

This shows how a mental fact C and a physical fact C' can determine an effect E without overdetermining it, even though C≠C' and neither C nor C' supervenes on the other in the sense given above.

Yet there is a weaker sense in which C and C' may indeed supervene on each other: each may in the circumstances have a zero chance of existing without the other. In particular, deterministic laws may link Kim's pain to her brain states both ways round, just as they link the determinate pressure $p$ and volume $v$ of any sample $g$ of a gas in equilibrium at a constant temperature [17.2]. And then, just as the gas laws give $pg$ and $vg$ a zero chance of existing in the circumstances without the other, so the laws linking pain to brain states will make C and C′ supervene on each other in this weaker sense. But this symmetrical supervenience, generated by psychophysical laws, is no use to physicalists, who need an asymmetrical supervenience of the mental on the physical, generated by purely physical laws. And while my account of causation is consistent with such supervenience, it does nothing to support it: nothing in my account implies that the efficacy of causation depends in any way on its linking physical as opposed to mental facts.

# 9 *Factual causes and effects*

## 1 Iterated causation

Now that we have seen how causation can be more or less effective, we can return to two of the questions postponed from chapter 1. The main one is what causation itself is: what is the nature of the causal link between causes and effects? But since the nature of this link depends on what it links, we must first consider the other question: what kind of entities are causes and effects – facts, or particulars [1.2]?

One advantage of the view that causes and effects are facts is that it lets causation be *iterated*: it lets the fact that C causes E have its own causes and effects. To see how this can happen, recall that facts by definition correspond to true sentences, like 'Don falls' and 'Don dies'. So if causes and effects are facts, causation is rightly reported by causal instances of

(1)   'E because C',
e.g.   'Don dies because he (Don) falls',

entailing the facts C and E, e.g. that Don falls and that he dies, which (1) says are linked as cause to effect.

On this view a true 'E because C' just states another fact, no different in that respect from C and E. In particular, this fact can also have causes and effects, i.e. there can be, and are, true instances of:

(1a)   '(E because C) because B',
e.g.   'Don dies because he falls, because his bones are brittle';
(1b)   'F because (E because C)',
e.g.   'The climb is halted because Don dies because he falls';

and so on to any degree of complexity.

In short, if a cause C and effect E are entities of the same basic sort – facts – as the fact that C causes E, then causation will be, as it seems to be, iterable. Moreover, as (1a) and (1b) show, the distinctive form of 'E because C' need not make the fact that C causes E differ in kind from its constituent facts C and E. For (1a), (1b), etc. are not new forms of causal sentence: they are simply instances of (1) in which 'C' or 'E' (or both) are also instances of (1).

This matters because there are many important examples of iterated causation that we need to make sense of: it is by no means a rare or trifling phenomenon. For even when 'C' and 'E' do not explicitly instantiate (1), the facts which correspond to them may still be causal facts. Take the fact that my mass is $M$, which is what makes any net force $F$ cause me to accelerate at $A=F/M$ [4.4]. This fact about me both embodies a causal link, between $F$ and $A$, and has its own effects. In particular, it has an effect on me whenever I perceive it indirectly by weighing myself, as when, by causing my bathroom scales to read '$M$', it causes me to believe truly that my mass is $M$ [6.3].

These perceptual examples of iterated causation, where our senses make a causal fact cause us to believe in it, are especially important in exploding the Humean myth that causation itself, as opposed to causes and effects, cannot be perceived:

> No object ever discovers, by the qualities which appear to the senses, either the causes which produced it, or the effects which will arise from it (Hume 1748 §23).

This myth, which has made many philosophers deny the very existence of singular causation, tacitly takes causal links to differ in kind from what they link and, in particular, to lack effects by which we could perceive them. Even Ducasse, who thinks we can and do observe the causal relation

> whenever we perceive that a certain change is the *only* one to have taken place immediately before, in the immediate environment of another [i.e. the effect] (Ducasse 1926 p. 132),

tacitly subscribes to this myth by equating seeing causation with seeing an effect's immediate cause. But we can do better than this if facts can be, and so have, causes and effects: we can see causal links directly. For then our senses can let us see not only C and E but also the fact that C causes E, by making that causal fact cause us to believe truly that C causes E.

Thus suppose that, to vary the example, I see that the sun is melting my snowman Fred. The fact that Fred is made of snow is among other things a causal fact, because it makes the sun's heat cause Fred to melt, just as my mass makes forces cause me to accelerate. This makes it true that

> Fred melts because he is heated, because he is made of snow,

which is an instance of (1a). And my seeing not only that Fred is heated and is melting, but also that he is made of snow, may make me believe that he melts *because* he is heated. If so, then I see an instance of causation, since my senses have made true a perceptual instance of (1b), namely that

> I believe 'E because C' because (E because C),

where 'E' is 'Fred melts' and 'C' is 'Fred is heated'.

But if all causes and effects are particulars, this account of how we see causation makes no sense, because iterated causation makes no sense. For a particular cause $c$, like Don's fall, and effect $e$, like Don's death, differ in kind from the fact that they are causally linked. That fact corresponds to a true sentence of the form

(2)    '$c$ causes $e$',

e.g.    'Don's fall causes his (Don's) death';

whereas $c$ and $e$ correspond only to referring terms, like 'Don's fall' and 'Don's death', which are neither true nor false. So if only particulars can have causes and effects, then the fact that $c$ causes $e$ cannot have them, and so in particular cannot cause us to believe in it: causal links cannot be seen.

Those who take all causes and effects to be particulars need not of course deny the existence of truths of mixed forms like:

(2a)    '($c$ causes $e$) because B',

e.g.    'Don's fall causes his death because his bones are brittle';

(2b)    'F because ($c$ causes $e$)',

e.g.    'the climb is halted because Don's fall causes his death';

and so on. But whereas (1a) and (1b) are instances of (1), (2a) and (2b) are not instances of (2). They are molecular sentences linking '$c$ causes $e$' to another sentence 'B' or 'F'. They are not, as (2) is, atomic sentences linking terms for particulars, because B and F are not particulars but facts, on a par with the fact that $c$ causes $e$. (2a) and (2b) do not therefore, as (2) does, report a relation between particulars. So if that is what causation is, then whatever makes (2a) and (2b) true, it is not causation.

This shows why we cannot even settle when causation occurs, let alone what it is, until we have settled whether causes and effects are facts or particulars. Now it may be that some causes and effects are facts and others are particulars, with correspondingly different causal links between them. But if so, then the two kinds of link must be far more closely related than (1) and (2) make them appear to be. For it can hardly be a coincidence that pairs of instances of these two forms, like

> 'Don dies because he falls' and
> 'Don's fall causes his death',

are true or false together. It is obvious in this and many other cases that whatever makes either member of each pair true will also make the other member true. So whichever of (1) and (2) we decide comes first, we must be able to derive the other from it. But first we must decide which comes first. Which does causation really link: facts or particulars?

## 2 The initial case for facts

The answer to this question may now seem obvious: causes and effects are facts. For a start, there are all the apparent and important cases of iterated causation given in §1. If causes and effects are facts, these really can be as causal as they seem to be; which it seems they cannot be if causes and effects are particulars.

On the other hand, my instances of the mixed forms (2a) and (2b),

'Don's fall causes his death because his bones are brittle' and
'the climb is halted because Don's fall causes his death',

appear to be no less uniformly causal than (1a) and (1b). So perhaps the causation in (2a) and (2b) can be taken to link particulars after all? Certainly we can recast these sentences, using 'causes' instead of 'because', to get, for example,

'Don's bones being brittle causes his fall to cause his death' and
'Don's fall's causing his death causes the climb to be halted'.

But this does not really show that causation between particulars is iterable, because the phrases 'Don's bones being brittle' and 'Don's fall's causing his death' do not refer to particulars. They are what even Davidson (1980 Essay 7), who argues that causation can only link particular events, calls 'occurrences of verb-nominalisations that are fact-like or proposi- tional' (p. 162n). In other words, they refer to whatever facts correspond to the true sentences 'Don's bones are brittle' and 'Don dies because he falls'. They are like the phrase 'Don's falling', which for this very reason I have been using to refer to the fact that Don falls, as opposed to the particular, his fall [1.4]. And just as 'Don's falling causes his dying' is a trivial variant of 'Don dies because he falls', so my recasting of these instances of (2a) and (2b) makes them trivial variants of my instances of (1a) and (1b),

'Don dies because he falls, because his bones are brittle' and
'The climb is halted because Don dies because he falls'.

In short, recasting these instances of (2a) and (2b) does nothing to show that causation between particulars can be iterated. Indeed nothing can show this, since nothing can alter the fact that only if causes and effects can be facts can the fact that *c* causes *e* have causes and effects. The many apparent examples of iterated causation therefore really do provide reason to think that some if not all causes and effects are facts.

Another reason to think this underlay my recasting in chapter 1.2 of instances of (2), '*c* causes *e*', as instances of '*e* exists because *c* exists' and thus of (1), 'E because C'. I did this recasting then merely to simplify the ensuing discussion, without begging the present question, by giving all causal statements a common form. And for that purpose I might as well have gone the other way, recasting instances of (1) as instances of (2) – except that this cannot always be done.

For what gives all instances of '*c* causes *e*' equivalent instances of 'E because C' is the fact that to every actual particular there corresponds the fact that it exists. But not all instances of 'E because C' correspond to instances of '*c* causes *e*', because not all causally related facts contain particulars. Obvious examples, which we shall consider later [11.1], occur whenever the cause or effect is that *no* particular of a certain kind exists. Thus it could be that Don does not die because he does not fall, Bill does not get cancer because he does not smoke, Kim does not recover because she does not take her medicine, and so on. In all these cases there is no particular of one kind because there is no particular of another kind. What particulars is the causation in these cases supposed to link?

There are admittedly answers to that question, even if in the end they will not do, as we shall see in chapter 11.1. But here I need only remark that in these and many other apparent cases of causation there are at least no obvious particulars for causation to link. There is no automatic or easy way of turning all causal truths of the form 'E because C' into truths of the form '*c* causes *e*', as there is the other way round. And that is another reason for taking some if not all causes and effects to be facts.

## 3 The identity of facts

Despite these reasons for taking at least some causation to link facts, many philosophers think it can only ever link particulars. They have two main grounds for thinking this. The first is an objection to facts taken, as I am taking them, to correspond to truths. The objection is that as a theory of truth (the correspondence theory) this is vacuous, because we have no independent way of saying what facts are. With this I agree: my claim that facts correspond to truths is meant to define facts, not truth [1.2]. A correspondence theory of truth will therefore have to say in other terms what *satisfies* this definition, i.e. what facts, so defined, are. It may say for example that facts are particulars having properties, like Bill having cancer. But then it will need an account of particulars and properties which does not make it viciously circular: it cannot for example just define a property $K$ as what any particular $x$ has iff '$x$ is $K$' is true.

These and other problems make it hard to devise a defensible correspondence theory of truth. But then that is not my job: my job is to devise a defensible theory of causation. And for this purpose I need not say much about the facts C and E that are entailed by true causal instances of 'E because C'. What I do need to say I shall say in chapter 13, where we shall see that causation is not really a relation at all. But that must wait until we have seen why facts must be what, if anything, causation relates. And in showing that this is so we can take for granted such pairs of facts as: Don falls and dies; Bill smokes and gets cancer; Sue visits the Bull and gets her gin; Kim takes her medicine and recovers; there is a spark and an explosion in a car engine's cylinder; and so on.

This is really all that needs saying here about facts. But one objection to them is so common that I shall have to deal with it now if I am to make what follows credible. The objection is that facts lack a clear *criterion of identity*. In other words, no clear and credible test will tell us when true sentences, statements or propositions 'P' and 'Q' correspond to the same fact, i.e. when P=Q. Tests that are clear are not credible, and tests that are credible are not clear.

Take the test which says that P and Q are identical iff the corresponding truths 'P' and 'Q' are identical, i.e. that

$$P=Q \text{ iff 'P'='Q'.}$$

This test may be credible enough if 'P' and 'Q' are propositions; but then it is not clear, since the identity conditions of true propositions are no clearer than those of facts. While if 'P' and 'Q' are sentences, then although the test may be clear enough, it is not credible, since it is obviously too strong, because languages admit different ways of stating the same fact. (No one thinks for example that the two sentences 'Bill is Kim's husband' and 'Kim is Bill's wife' state two different facts.) Moreover, one and the same fact can be and usually is statable, by different sentences, in different languages: factually accurate translation may often be difficult, but it is not always impossible.

Another clear test for the identity of facts, that

$$P=Q \text{ iff 'P' and 'Q' are both true,}$$

is not credible because it is too weak. For suppose that Don falls and dies, i.e. that 'Don falls' and 'Don dies' are both true. These are obviously two facts, not one: the fact that Don falls is not the same as the fact that he dies.

The view that all truths correspond to the same fact, i.e. that there is really only one fact, may well seem too bizarre to be taken seriously. Unfortunately there is an argument for it whose influence requires us to discuss and rebut it. For reducing the number of facts to one would immediately refute the idea that causation links facts: since the world's many causes are obviously not identical either to each other or to their effects.

The argument in question is at the core of Davidson's (1980 Essay 7 pp. 152–3) well-known attack on the idea that causation links facts, an attack which provides the other main reason to reject the idea. In §4 I shall defend the idea at length against this attack. But before doing so I have three points to make about the common cry of colleagues for a criterion of identity for facts.

First, even if some such criterion is needed, I need not supply it. I have said already that the causation reported by a true 'E because C' can link whatever makes 'C' and 'E' true. In other words, our theory of causation can help itself to whatever the right theory of truth uses to account for the truth of 'C' and 'E'. That, whatever it is, will be good enough for us.

Second, there may indeed be no one criterion of identity for all the diverse facts that causation links. But why should there be? Consider the diversity of particular things, ranging from quarks, through molecules, cells, organisms, mountains and planets, to galaxies. Why must there be a single identity criterion for things of all these kinds: why may not each kind have its own? If it does, surely no one will take that fact to disprove the existence of particular things. But why then should the lack of a single identity criterion for all facts cast wholesale doubt on their existence?

Third, if contingent facts of all kinds do need a single identity criterion, there is a far more credible candidate than the two I have so far mentioned. It is the criterion Davidson himself (1980 Essay 8 p. 179) offers for the identity of events, namely that, for any events $d$ and $d'$,

> $d=d'$ iff $d$ and $d'$ have all the same causes and effects.

That is, $d=d'$ iff for no 'c' or 'e' does replacing 'd' by 'd'' make a true 'c causes $d$' or '$d$ causes $e$' false or a false one true. Take a spark causing an explosion in a car engine's cylinder. Is the spark the same event as the short circuit? The test says that it is iff replacing 'the spark' by 'the short circuit' in any sentence of the form 'the spark causes ...' or '... causes the spark' (where 'the spark' refers to this particular spark) would never make a true sentence false or a false one true.

Now at least half of this test will certainly apply to facts, since it applies trivially to everything. For one and the same entity, whether it be a fact or a particular or anything else, cannot both have and not have a given cause or effect. This half of the test tells us nothing, either about causation or about events. The other half of the test is the serious half: the thesis that events are identical *if* they have all the same causes and effects. But this thesis also applies just as well to facts – or at least to those facts that have, and therefore are, causes or effects. For of any such facts D and D' we can say just as credibly that

D=D' if D and D' have all the same causes and effects;

i.e. that D=D' if for no 'C' or 'E' does replacing 'D' by 'D'' make a true causal 'D because C' or 'E because D' false or a false one true.

Facts that are causes and effects can therefore pass the causal test of identity as easily as events can. And for what it is worth, they can also pass the spatiotemporal test (Quine 1985 p. 168), which says that

$d=d'$ iff $d$ and $d'$ occupy the same region of spacetime.

For as we noted in chapter 1.2, a fact P can be located in space and time, if

'P at $s$ at $t$' [is] true, everywhere and always, for some but not all places $s$ and times $t$, with a smallest such $s$ and $t$ ..., included in all the others, which is P's location.

Thus if located events can be identified by their locations, so too, rightly or wrongly, can located facts. In short, neither the spatiotemporal nor the causal test of identity, nor any other test I know of, shows facts to be less acceptable than particulars as entities capable of being causes and effects.

## 4 The argument that causation links all facts or none

It is however one thing to admit the existence of facts, quite another to admit that causation links them. So we must now see what is wrong with the argument, mentioned above, which purports to prove that causation cannot link facts, i.e. that 'E because C' cannot be the form of any true causal statement.

The first assumption of this argument, that causation does not link all facts, is undeniable [1.3], since no one can deny that there are true 'C' and 'E' for which 'E because C' is false. What the argument then tries to show is that, if 'E because C' were true for any true 'C' and 'E', it would have to be true for all. If that were so, then since 'E because C' is *not* true for all true 'C' and 'E', it could never be true for any true 'C' and 'E'. And then, since it is certainly never true for any false 'C' or 'E' [1.3], it could never be true at all: there would be no true causal statements of the form 'E because C'.

The flaw here lies in one of the two assumptions which this *reductio* argument needs in order to reach its absurd conclusion that when 'C' and 'E' are true 'E because C' must be either always false or always true. These assumptions are that

(i)     a true 'E because C' cannot be falsified by replacing 'C' or 'E' by logically equivalent sentences, and

(ii)    a true 'E because C' cannot be falsified by replacing a referring term in it by a co-referring one, i.e. one referring to the same entity.

The argument then runs as follows:

(a) Assume that 'E because C' is true for some true 'C' and 'E'.

(b) Any sentence 'P' is logically equivalent to '$\{x{:}x{=}x\&P\}{=}\{x{:}x{=}x\}$'. ($\{x{:}x{=}x\}$ is the set of entities that are identical to themselves, which is the set of everything. $\{x{:}x{=}x\&P\}$ is the set of entities such that they are self-identical and 'P' is true. So, necessarily, this set *is* the set of everything iff 'P' *is* true: hence the logical equivalence of '$\{x{:}x{=}x\&P\}{=}\{x{:}x{=}x\}$' and 'P'.)

(c) It follows from (i), (a) and (b) that we may replace 'C' and 'E' in 'E because C' by '$\{x{:}x{=}x\&C\}{=}\{x{:}x{=}x\}$' and '$\{x{:}x{=}x\&E\}{=}\{x{:}x{=}x\}$' to get

(19)    '$\{x{:}x{=}x\&E\}{=}\{x{:}x{=}x\}$ because $\{x{:}x{=}x\&C\}{=}\{x{:}x{=}x\}$'.

(d) It follows from (b) that for *any* true sentences 'Q' and 'R', including 'C' and 'E', the referring terms '$\{x{:}x{=}x\&Q\}$' and '$\{x{:}x{=}x\&R\}$' refer to the same entity, namely $\{x{:}x{=}x\}$, the set of everything.

(e) Given (ii) and (d), we may replace '$\{x{:}x{=}x\&C\}$' and '$\{x{:}x{=}x\&E\}$' in (19) by the co-referring '$\{x{:}x{=}x\&Q\}$' and '$\{x{:}x{=}x\&R\}$' to get

(20)    '$\{x{:}x{=}x\&R\}{=}\{x{:}x{=}x\}$ because $\{x{:}x{=}x\&Q\}{=}\{x{:}x{=}x\}$'.

(f) Finally in (20), given (i), we may replace '$\{x{:}x{=}x\&Q\}{=}\{x{:}x{=}x\}$' and '$\{x{:}x{=}x\&R\}{=}\{x{:}x{=}x\}$' by 'Q' and 'R' to get

'R because Q'.

In short, on the assumptions (i) and (ii), any true causal 'E because C' entails 'R because Q' for all true 'Q' and 'R': if causation links any facts it links all facts. But it does not link all facts. So it links none. 'E because C' is not the form of any true causal statement: causation links no facts.

## 5  How causation can link facts

What is wrong with this argument? Nothing, given (i) and (ii). So for causation to link facts, one of these assumptions must be false. Let us take them in turn.

(i) says that a true 'E because C' cannot be falsified by replacing 'C' or 'E' with a logically equivalent sentence. I think this may well be true. In particular, the objectivity of the chances that causes give their effects stops

(16)  $ch_C(E) > ch_{-C}(E)$,

which 'E because C' entails, being falsified in this way. For as there is no way in which 'E' can be true and a logically equivalent 'E'' false, any chance $ch(E)$ that E is a fact must equal the corresponding $ch(E')$. And if E' must conform to (16) iff E does, then replacing 'E' by 'E'' cannot falsify 'E because C' by falsifying (16); and I can see no other reason to deny assumption (i).

But I can see every reason to deny assumption (ii), which seems to me credible only when confused with the fact that, as I shall put it,

(ii')  'C causes E' is always *transparent for* C and E.

'C causes E' is the form (1'), equivalent by definition to 'E because C', but in which 'C' and 'E' are used as singular terms abbreviating 'the fact that C' and 'the fact that E' [1.4]. Then to say that 'C causes E' is always transparent for C and E is to say that no true instance of it can be falsified by replacing 'C' or 'E' by a term referring to the same fact.

To see why (ii') must be true, first consider its analogue for particulars:

(ii'')  'c causes e' is always transparent for c and e.

This says that no true 'c causes e' can be falsified by replacing 'c' or 'e' by any term referring to the same particular. In other words, the truth of any 'c causes e' depends only on whether the particulars it refers to are linked as cause to effect, not on how it refers to those particulars. And it is easy to see that this must be so.

For suppose it was not. Then there could be two pairs of co-referring terms 'c'/'c'' and 'e'/'e'' such that 'c causes e' is true but 'c' causes e' and 'c causes e'' are false. But this means that c and c' could have different effects, and e and e' different causes, even though c is c' and e is e'. And this cannot be. For whatever causes and effects are, a single cause c (=c') cannot both have and not have an effect e, and a single effect e (=e') cannot both have and not have a cause c. So if replacing 'c' by 'c'' falsifies a true 'c causes e', 'c' and 'c'' must refer to different particulars, and similarly for 'e' and 'e''. This is why 'c causes e' must be transparent for c and e.

Take our car engine cylinder [6.2]. If the spark in the cylinder *is* the short circuit, and the explosion *is* the rapid expansion of the gas, then if

'the spark causes the explosion'

is true, so are

> 'the short circuit causes the explosion',
> 'the spark causes the rapid expansion of the gas' and
> 'the short circuit causes the rapid expansion of the gas'.

This argument for the transparency of '*c* causes *e*' is unanswerable. And since it assumes nothing about what kind of entity *c* and *e* are, it applies equally well to facts. We can therefore use it to prove (ii'), in which 'C' and 'E' are used to refer to the facts that correspond to the true sentences 'C' and 'E' in a true 'E because C'. 'C causes E' thus has the very same form as '*c* causes *e*', differing from it only in referring to facts rather than particulars. But that cannot stop the above argument showing that 'C causes E' must also always be transparent for C and E.

For suppose it was not. Then there could be two pairs of co-referring terms 'C'/'C'' and 'E'/'E'' such that 'C causes E' is true but 'C' causes E' and 'C causes E'' are false. But this means that C and C' could have different effects, and E and E' different causes, even though C *is* C' and E *is* E'. And this cannot be. For whatever facts are, a single fact C (=C') cannot both have and not have an effect E, and a single fact E (=E') cannot both have and not have a cause C. So if replacing 'C' with 'C'' falsifies a true 'C causes E', 'C' and 'C'' must refer to different facts, and similarly for 'E' and 'E''. 'C causes E' must therefore be as transparent for C and E as '*c* causes *e*' is for *c* and *e*, and for the same reason.

Thus, taking the same example, if there being a spark in the cylinder is the same fact as there being a short circuit in it, and if there being an explosion is the same fact as the gas expanding rapidly, then if

> 'there is an explosion because there is a spark'

is true, so are

> 'there is an explosion because there is a short circuit',
> 'the gas expands rapidly because there is a spark' and
> 'the gas expands rapidly because there is a short circuit'.

(ii') is therefore as demonstrably true as (ii'') is. And if (ii'') is all that is meant by saying that causation links particulars regardless of how they are referred to, (ii') must equally be all that is meant by saying that causation links facts regardless of how they are referred to. Those of us who take causation to link facts cannot therefore be committed thereby to anything stronger than (ii').

In particular, we cannot be committed to (ii), since the argument for (ii') does not entail (ii). For what (ii) says is that 'E because C' is transparent not only for the facts C and E but also for any particular referred to within the sentences 'C' and 'E'. But this does not follow from (ii'), and is not true, as we shall now see. Some true causal instances of 'E because C' can be falsified by replacing referring terms within 'C' and 'E' by co-referring terms. And this is why the argument given in §4 fails to show that causation cannot link facts.

To see why (ii) is false, suppose that several climbers fall off Castle Rock, but that Don falls first because he has the weakest rope, so that

(21)   'Don's fall is the first because his rope is the weakest'

is true. Now (21) is an instance of 'E because C', which entails both 'C' and 'E'. That is, it entails both that Don's rope *is* the weakest and that Don's fall *is* the first. In other words, it entails that 'Don's rope' and 'the weakest rope' refer to the same thing, and that 'Don's fall' and 'the first fall' refer to the same event. So if, as (ii) says, (21) were transparent for Don's fall and Don's rope, it could not be falsified by replacing either member of either of these pairs of terms by the other member.

But it can, since the results of two such replacements,

(21')   'Don's fall is Don's fall because his rope is the weakest' and
(21")   'Don's fall is the first because his rope is his rope',

are both obviously false. The necessary fact that Don's fall is Don's fall does not depend, causally or otherwise, on the contingency of his having the weakest rope. And Don's falling first is not caused by the necessary fact that his rope is his rope. (We can ignore the readings of 'Don's fall is Don's fall' and 'Don's rope is Don's rope' in which they are not necessarily true: in those readings (21') and (21") may well be true [12.6].)

Although the falsity of (21') and (21") seems to me self-evident, it can also be derived from and explained by the need for causes to raise their effects' chances, i.e. for any cause C and its effect E to be such that $ch_C(E) > ch_{\sim C}(E)$. For 'E' in (21') is 'Don's fall is Don's fall' which, being necessarily true, has a chance 1 of being true whether or not Don's rope is the weakest, so that $ch_C(E) = ch_{\sim C}(E) = 1$. Thus the reason (21') is false is that E here is a necessary fact, and nothing can raise a chance of 1.

(21") is false for a different reason. Here the necessary fact, that Don's rope is his rope, is not E but C. So the question here is what $ch_{\sim C}(E)$ is, i.e. what chance Don has of falling first in worlds where this necessary fact is not a fact. But since no such worlds exist, this question has no answer. There is no such thing as Don's chance of falling first when his rope is not his rope: when 'C' is a necessary truth $ch_{\sim C}(E)$ does not exist, i.e. it has no value. But if it has no value, then in particular it has no value less than

$ch_C(E)$, thus making '$ch_C(E)>ch_{\sim C}(E)$' false yet again. This explains why necessary facts can no more have effects than they can have causes.

In short, what makes (21) *opaque for* (i.e. not transparent for) Don's fall and his rope is that it is an instance of 'E because C' in which 'C' or 'E' is an identity statement. For whenever 'C' or 'E' is a true identity statement of the form '$a$ is the $K$', or 'the $K$ is the $K'$', it can always be turned into a necessary truth, by replacing 'the $K$' with the co-referring term '$a$' or 'the $K'$' (or *vice versa*), thus making '$ch_C(E)>ch_{\sim C}(E)$' false. And this is what stops the argument of §4 showing that causation links all facts if it links any: because it makes that argument's assumption (ii) fail just when the argument needs it.

We can show this as follows. Let us grant the argument's assumption (i) and hence its steps (a)–(d). That is, let us agree that 'E because C' entails

(19)   '$\{x{:}x{=}x\&E\}{=}\{x{:}x{=}x\}$ because $\{x{:}x{=}x\&C\}{=}\{x{:}x{=}x\}$'.

The next step, (e), is where the argument fails. For the fact that the truth of 'C', 'E', 'Q' and 'R' makes '$\{x{:}x{=}x\&C\}$', '$\{x{:}x{=}x\&E\}$', '$\{x{:}x{=}x\&Q\}$' and '$\{x{:}x{=}x\&R\}$' all refer to $\{x{:}x{=}x\}$ cannot make (19) entail

(20)   '$\{x{:}x{=}x\&R\}{=}\{x{:}x{=}x\}$ because $\{x{:}x{=}x\&Q\}{=}\{x{:}x{=}x\}$'.

For if it did, i.e. if (19) were transparent for $\{x{:}x{=}x\}$, then since '$\{x{:}x{=}x\}$' also refers to $\{x{:}x{=}x\}$, (19) would also have to entail both

'$\{x{:}x{=}x\}{=}\{x{:}x{=}x\}$ because $\{x{:}x{=}x\&Q\}{=}\{x{:}x{=}x\}$' and
'$\{x{:}x{=}x\&R\}{=}\{x{:}x{=}x\}$ because $\{x{:}x{=}x\}{=}\{x{:}x{=}x\}$'.

These, by (i), replacing '$\{x{:}x{=}x\&Q\}{=}\{x{:}x{=}x\}$' and '$\{x{:}x{=}x\&R\}{=}\{x{:}x{=}x\}$' with their equivalents 'Q' and 'R', then entail the following analogues of (21') and (21''):

(20')   '$\{x{:}x{=}x\}{=}\{x{:}x{=}x\}$ because Q';
(20'')   'R because $\{x{:}x{=}x\}{=}\{x{:}x{=}x\}$'.

But (19) can no more entail (20') and (20'') than (21) can entail (21') and (21''). For since 'Q' is any true sentence, what (20') says is that *any* fact – say that Don has the weakest rope – will cause the set of everything to be the set of everything. This is obviously false, and for the same reason that (21') is false: $\{x{:}x{=}x\}{=}\{x{:}x{=}x\}$ is a necessary fact which cannot be caused by any Q, because its chance, 1, would be no less if 'Q' were false. Similarly with (20''), which says that *every* fact – say that Don falls first – is caused by the fact that the set of everything is the set of everything. This is obviously false too, for the same reason that (21'') is: the necessary fact

$\{x:x=x\}=\{x:x=x\}$ can no more have effects than it can have causes. That is what makes (20″) false for all 'R'.

In short, step (e) fails because it requires (19) to be both transparent for the particular, $\{x:x=x\}$, to which it refers and an instance of 'E because C' in which 'C' and 'E' state identities. But as we have seen, it cannot be both, because when C or E is a fact of identity the '$ch_C(E)>ch_{-C}(E)$' which 'E because C' entails is opaque.

The fact that causes must raise their effects' chances does more than tell us why a necessary fact like $\{x:x=x\}=\{x:x=x\}$ cannot have the causes and effects which (20′) and (20″) say it has. It tells us why the inference from (19) to (20), and hence to 'R because Q', need not preserve the truth of 'E because C'. The reason is that the values of $ch_C(E)$ and $ch_{-C}(E)$, and hence the fact that $ch_C(E)>ch_{-C}(E)$, depend on more than the truth of 'C' and 'E', because different facts can and often do have different chances. This is what makes '$ch_C(E)>ch_{-C}(E)$' and thus 'E because C' false for some true 'C' and 'E' and true for others. This shows both why Davidson's argument fails – by showing why its assumption (ii) fails – and why its conclusion is false. In short, it is because causes must raise the chances of their effects that causation can and does link some facts without linking all of them.

All this reinforces the already overwhelming case for making causation conform to (16), $ch_C(E)>ch_{-C}(E)$: nothing else I know of can explain why the inference from (19) to (20) fails where it does fail. But strong though the case for this constraint on causation is, I must emphasise that it is not needed to refute Davidson's argument against causation linking facts. To do that we need only show *that* (19) is opaque for $\{x:x=x\}$, not *why* it is. And what shows this is the proof I have given that, if (19) were transparent for $\{x:x=x\}$, it would entail the obviously false (20′) and (20″). This proof, which does not assume that causes raise their effects' chances, is enough to demolish the case against causation linking facts.

## 6 Facts and events

We have seen that the arguments considered in §3–5 fail to show either that there are no facts or that causation does not link them. Nor does any other argument I know of show either of these things. Nothing stops causes and effects being facts. And this being so, we have already seen good reasons to suppose that many of them are facts.

But this does not settle the question of what in general causes and effects are. For if there are good reasons for taking some causes and effects to be facts, there are equally good reasons for taking others to be particulars, especially particular events, like Don's fall and his death. Moreover, as we have seen, many if not all of these events correspond to factual causes and effects, like the facts that Don falls and that he dies. But how, if Don's fall and the fact that he falls are both causes, and his death and the fact that he dies are both effects, are the causal links between these two pairs of entities related? That is the next question we must answer. But before we can answer it we need to know more about what these peculiarly causal kinds of particulars – events – are.

# 10 *Events*

## 1 Events and things

In discussions of causation the word 'event' has become a term of art which different artists use in different ways, not all of which will serve our turn. In particular, calling causes and effects 'events' will tell us nothing about what they are if, like many philosophers, we call all singular causes and effects 'events' whatever we think they are. Doing this is indeed worse than useless: it is positively misleading, because it obliterates the important distinction between causes and effects that are facts and those that are particulars.

This is why I follow Davidson (1980 Essay 8) in reserving the term 'event' for a sort of particular. By this I mean that, like people, animals, plants and inanimate things, events correspond only to names and other referring terms, not to true sentences [1.2]. But we need to know more about particulars than this, since this fact about them does not distinguish them from entities of other sorts which I shall also need to invoke later in this account of causation. Specifically, it does not distinguish them from universals, i.e. from properties, like having a certain mass, and relations, like being a certain distance apart. For properties and relations can also be referred to by names and other terms, such as '1 kilogramme' and 'the mass of the sun', or '25 kilometres' and 'the distance between Cambridge and London'; and they too do not correspond to true sentences.

The obvious way of distinguishing particulars from universals, by taking them to be localised in space and time, may not work in all cases. The reason is that some unlocalised entities, like numbers and some or all sets, may also be particulars. However, all the particulars which might be singular causes or effects will certainly have more or less restricted locations in space and time [1.1]. So this constraint will at least distinguish all the particulars that concern us from universals.

I shall need to say more about particulars and universals later; but not yet. What I must say more about now are events, which is what most particular causes and effects are, since both the nature and the existence of events are controversial [1.2]. Yet if most or even much causation is to link

121

particulars, particular events must exist, or there will be too few particulars to go round. If for example there were no such events as Don's fall and Don's death, the causation which appears to link these particulars could really only link the facts that Don falls and that he dies. For here there is only one other relevant particular, Don, and causation needs two: one to be the cause and the other to be the effect. The same goes for our other examples: Sue's visiting the Bull causing her to get her gin; Kim's taking her medicine causing her to recover; the spark in a car engine's cylinder causing an explosion. In these and many other cases causation can only link particulars by linking particular events.

What then are events, and what in particular distinguishes them from particulars of the other and less contentious kinds that I am calling 'things'? There must be answers to these questions, since everyone can divide particulars into these two sorts, and will moreover agree on which kinds of particulars each sort includes. Take the following lists of kinds of events and of related things:

> *Events*: Lightning flashes, eruptions, tides, falls, meals, speeches, birthday parties, elections, battles, ...
>
> *Things*: Electrons, volcanoes, oceans, bodies, omelettes, books, babies, political parties, armies, ...

Whatever we think events and things are, we will all agree which of the two lists these and many other kinds of particulars should be put in. And we will also all agree that the particulars in the first list are more often and more obviously causes and effects than the particulars in the second. But we still need to say what we are agreeing on, and why. For while our obvious and remarkable agreement on examples strongly suggests the existence of a generic difference between events and things, it does not of course tell us what that difference is.

## 2  The temporal parts of events

The difference between events and things, I and many others have argued (Simons 1987 chs 4.1, 5.1; Mellor 1998 ch. 8.1), is this. Every particular that is extended in space, whether it is a thing or an event, has spatial parts. An omelette, for example, which is a thing, obviously has spatial parts. And so does a family meal, which is an event, its spatial parts being the meals eaten on that occasion by each member of the family. But not every particular that is extended in time has temporal parts. Events do: each course of a meal is a temporal part of it. But things do not. An omelette has no temporal parts, only spatial ones. And this I maintain is why things, such as omelettes and their spatial parts, are wholly present at any instant of time at which they exist at all. Whereas extended events, like meals and the courses that are their temporal parts, are never wholly present at any instant.

This distinction does not of course apply to the degenerate case of particulars which are not extended in time, like spacetime points. Space-time points and regions are however peculiar particulars, which we shall need to distinguish later on from the things and events that are located at them [16.7]. But there may also be instantaneous particulars that are not spacetime points. If so, I shall call them events and not things, in order to preserve two appealing if inessential implications: (i) that events are not things, and (ii) that things are wholly present at more than one time and so can be reidentified as such from time to time (Strawson 1959 ch. 1).

Even with these qualifications, this account of the distinction between events and things is contentious. It depends, for one thing, on a substantial concept of a part. For if all parts needed were spacetime boundaries, then things too would have temporal parts, like Kim–in–1990. But I mean more than this by parts of things and events. I mean what we all mean by spatial parts, such as parts of our bodies: I mean things or events whose existence is logically independent of the wholes they are parts of. Kim–in–1990 is not in this sense a temporal part of Kim because, unlike her arms and legs, it cannot exist apart from her. Each step of her walk to her medicine chest, on the other hand, could exist on its own: it is as substantial a temporal part of her walk as her limbs are spatial parts of her body.

As for parts, so for wholes. They too must be things or events in their own right: their existence cannot be entailed merely by the existence of the things or events which are in fact their parts. This means in particular that a thing or event must be something more than the so-called *mereological sum* of the things or events that are its parts, an entity which exists if they do by mere definition (Simons 1987 p. 1).

With these substantial concepts of part and whole the temporal-parts test distinguishes all the located but non-instantaneous kinds of events and things I can think of. Take flashes of lightning, which are obviously events. It is equally obvious that, however short the interval [$t$] of instants that is the duration of a flash, only a part of it is wholly present in any shorter interval within [$t$], and no part of it is wholly present at any instant within [$t$]. The electrons in the flash, on the other hand, are wholly present at every instant within [$t$].

Similarly for the other items in my lists of events and things. Only temporal parts of eruptions, tides, falls, speeches, birthday parties, elections and battles are wholly present in any time interval within their full durations, and no non-instantaneous event is ever wholly present at an instant. Whereas volcanoes, oceans, bodies, books, babies, political parties and armies are all wholly present at every instant of their lives. And similarly for all other temporally extended kinds of particulars which have locations in spacetime but are not spacetime regions. I can think of none that we would both put in my list of events and take to be wholly present at an instant. Nor can I think of any that we would put in my list of things while denying that they are wholly present at some instant.

The only philosophers who will deny this, because they do credit things with temporal parts, are those who, like Quine, deny the significance of the distinction between things and events:

> Physical objects, conceived thus four-dimensionally in spacetime, are not to be distinguished from events ... (Quine 1960 p. 171).

But to say this is not to deny that our distinction between events and things is that between particulars with and without temporal parts: it is simply to deny that this distinction has any basis in reality. But this is not to deny the existence of the particulars we call events: far from it. For Quine, Don's fall and death are as available as Don to be particular causes and effects. So even though I think Quine is wrong to deny the reality of our distinction between events and things, that is not a point I need to argue here.

The only philosophers to whom I really need to sell the temporal-parts test for events are those who deny that events exist, thereby denying the existence of most if not all particular causes and effects. This scepticism about events is sufficiently common to make the test worth selling, since the test shows why the existence of events is apt to be overlooked: precisely because, unlike things, they are never wholly present at any instant. This is why anyone asked to list presently existing entities will be far more likely to list things (volcanoes, oceans, bodies, books, babies, political parties, armies, ...) than events (eruptions, tides, falls, meals, speeches, birthday parties, elections, battles, ...). Hence the widespread feeling that events are in some way less real than things, a feeling which our test can explain away as a natural consequence of the difference between events and things.

This basic source of scepticism about events may be further reinforced by the equally widespread and mistaken view that the present is more real than the future, if not than the past. This view requires things and events to be not merely earlier or later than each other but also past, present or future: respects in which everything in time changes as it 'flows' from the future to the past *via* the present. This so-called *tensed* theory of time has several variants, differing in what they take being past, present or future to entail. Some claim that only the present is real, i.e. exists in the atemporal sense of 'exist' that is needed to stop this claim being a trivial tautology

[1.2]. Others take the past to be as real as the present. But most tensed views of time agree that the future is in some way less real, or less fixed, than the present. And in whatever way a tensed theory favours the reality or fixity of the present and perhaps the past, it will naturally favour present things over present events with future parts. Thus it will favour a wholly present falling Don over his partly future fall, and similarly in other cases.

But as I remarked in the Introduction, the tensed theory of time is provably false (see my 1998 chs 1–7), which is why it can give no reason to doubt the reality of events. And on the demonstrably correct *tenseless* view of time, the reality of a thing or event never depends on its temporal location. The actual future, like the actual past, is no less real than the actual present. So the existence of an event like Don's fall is no more impugned by its being never wholly present at a point in time than the existence of Don himself is impugned by his being nowhere wholly present at a point in space.

## 3  The identity of events

There are however other objections to events, which do not depend on their having temporal parts, or on a mistakenly tensed view of time. One is that the identity criteria of events are less clear than those of things. That is, if '*d*' and '*d'*' refer to events and '*b*' and '*b'*' refer to things, it is less clear what makes $d=d'$ than it is what makes $b=b'$.

This objection to events is the same as the objection to facts discussed in chapter 9.3, and part of my answer to that objection will serve to answer this one. For first, we may admit that no one identity criterion will apply to events of all kinds, any more than one applies to facts of all kinds. But equally no one such criterion applies to things of all the kinds listed in §1, nor to those listed earlier: quarks, molecules, cells, organisms, mountains and planets, clusters of galaxies [9.3]. Things of these very diverse kinds have equally diverse criteria of identity, which are generally no clearer than those of comparably specific kinds of events. For example, whatever fixes the identities (and hence the number) of armies in a war, or of mountains in the Himalayas, it certainly delivers no clearer answers to those questions than whatever fixes the identities and hence the number of battles in a war, or of tremors in an earthquake.

Moreover, even if all events had to have the same identity criterion, they would be no worse off in that respect than things are. For both of the standard tests of identity mentioned in chapter 9.3 apply at least as well to events as to things. Take the spatiotemporal test, which says of any events *d* and *d'* just what it says of things, namely that $d=d'$ iff *d* and *d'* occupy the same region of spacetime. This test is indeed contentious, and I think it is wrong, but it is no less credible for events than for things. And the other test is more credible for events – not surprisingly, since it was devised for them. This is the causal test, which says that $d$ and $d'$ are identical iff they have all the same causes and effects. That is far more credible as a thesis about events than it is as a thesis about things, if only because it is far less obvious that causation links things than that it links events. But this being so, it is if anything things rather than events which lack a clear criterion of identity.

## 4 Events and changes

Other objections to events rest less on differences between things and events than on their obviously close connections, which suggest that one of these two types of particular might be reducible to the other; and reductions have in fact been proposed in both directions. However we need not consider here how things might be reduced to events, e.g. by crediting them with temporal parts [§2]. For that, as we noted in §2, would not deprive us of particular causes and effects: only a reduction of events to things would do that.

The obvious way to reduce events to things is to identify them with changes in things (Lombard 1986). A change is some thing having one property at one time and another, incompatible, property later: e.g. being first alive and then dead, or first hot and then cold – pairs of properties which no one thing can have simultaneously. Changes thus correspond to conjunctions of true sentences saying that the things in question do have those properties at those times. In other words, changes, and *a fortiori* any events identified with them, are really not particulars but facts.

Most of the apparently particular events in our examples do indeed involve changes. Don's fall entails a change in his position, and his death entails a change in his bodily state. Bill's getting cancer includes a change in his body, and his smoking involves a sequence of changes in the contents of his lungs. Similarly, obviously, for Sue visiting the Bull and getting her gin and for Kim taking her medicine and recovering from her illness. Similarly again when a spark causes an explosion in a car engine's cylinder: the gas mixture through which the spark passes first changes in temperature and then and therefore changes in pressure. One way or another, many if not all causally linked events involve changes in things.

But not all events are changes in things. For a start, the beginning or end of a thing is not always a change. It obviously cannot be a change in that thing, and it will not always be a change in anything else. An animal's death, for example, may indeed be just a change in its body. But not if the animal is killed by being vaporised, or otherwise destroyed by the destruction or scattering of its bodily parts. For even when a thing's parts survive it, they may no longer be parts of any other thing in which its demise could be a change. Some events, moreover, are not even the beginnings or ends of things: they are no part of the history of any thing. Of what thing's history, for example, is a flash of lightning a part?

Things could perhaps be postulated *ad hoc* for events to be changes in: as a last resort, the whole universe, construed as a single thing which has all other things as its spatial parts. But that would be a poor way of making events changes, and no way of reducing them to independently identified things. Nor would it work for the beginning or end of the universe itself – a fact which can hardly be taken as an *a priori* disproof of the Big Bang.

Moreover, even if all events were changes, it would still not follow that all particulars located in space and time are things. For changes need more than things with changing properties and relations. Since changes are things having incompatible properties at different times, they also need times. And times – or points or regions of spacetime – are particulars in their own right [16.7], which are certainly not reducible to changes in things.

## 5 Davidson's argument for events

There is yet another reason for taking changes to require events as well as things. This is that even when statements of change do not refer explicitly to particular events, they may still entail the existence of events. The reason is that many such statements have entailments of which, as Davidson (1980 Essay 6) has argued, the best explanation is that changes are, or at least entail, particular events.

Take the following state of affairs:

(a)   Don falls fifteen metres onto rocks.

This obviously entails that

(b)   Don falls,
(c)   Don falls fifteen metres, and
(d)   Don falls onto rocks.

If it is obvious *that* these entailments hold, it is not at all obvious *why* they hold unless (a) entails the existence of a particular event which is

(i)    a fall,
(ii)   of Don,
(iii)  fifteen metres long, and
(iv)   onto rocks.

For obviously any particular that satisfies all the four conditions (i)–(iv) must satisfy any two or three of them: hence the entailments (b)–(d). These therefore, by the principle of inference to the best explanation [6.4], give us reason to infer the existence of such a particular, namely Don's fall. But then this particular, Don's fall, is as good a candidate for being the change in Don as is the fact that Don falls.

Similarly for most and perhaps all other cases of change. Taking changes to be particulars is no less credible than taking them to be facts. So even when an apparent event *is* a change, it may still be the particular it appears to be: distinct from the thing in which it is a change, but not just a fact about that thing.

This view of change explains away another source of scepticism about particular events. This is the fact that we use relatively few names for them, as opposed to definite descriptions which rely on names for things, like 'Don's death' and 'Kim's recovery'. We do admittedly use some names for events, like 'the Big Bang', 'World War II' and 'the 1992 Olympics', but far fewer than for things like people and places. Yet if changes are particular events, then since most things change many times, particular events must far outnumber particular things. Why then, if all these events exist, do so few of them have names?

The reason is probably that, as Strawson (1959 ch. 1) observes, we use names mainly to *re*identify particulars which are wholly present at more than one time. If so, then since temporally extended events are never wholly present at even one time, never mind several, we lack this reason to name them. But Davidson's account of change shows how we can commit ourselves to the existence of events without identifying them even once. For on this account, although 'Don falls' and 'Don dies' do not refer to any particular event, they do entail that some such particulars – a fall of Don and a death of Don – exist. But because these particulars are events, there will be less need to reidentify them later than there would be if they were things, and thus less reason to name them. So when, as here, we want to refer to them, we use definite descriptions constructed from the names we use to reidentify the things they are changes in. But if this is why we rarely name events, we must not infer, from our lacking names for events, that they do not exist.

## 6 Events for the sake of argument

These and other arguments persuade me that many of the particular events which causation seems to link do in fact exist. The arguments for the existence of these events are not indeed conclusive, and many philosophers reject them. But the idea that there are particular events needs no more defence from me. It might need more defence if I were going to argue that causation only linked particulars: since if it did, it would certainly need to link particular events. But since I shall argue no such thing, I need not be too concerned to rebut objections to events.

In the next chapter we shall see that causation mostly links facts, and that if and when it does link particulars, it does so only by linking facts in which those particulars figure. So no causation would be lost even if there were no particular events. Even if the apparent particulars, Don's fall and Don's death, did not exist to be linked as cause to effect, Don could and would still die because he falls. But I believe these events do exist and so could be linked by causation, as they appear to be. I shall therefore, if only for the sake of argument, grant their existence in order to see whether, and if so how, causation can link them as well as the corresponding facts that Don falls and that he dies.

# 11 *Particular causes and effects*

## 1 Causation and causal explanation

If there are particular events, causation might well be able to link particulars whenever it seems to do so. In other words, every causal truth whose apparent form is (2), '*c* causes *e*', might really be made true, as it appears to be, by causation linking the particulars *c* and *e*. Don's fall might really be what causes his death; the spark in a car engine's cylinder might really be what causes the explosion that follows it; and so on. Why should we doubt that this is so, now we have granted the existence of particular events?

The reason some doubt must remain is that it remains to be seen how causation between particulars is related to the causation between facts which is reported by corresponding instances of 'E because C'. How *is* the fact that Don's fall causes his death related to the fact that Don dies because he falls? These two causal facts must be related because, as we noted in chapter 9.1, they are obviously not independent: they stand or fall together. Don will only die because he falls if his fall causes his death, and *vice versa*. So there cannot really be two independent causal links here, one between particulars and the other between facts. One of these links must reduce in some way to the other. The only question is how, and which way, the reduction goes. Which of these two types of entity does causation really link, particulars or facts?

Let us start by looking at some consequences of taking causation to link particulars. Davidson (1980 Essay 7), who does this, therefore takes 'E because C' to give the logical form not of causal statements but of causal explanations [5.6]. So for him my form (1'), 'C causes E', which by definition is equivalent to 'E because C' [1.4], should really read

'C causally explains E'.

In short, what I call facts are for Davidson linked not by causation itself but only by causal explanation.

How can this be? How can facts explain other facts causally without causing them? There is indeed more to causation than explanation, since

130

factual causes do more than explain their effects: they provide evidence for them, and more or less useful means of bringing them about [4–6]. But Davidson needs more than a distinction between causation and causal explanation: he needs a dichotomy. For, as I noted in chapter 5.6, 'it takes more than a referring term to be an *explanans* or an *explanandum*: it takes a true sentence'. This means that, in the sense in which a cause might be an explanation, explanations must be facts, not particulars; and so must what they explain. But this entails that if all causes had to be particulars, none could ever explain its effects – or anything else – because explanations, being facts, could not be causes. Similarly, if all effects had to be particulars, they could never be explained, by causes or by anything else, because only facts can be explained.

This dichotomy is very hard to accept. It is, as we have seen, a strong connotation of causation that causes explain their effects [5.6]. Why else, after all, should we use 'be*cause*' as an explanatory connective? Why else should we take 'C causes E' to entail 'C explains E' – an entailment which is presupposed by Davidson's interpretation of 'C causes E' as 'C causally explains E'? In short, Davidson's dichotomy between causation and causal explanation is a most unwelcome consequence of his view that causation only links particulars. It is certainly not a consequence which recommends the view.

Nor of course does anybody think it is. Davidson's own reason for taking causation to link no facts is not this dichotomy but his argument that causation cannot link some facts without linking all of them. But since that argument fails [9.4], it can give us no reason to deny that causation can do what it often seems to do, namely link facts, thus allowing factual causes to explain their factual effects.

## 2  Negative causes and effects

However, showing that causation can and does link facts does not of course show that it always links facts. Nor does it show that facts rather than particulars are what causation primarily links. It could be the other way round: it could be that Don dies because he falls only because his fall causes his death, and similarly in other cases. It could be that whenever causation links or seems to link facts, what it primarily or really links are particular constituents of those facts. But is this really so? Does causation between facts always entail and derive from causation between particulars?

To show that it does, we should first have to show that suitable causally linked particulars exist in every case of apparently factual causation. Such particulars are indeed often easy enough to find, as they are in our examples: 'Don dies because he falls' could easily be made causal by a causal link between Don's fall and his death. In this and many other cases causally linked facts do entail the existence of causally linked particulars. For as Ramsey (1990 ch. 3 p. 37) remarks,

> 'Caesar died' is really an existential proposition, asserting the existence of an event of a certain sort, thus resembling 'Italy has a king', which asserts the existence of a man of a certain sort. The event which is of that sort is called the death of Caesar, and should no more be confused with the fact that Caesar died than the King of Italy should be confused with the fact that Italy has a king.

Similarly for the facts, if they are facts, that Don falls and that he dies. These are singular facts about Don, but not about events: the sentences 'Don falls' and 'Don dies' contain no names or other terms referring to the events that are Don's fall and Don's death. Nevertheless, for the reasons given in chapter 10.5, I follow Davidson in taking these sentences to entail the existence of *some* such particulars, namely of a fall of Don and of a death of Don. So if Don falls and dies, these facts, like the fact that Caesar died, are existential facts about events.

This being so, then perhaps what makes 'Don dies because Don falls' a true causal instance of 'E because C' is the fact that these particular events are linked as cause to effect, i.e. the fact that Don's fall causes his death. In this way the causation which appears to link the facts, that Don falls and that he dies, may be reducible to causation linking the particulars on whose existence those facts depend.

That reduction might work in cases like this. But it could not possibly work in all cases of causation between facts. For the 'C' and 'E' in a true causal 'E because C' need not assert the existence of particulars. They may deny it. Thus suppose that Don manages to hold on when his rope breaks, and so does *not* die, because he does *not* fall, thus making

'Don does not die, because he does not fall'

true. This instance of 'E because C' is obviously no less causal than 'Don dies because he falls'. But here 'C' and 'E' assert that there is no fall or death of Don. They are negative existential statements, made true by the *non*-existence of such particulars, and *a fortiori* of causally linked ones. Where now are the causally linked particulars which, if causation only links particulars, are needed to make this a case of causation?

The obvious way to answer this question is to rephrase the statement of this causation to remove its explicit negation. We could say for example that Don *survives* because he *holds on*, where 'survives' just means 'does not die' and 'holds on' just means 'does not fall'. This rephrasing may well seem to reveal the causally linked particulars – Don's holding on, and his survival – which Davidson needs in order to make this instance of 'E because C' causal. In fact it reveals no such thing, as we shall now see.

These apparent particulars would of course be events: Don's holding on and his survival would, if they existed, have temporal as well as spatial parts. They are however *negative* events, i.e. events which exist by definition just in case some corresponding positive events, in this case Don's fall and his death, do not exist. Now although no one believes in negative things (like not-Don, who exists by definition just in case Don himself does not), negative events may seem at first sight more credible. But this is really only because the term 'event' is often applied to entities – like things having properties at times (Kim 1976) – that are not particulars at all but facts. Real negative particulars are no more able to exist if they are events than if they are things. So 'Don survives because he holds on' could not, if true, be made causal by a causal link between his holding on and his survival, i.e. between his not falling and his not dying, since no such particulars can exist for causation to link.

To show this, I shall first use Ramsey's example, 'Italy has a King', to show why there can be no negative things. The proof goes as follows. The existential statement 'Italy has a married King' entails 'Italy has a King', obviously because no one can be both married and a King of Italy without being a King of Italy. However, the entailments of negative existential statements go the other way: 'Italy has no King' entails both 'Italy has no married King' and 'Italy has no unmarried King'. Again, the reason is obvious: if no particular person is King of Italy, no married one is, and no unmarried one is. But now suppose instead that 'Italy has no King' is made true by a single *negative person*, the non-King of Italy, who exists just when Italy has no King. To make 'Italy has no King' entail both 'Italy has no married King' and 'Italy has no unmarried King', this non-King will have to be both married and unmarried. But he cannot be both; so he does not exist.

As for particular things, so for particular events. If 'Don dies' asserts the existence of a death of Don, the reason it is entailed by 'Don dies quickly' is that nothing can be both quick and a death of Don without being a death of Don. But here too the entailments of negative existential statements go the other way: 'Don does not die' entails both 'Don does not die quickly' and 'Don does not die slowly'. Again the reason is obvious: if no particular event is a death of Don, then no quick one is, and no slow one is. But now suppose instead that 'Don does not die' is made true by a single *negative event*, Don's survival, which exists just when Don is not dying. To make 'Don does not die' entail both 'Don does not die quickly' and 'Don does not die slowly', Don's survival will have to be both quick and slow; but it cannot be both, so it does not exist.

In short, if Don's fall and death are particulars, his non-fall and his non-death cannot be, whatever we call them: giving negative particulars positive names, like 'Don's holding on' and 'Don's survival', cannot turn them into positive ones. The fact is that, whatever they are called, these negative entities can only exist if they are negative existential *facts*: Don's holding on the fact that he does not fall; his survival the fact that he does not die.

Now we could admittedly debate which the real particulars are in this case – deaths or survivals, falls or holdings on – but it would not help the cause of causation between particulars. For whichever the real particulars are, only one of the pair of statements

> 'Don dies because he falls' and
> 'Don survives because he holds on'

could, if true, be made causal by a causal link between particular events. Yet each is as obviously causal as the other: if either of them is a causal statement, both are. And as in this case, so in general: many pairs of statements of the forms

(1)    'E because C' and
(1~)   '~E because ~C'

are obviously equally causal. Yet if all causes and effects were particulars they could not be.

If, on the other hand, the causes and effects here are facts, (1) and (1~) can easily both be causal. In my liberal sense of 'fact', 'Don dies because he falls' and 'Don survives because he holds on' can both report causal links between facts. For since any statement, whether 'P' or '~P', will if true correspond by definition to a fact [1.2], *negative facts* are still facts. The fact, if it is a fact, that C causes E cannot therefore stop the states of affairs ~C and ~E being causally linked when they are facts, i.e. when 'C' and 'E' are false. If C and E can be causally linked when they are facts, so too can ~C and ~E.

This is not of course to say that (1) and (1~) can be true together. They cannot, but only because 'C&E' and '~C&~E' are contraries. Nothing stops (1) being true if C and E are facts and (1~) being true if ~C and ~E are. Thus although 'Don dies because he falls' and 'Don survives because he holds on' cannot both be true, Don may well die because he falls if he falls, and survive because he holds on if he holds on.

And most importantly, both of these states of affairs can be *causal*: each can be made actual, if it is actual, by a causal link between the facts that it would then entail. It therefore makes no odds which are the positive states of affairs: Don's falling and his dying, or his holding on and his surviving. In other words, it is immaterial whether 'Don dies because he falls' or 'Don survives because he holds on' instantiates 'E because C' as opposed to '~E because ~C', or even whether there is no answer to that question. For either way the causation will be the same: as a form of causal statement, (1~) is no different from (1).

## 3  Existential and particular causes and effects

Since therefore causation cannot always link particulars, factual causes and effects cannot all be reduced to particular ones. The reduction, if any, will have to go the other way. The question is how: how can causal links between particulars reduce to causal links between facts? How in particular can truths of the form 'E because C', some of which we have seen to be opaque for particulars referred to in 'C' or 'E' [9.5], yield transparent truths of the form '*c* causes *e*'?

Part of the answer to this last question is simple enough. A true 'E because C' always yields a true 'C causes E' that is transparent for C and E, the facts that correspond to the true sentences 'C' and 'E'. But it does not always yield a true and transparent '*c* causes *e*', where *c* and *e* are particulars. In particular, as we have just seen, it does not do so when 'C' or 'E' or both assert the non-existence of particulars of certain kinds, like a fall or a death of Don.

Moreover 'E because C' can fail to entail a transparent '*c* causes *e*' even when *c* and *e* are referred to in 'C' and 'E'. Take our example from chapter 9.5:

(21)  'Don's fall is the first because his rope is the weakest'.

The closest we can get here to the form '*c* causes *e*' is something like

'Don's rope's being the weakest causes his fall to be the first'.

But just as, in

'Don's bones being brittle causes his fall to cause his death'

[9.2], 'Don's bones being brittle' refers not to a particular but to the fact that Don's bones are brittle, so 'Don's rope's being the weakest' refers, if to anything, to the fact that his rope is the weakest; and similarly for 'his fall to be the first'. We have turned (21) into an instance not of '*c* causes *e*' but only of 'C causes E', where C and E are facts.

And this is unavoidable, because the cause and effect in this case could not be particulars. For what (21) says is that each of two particulars satisfies two different definite descriptions ('Don's fall' and 'the first fall', 'Don's rope' and 'the weakest rope'), and that the first one does so because the second one does so. That inevitably makes the truth of this instance of 'E because C' depend not only on the particulars it refers to but on how it refers to them. And this is why, whenever 'C' or 'E' state identities, 'E because C' is opaque for the particulars involved and thus fails to yield a transparent '*c* causes *e*'.

But how then *can* a true 'E because C' yield a true '*c* causes *e*'? It must be possible, because it obviously happens in at least two of our original examples: 'Don dies because he falls' and 'there is an explosion because there is a spark' obviously entail 'Don's fall causes his death' and 'the spark causes the explosion'. The other examples are perhaps less obvious: 'Bill's smoking causes him to get cancer', 'Sue's visiting the Bull causes her to get her gin' and 'Kim's taking her medicine causes her recovery' look more like instances of 'C causes E' than of '*c* causes *e*'.

Yet even in these cases the causation may still link particulars. For example, whenever Bill smokes a cigarette, there will be a particular event that is his smoking of it, and the sequence of all these events may also be a particular, say *c*. Bill's being a smoker certainly entails that there is some such sequence, and his getting cancer arguably entails that there is an event, *e*, that is the onset of his cancer. If so, 'Bill's smoking causes him to get cancer' may well entail that the particular *c* causes the particular *e*.

Similarly in the other cases: 'Kim's taking her medicine causes her recovery', for example, may also be or entail an instance of '*c* causes *e*'. But even if it does not, that will not matter. For on the one hand I am not trying to argue that causation always links particulars: far from it. And on the other, even if these examples are doubtful, many others, like Don's fall causing his death, and the spark causing the explosion, are not. And this is all that matters here. For the question here is not how often a true 'E because C' yields a true '*c* causes *e*', nor whether it does so in a particular case, but *how* it does so when it does.

To see how it does so, the first thing to note is that, with exceptions to be discussed in chapter 12, 'E because C' only entails '*c* causes *e*' when 'C' and 'E' are *existential* statements. In the car engine example this is explicit: 'there is an explosion because there is a spark'. In the other examples it is implicit, as we noted in §2: 'Don falls' and 'Don dies' may not entail the existence of Don's fall and Don's death by referring to those particular events, but they do entail that events of these sorts, a fall of Don and a death of Don, exist. Similarly in the other cases, if indeed they are cases.

'Kim takes her medicine' and 'Kim recovers' need not refer to the particular events that are her taking of her medicine and her recovery to entail that some such events exist. Similarly again for 'Bill smokes' and 'Bill gets cancer', and for 'Sue visits the Bull' and 'Sue gets her gin'.

In short, all these instances of 'E because C', if they do yield instances of '*c* causes *e*', take the special form 'there is at least one particular that is *L* because there is at least one particular that is *K*', where '*K*' and '*L*' are predicates like 'a fall of Don' or 'a death of Don'. This form I shall usually abbreviate to 'there is an *L* because there is a *K*'. Unfortunately however, 'there is a *K*' is ambiguous, since it can also mean 'there is a property *K*', a reading we shall need later on. So to prevent this misreading I shall sometimes use the standard symbolism for the so-called *first order existential quantifier* 'there is a *K*-particular', namely '$(\exists x)(Kx)$'.

I shall also, for brevity, use '$(\exists x)(Kx)$' both as a sentence and also as a term referring to the fact that there is a *K*-particular, just as I use 'C' and 'E' both as sentences (in 'E because C') and as referring terms (in 'C causes E'); and similarly of course for '$(\exists x)(Lx)$'. We may then write this special case of (1), 'E because C', either as

(22)  '$(\exists x)(Lx)$ because $(\exists x)(Kx)$'

or as the corresponding case of (1′), 'C causes E', namely

(22′)  '$(\exists x)(Kx)$ causes $(\exists x)(Lx)$',

i.e. 'there being a *K*-particular causes there to be an *L*-particular'.

Next, we may take it in all our examples that the descriptions '*K*' and '*L*' are, in context, definite. That is, they are such that in the stated or assumed circumstances S one and only one particular satisfies each of them. If more than one particular does so, if for example Don falls twice, no '*c* causes *e*' will follow until we make the description definite, for example by saying that Don dies because he falls *off Castle Rock*. Once this is done, there will be one and only one particular that is *K*, such as Don's one and only fall off Castle Rock, and one and only one particular that is *L*, such as Don's one and only death. These particulars I shall call respectively 'the *K*' and 'the *L*'. But again, to avoid confusion with the other possible meaning of 'the *K*', namely 'the property *K*', I shall sometimes use the standard symbolism, introduced in chapter 2.3, to abbreviate 'the one and only *K*-particular' to '$(\imath x)(Kx)$'; and similarly for 'the *L*'.

Now let the particulars *c* and *e* be the *K* and the *L* respectively, so that

(23)  '$c = (\imath x)(Kx)$' and
(24)  '$e = (\imath x)(Lx)$'

are both true. Then I say that, provided being $L$ is an essential fact about $e$
[12.2], (22), (23) and (24) together entail

(2)    '$c$ causes $e$'.

This I maintain is how 'Don dies because he falls' entails 'Don's fall causes
his death', and similarly in other such cases.

The reverse entailment however does not hold. The fact that, for a
given '$K$' and '$L$', $c$ is the $K$, $e$ is the $L$ and $c$ causes $e$ does not entail that
there is an $L$ because there is a $K$. This is because the particulars $c$ and $e$
will generally satisfy many pairs of definite descriptions '$K'$' and '$L'$' for
which 'there is an $L'$ because there is a $K'$' is false. Thus suppose that
Don's is the only fall from Castle Rock on 4 June 1988, and that his fame
makes his death the most newsworthy event of that week. Taken in the
context of that place and time, 'the fall' and 'the most newsworthy event'
will then be definite descriptions of Don's fall and of Don's death. But it
does not follow from this that there is a most newsworthy event because
there is a fall, and it is probably not true. For the chance of there being a
most newsworthy event that week would almost certainly have been no less
had Don not fallen and therefore not died: it just would not have been
Don's death.

What I maintain '$c$ causes $e$' does entail is that (22), (23) and (24) are all
true for *some* possible predicates '$K$' and '$L$'. And this makes '$c$ causes $e$'
transparent for $c$ and $e$, as we saw in chapter 9.5 that it must be. For
suppose that '$c'$' and '$e'$' are any other terms referring respectively to $c$ and
$e$. Then the self-evident transparency of identity statements like (23) and
(24) makes them entail

$$'c' = (\imath x)(Kx)' \text{ and}$$
$$'e' = (\imath x)(Lx)',$$

which, together with (22), '$(\exists x)(Lx)$ because $(\exists x)(Kx)$', then entail

'$c'$ causes $e'$'.

This is why, if Don's fall does cause his death, his fall is the only fall and
his death is the most newsworthy event, then 'the fall causes the most
newsworthy event' is true, even though 'there is a most newsworthy event
because there is a fall' is false.

This shows how existential instances of 'E because C' can and do yield
instances of the transparent '$c$ causes $e$'. But it also shows how and why
what causation really links in these cases are not the particulars $c$ and $e$ that
are the $K$ and the $L$ but the corresponding facts, $(\exists x)(Kx)$ and $(\exists x)(Lx)$.
For all $c$ and $e$ do here, by being $K$ and $L$, is supply the facts which the

causation links, by making '$(\exists x)(Kx)$' and '$(\exists x)(Lx)$' true. But they do not thereby supply the causation that links those facts. For $(\exists x)(Kx)$ and $(\exists x)(Lx)$ need not be linked as cause to effect, and if they are so linked, it will not be because $c$ and $e$ are. It is the other way round: $c$ and $e$ merely inherit the causal link between the corresponding existential facts.

Furthermore, the facts $(\exists x)(Kx)$ and $(\exists x)(Lx)$ will rarely require the $K$- and $L$-particulars that inherit their causation to be the particulars $c$ and $e$ which actually inherit it. For 'the $K$' and 'the $L$' will rarely be *rigid designators* (Kripke 1980 Lect. 1): that is, most of them will, in some other possible world, refer to different particulars. Thus Don could die because he fell even if he fell and died so differently that his fall and death were quite different events from those that in this world are his fall and his death. In that case '$(\exists x)(Lx)$ because $(\exists x)(Kx)$' would still be true, but the $K$- and $L$-particulars that inherited the causal link between $(\exists x)(Kx)$ and $(\exists x)(Lx)$ would not be the events, $c$ and $e$, that inherit it in our world.

## 4  Facts first?

It looks then as if all singular causation either is or reduces to causation between facts. For first, it often links facts without linking particulars at all: as it does (a) when it links facts of identity, as when Don falls first because his rope is the weakest, and (b) when it links negative existential facts, as when Don does not die, because he does not fall. And second, even when one particular does cause another, it does so only because those two particulars satisfy some possible definite descriptions '$K$' and '$L$' such that there is an $L$ because there is a $K$.

Discovering what makes one fact cause another will thus show us what makes one particular cause another. Since all causes and effects are either particulars or facts [1.2], this may seem to cover the whole subject. Yet it may not, for it may not cover another, oddly neglected, kind of causation, where particulars do not *cause* but only *affect* each other, which we have not yet discussed. We cannot safely conclude that all causation really links facts until we know whether, and if so how, it does so whenever particulars affect each other. That therefore is the question to which we now turn.

# 12 *Affecting particulars*

## 1 Causing and affecting

How does affecting a particular event or thing differ from causing it? Both are obviously cases of causation and yet also obviously distinct. Thus suppose Kim gives her father-in-law, the fallen Don, an injection to make his death painless. The injection affects his death, but does not cause it. Here the affected particular is an event. But things too, including people, can be affected. In perception, for example, we are affected but not caused by the things we see and hear. What is the difference? And what, given the difference, makes affecting something a case of causation?

The second question is the easier. First, to affect a particular *event* is to cause some fact about it: Kim's injection affects Don's death by causing it to be painless. Second, to affect a particular *thing* is to cause either a fact about it or a change in it, which may be a fact or an event. Thus when I see a thing stay put, it affects me by causing me to keep my previous belief about where it is, a fact that is not a change in me. When I see a thing move, on the other hand, it affects me by causing a change in my belief about where it is. This is why affecting a particular, whether it be an event or a thing, is always a causal matter: it is always a case of causing either a fact about the affected particular or a change in it.

Our first question is harder to answer. But we must answer it, precisely because affecting a particular involves causing something, but not the particular itself. So the form (2), '*c* causes *e*', which I have so far used to report causal links between particulars, will not cover all cases, because it will not cover instances of '*c* affects *e*'. This is why I said in chapter 1.2 that the general form of statements of causation between particulars should really be not (2) but

(2′)  '*c* causes or affects *e*'.

I added however that in what followed we could, for simplicity, ignore (2′) and consider only (2), on the grounds that the difference between causing a particular and affecting it is not a causal one. This is the claim which I must now make good.

140

## 2 Essential and inessential facts

The difference between causing and affecting a particular is this: causing a particular is causing it to exist and affecting it is not. More precisely, affecting a particular is causing some fact about it that is not *essential* to it. Thus our parents cause us, by causing us to exist. Other particulars only affect us, by causing facts about us that are *inessential* to us: facts without which we should still exist. Similarly for events. Don's fall causes his death by causing that event to exist. Kim's injection, on the other hand, only affects Don's death by causing it to be painless, since that is an inessential fact about it: Don's death would have existed even if it had been painful.

This description of that example is not quite right, as we shall shortly see. But the basic idea is right, namely that the distinction between causing and affecting particulars is the distinction between causing essential and inessential facts about them. This distinction does not however require essential and inessential facts about particulars to differ in kind: it can be a matter of degree, e.g. of *how* different Don or his death could be without being a different particular, a question whose answer may indeed be somewhat arbitrary. But this does not matter: for, as we shall see, since the distinction does not depend on any causal fact, it is not one we need to account for. However, before showing that this is so, I must show how the distinction between causing a particular and affecting it rests on the distinction between essential and inessential facts.

We have seen that '$c$ causes $e$' entails that, in the relevant circumstances S, for some $K$ and $L$ such that $c$ is the $K$ and $e$ is the $L$, there is an $L$ because there is a $K$ [11.3]. But for '$c$ causes $e$' to imply that $c$ causes $e$ to *exist*, it must entail more than this. It must also entail that being $L$ is an essential fact about $e$, i.e. is such that if $e$ were not $L$ it would not exist. This is why Don's fall causes his death: being a death of Don is an essential fact about Don's death. If Don had not died, this particular event would not merely have been different, it would not have existed at all.

This is consistent with the fact that, because falling can kill people in very different ways, the fact that Don dies because he falls does not fix the identity of the event that is in fact his death [11.3]. Other ways of dying (cancer, poison, drowning) make it even more obvious that different events could satisfy the description 'a death of Don'. But being a death of Don may still be an essential fact about any event $e$ that *is* Don's death. In other words, if Don did not die, then whatever other facts about $e$ remained facts – e.g. that Don broke his back – the event they were facts about would not be $e$. This is why Don's fall *causes* his death, i.e. causes that very event to exist, rather than *affecting* it by causing it to be – among other inessential facts about it – a death of Don.

It may now seem obvious how '*c* affects *e*' differs from '*c* causes *e*': it entails that being *L* is an *in*essential fact about *e*, that *e* would exist even if it were not *L*. This is why the injection which causes Don's death to be painless only affects it: its being painless is an inessential fact about it. But this is not quite right. For suppose that, without raising Don's chance of dying, Kim's injection did alter the way in which Don died enough to make his death a different event. We should still not say that the injection caused his death. And this looks like a counter-example to the claim that if *c* causes *e* to exist then *c* not merely affects *e* but causes it.

Not so. This is not really a counter-example, merely one of many apparent instances of '*c* causes the *L*' which really instantiate the mixed form '*c* causes $(\exists x)(Lx)$', i.e. '*c* causes there to be an *L*'. When we credit Don's fall with causing his death, all we mean is that it causes him to die: we do not care about the identity of the event that is his death. Similarly, when we deny that Kim's injection causes Don's death, what we mean is that it does not cause him to die: we do not care if it causes his death to be a different event from the death he would otherwise have died. This is why, when we say that Kim's injection only affects Don's death, we are not really raising tricky if trivial questions about what the identity of a particular event depends on. We are simply saying that the injection, because it did not raise Don's chance of dying, did not cause him to die.

As this case is not really an instance of '*c* affects *e*', it does not refute my thesis that *c* affects *e* iff *c* causes an inessential fact about *e*. That thesis stands – and not because '*c* affects *e*' has no true instances. On the contrary: it has many, even when *e* is an event. To take an obvious example, the identity of sporting contests does not depend on who wins them. This is why a player can affect a soccer match, by scoring the goal that causes his team to win, without causing the match, i.e. without causing it to exist. The reason he can do this is that the final score, however important to the fans, is not, in the sense that matters here, an essential fact about a soccer match.

This is even more obvious when the affected particular *e* is a thing, such as a person. I have already mentioned perception, where we are affected, but not caused, by the things and events we perceive. Other examples include the actions in which, by causing events, we affect other things, such as the people we affect by speaking to them. These effects – the facts about people that are caused by the things and events they perceive, including us when we talk to them – are of course very various. But they all have one thing in common. None of them is essential to the person thereby affected: he or she would still exist, would still be the very same person, without that fact. That is why these effects on people affect but do not cause them.

## 3 Identity criteria

In these and many other cases it is obvious whether a fact, thing or event causes or merely affects a particular $e$. On the above account, this requires it to be obvious whether the effect on $e$, that it is $L$, is an essential or an inessential fact about $e$, i.e. whether $e$'s identity and thus existence requires it to be $L$. So we must after all consider the question of what the identity of particulars depends on, if only to show that whatever it depends on is not causation and is thus not something we need to explain.

The reason this is not self-evident is that causation has, as we have seen, been used to provide an identity criterion for particular events [9.3; 10.3]. But that causal test does not address the present question. For all it says is that, for all $L$ and $L'$, the $L$ is the same particular as the $L'$ iff the $L$ and the $L'$ have all the same causes and effects. Thus Don's fall is the first fall (off Castle Rock that day) iff all causes and effects of Don's fall are also causes and effects of the first fall. But all this tells us is whether the event that is in fact Don's fall is also in fact the first fall. It does not tell us whether that event would not exist if it were *not* a fall of Don, or *not* the first fall. That is, it does not tell us whether these facts about it are essential to it. To answer that question we need something which a test of actual identity does not automatically supply: namely, a test of what is often called 'transworld' identity but which, to avoid raising irrelevant questions about other possible worlds, I prefer to call *counterfactual* identity.

Once we distinguish these questions, it is obvious that neither of the tests discussed in chapters 9.3 and 10.3 will answer questions of counterfactual identity. The spatiotemporal test, which would make every particular's exact location and extension in space and time essential facts about it, is obviously far too strong. It may work for spacetime points and regions, but not for anything else. My having stood up a minute ago would not for example have – literally – made a different man of me.

The causal test is also far too strong. For almost any variation in a particular that has causes and effects will alter some of them. The injection which makes Don's death painless will automatically alter that event's causes (since we must obviously now take these to include entities that affect it) and almost certainly its effects: thus, by the causal test, making Don's death a different event. By making almost all facts about causal particulars essential to them, the causal test will make it almost impossible to affect particulars rather than to cause them, which is absurd.

Nor can we make the causal test work by weakening it to say merely that $e = e'$ *if* (but not *only* if) $e$ and $e'$ have all the same causes and effects. That only makes the test useless. For as we have just seen, if $e$ and $e'$ are alternatives like Don's painful and painless deaths, their causes and effects will almost certainly differ. But then the weakened causal test will rarely if ever apply and so will rarely if ever tell us whether $e=e'$ or not.

I know of no one general test for counterfactual identity and suspect indeed that there is none. But we need none. For once we have seen that whatever distinguishes essential from inessential facts is not causation, it need not matter to us what it is. We can use the distinction to distinguish causing a particular from affecting it without begging any of the questions about causation which must matter to us.

Our account of causation need not therefore distinguish instances of '*c* causes *e*' from instances of '*c* affects *e*'. All it need do is apply to both, as we have already seen that it does. For what makes both '*c* causes *e*' and '*c* affects *e*' *causal* is their entailing that, in the relevant circumstances S, for some $K$ and $L$, $c$ is the $K$, $e$ is the $L$, and $(\exists x)(Lx)$ because $(\exists x)(Kx)$. But all that this causation linking $(\exists x)(Kx)$ and $(\exists x)(Lx)$ entails about particulars is that the $K$ *either* causes the $L$ *or* affects it. Which it does depends not on causation but on whether being $L$ is an essential fact about the $L$: an interesting question, perhaps, but not a question about causation.

## 4  How particulars cause and affect each other

The distinction between $c$ causing $e$ and affecting it thus raises no problem for our account of causation. But saying *how* $c$ affects $e$, namely by being $K$, and thereby causing $e$ to be $L$, does raise one. It does so because it requires the factual cause and effect here to be more than the existential facts, $(\exists x)(Kx)$ and $(\exists x)(Lx)$, entailed by the true

(22)   '$(\exists x)(Lx)$ because $(\exists x)(Kx)$'

from which we have derived

(2′)   '$c$ causes or affects $e$'.

The reason the merely existential cause, $(\exists x)(Kx)$, and effect, $(\exists x)(Lx)$, are inadequate here is that, for $e$ to be the particular which $c$ affects, $c$'s factual effect must be that $e$ itself is $L$: no other $L$-particular will do. Thus suppose Bill sees that he has a match in his matchbox, i.e. suppose a match in it affects him, by causing him to believe that it contains a match [6.3]. The match's factual effect here is not just that *someone* is caused to believe this, but that Bill is. Similarly with the injection that Kim gives Don: its factual effect is not just that *some* death is made painless, but that Don's is.

In other words, the 'E because C' here must be not '$(\exists x)(Lx)$ because C' but an '$Le$ because C' which, even if it is opaque for particulars referred to in 'C', must be transparent for $e$ [9.5]. That is, a true '$Le$ because C' must not be falsified by replacing '$e$' with any other term for $e$. Otherwise the effect would not be the fact, specifically about *e*, which it must be if it is to entail a 'C affects *e*' that is transparent for *e*. Thus if Bill is Don's son, then substituting 'Don's son' for 'Bill' in a true 'Bill believes he has a match because C' must never falsify it, just as replacing 'Don' with 'Bill's father' must never falsify a true 'Don's death is painless because C'.

Similarly, when 'E because *Kc*' states the fact, *Kc*, that makes *c* cause E, it must be transparent for *c* if the cause is to be the fact, specifically about *c*, which it must be to entail a '*c* causes E' that is transparent for *c*. Thus 'the match that Bill sees is the only thing in the box' and 'Bill believes he has a match because the match he sees looks like a match' must entail 'Bill believes he has a match because the only thing in the box looks like a match'; and likewise in other cases.

These two conditions require the transparency for *c* and *e* of any true

(25)   '*Le* because *Kc*'

which says how *c* causes or affects *e*. And here lies the problem, since when '*L*' or '*K*' is what I shall call an *identity predicate*, as in chapter 9.5's

(21)   'Don's fall is the first because his rope is the weakest',

(25) is transparent for neither *c* nor *e*. For even though (21) entails that 'Don's fall' and 'the first fall' refer to the same event, and that 'his rope' and 'the weakest rope' refer to the same thing, substituting either term for the other makes (21) false [9.5]. In other words, (21), which is an instance of '*Le* because *Kc*', is opaque for both *c* and *e*. Why?

The reason is quite obvious, as we saw in chapter 11.3: (21) says that 'Don's fall' and 'the first fall' refer to the same event because 'Don's rope' and 'the weakest rope' refer to the same thing. This is what makes (21)'s truth depend not just on the particulars it refers to but on how it refers to them; and this is why (21) can no more entail a transparent '*c* affects *e*' than it can entail a transparent '*c* causes *e*'.

If this is what makes (21) opaque, can we not make (25) transparent by excluding identity predicates? We can admittedly not do this formally, by ruling out predicates containing identity signs: that ruling is too easily evaded by artificial predicates like Quine's (1948) 'pegasizes', which by definition applies only to Pegasus and is thus an identity predicate in content if not in form. But this is not a real problem. For what matters here is not the form of the predicates we use to say how *c* causes or affects *e* but their content: what makes *c* and *e* satisfy those predicates.

The real problem is that (25), '*Le* because *Kc*', can be opaque for *c* and *e* even when '*K*' and '*L*' are not identity predicates. For suppose that, in the relevant circumstances S, $c$ and $e$ are respectively not just $K$ and $L$ but the *only* particulars to be $K$ and $L$. This makes both

(23)  '$c = (\imath x)(Kx)$' and

(24)  '$e = (\imath x)(Lx)$'

true. But then, since 'the $K$' refers to $c$ and 'the $L$' refers to $e$, the truth of a transparent (25) would have to survive replacing '$c$' in it by 'the $K$', or '$e$' by 'the $L$', to yield

'$Le$ because the $K$ is $K$' or

'the $L$ is $L$ because $Kc$'.

Yet if 'the $K$ is $K$' and 'the $L$ is $L$' are the necessary truths they seem to be, (25)'s truth can survive neither of these replacements. For necessary facts, like the facts that the $K$ is $K$ and the $L$ is $L$, can no more be causes and effects than the facts of identity, that the $K$ is *the K* and the $L$ is *the L*, discussed in chapter 9.5. For as we saw there, what stops these identities being causes and effects is not that they are identities but that they are necessary. That is what stops them raising the chances of other facts, or having their own chances raised by other facts.

So if 'the $K$ is $K$' and 'the $L$ is $L$' are indeed necessarily true, then (25), '$Le$ because $Kc$', will be opaque for $c$ and $e$ for all '$K$' and '$L$', not just for identity predicates. But how then can (25) possibly entail a transparent (2′), '$c$ causes or affects $e$', and tell us transparently what it is about $c$ – namely $Kc$ – that causes or affects $e$, and what it is about $e$ – namely $Le$ – that is thereby caused? That is the problem.

## 5  Opaque causation

The problem would be easier to solve if '$Le$ because $Kc$' could be falsified only by replacing '$c$' or '$e$' with a co-referring term '$c'$' or '$e'$' which, like 'the $K$' or 'the $L$', makes '$Kc'$' or '$Le'$' necessarily true. For then we might try excluding such replacements by fiat. But that will not do the trick. For '$Le'$ because $Kc'$' can also be false when $Kc'$ and $Le'$ are contingent facts, which could be related as cause to effect, but are not, even though $Kc$ and $Le$ are so related and $c'=c$ and $e'=e$.

The best-known examples of this occur when $Kc$ or $Le$ or both are mental facts. Take Kim's belief that Don is dying, caused by her seeing him fall off Castle Rock. Let '$Kc$' be 'Kim sees Don fall off $c$', where '$c$' is 'Castle Rock', and '$Le$' be 'Kim believes that $e$ is dying', where '$e$' is 'Don'. Then '$Le$ because $Kc$' is true. But suppose Don is M, the head of MI5 ($e'$). Kim may not believe that M is dying because she sees Don fall off Castle

Rock, because she may not know that Don is M: '*Le'* because *Kc*' may be false, even though '*Le* because *Kc*' is true and *e'=e*. How can this be?

On our account of causation, this instance of '*Le'* because *Kc*' may be false for one of two reasons, one more obvious than the other. The obvious one is that '*Le''* is false: the reason Kim's seeing Don fall does not cause her to believe that M is dying is that she does *not* believe that M is dying. Here the opacity for *e* of '*Le* because *Kc*' follows simply from the fact that it entails '*Le*' and '*Le*' is opaque for *e*.

But '*Le'* because *Kc*' may also be false even if '*Le''* is true: Kim may for example believe that M is dying, without believing that Don is M, because she hears it on the news. But then it is not because she sees Don fall that she believes that M is dying. Why not, on my account?

The answer is of course that Kim's chance of believing that M is dying in these circumstances – she hears it on the news, she does not believe that Don is M – will be the same whether or not she sees Don fall off Castle Rock. Here what makes (25), '*Le* because *Kc*', opaque for *e* must be the opacity for *e* of the special case of (16), $ch_C(E) > ch_{\sim C}(E)$, that (25) entails:

(26)  $ch_{Kc}(Le) > ch_{\sim Kc}(Le)$.

Similarly for *c*, for which (26) and hence (25) must also be opaque, as readers can see for themselves by considering the two ways in which 'Kim believes that Don dies because she sees him fall off the rock that looks like a castle' can be false.

The question then is this: how can (26) be opaque for *c* and *e*? To see how, and to dispel the common but mistaken idea that causal opacity occurs only with mental causes and effects, imagine a device that tosses a coin *j*, *Tj*, giving it a chance $ch(Hj)=1/2$ of landing heads, *Hj* [2.1]. If *j* lands heads, the device (with chance 1) stops; otherwise (with chance 1) it tosses another coin *k* with $ch(Hk)=1/2$ and then stops. All this is shown below in Figure 14.

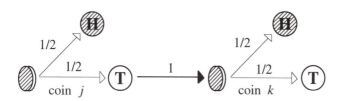

Figure 14: Opaque and transparent chances

Now consider the chance, before $j$ is tossed, that *the last coin tossed lands heads*. This is the chance that $j$ lands heads (making it the last coin tossed), *plus* the chance that $j$ does not land heads *times* the chance, if $k$ is tossed, that $k$ lands heads. In symbols, writing '$l$' for 'the last coin tossed':

(27)   $ch(Hl) = ch(Hj) + ch(\sim Hj) \times ch_{Tk}(Hk) = 1/2 + 1/2 \times 1/2 = 3/4.$

Finally, suppose that $j$ does land heads, and so *is* the last coin tossed, so that $j=l$. Yet (27) shows that, despite this identity, $ch(Hl)$ differs by 1/4 from $ch(Hj)$: replacing '$j$' with the co-referring '$l$' makes the true '$ch(Hj)=1/2$' false, thus showing it to be opaque for $j$.

We cannot evade this conclusion by denying the reality of the chance, $ch(Hl)$, that the last coin tossed lands heads. $ch(Hl)$ is as real a property of facts about the device before $j$ is tossed as $ch(Hj)$ is. It also, as readers can easily verify, meets all the conditions – Necessity, Evidence and Frequency – imposed on chances in chapter 4.

Both $ch(Hj)$ and $ch(Hl)$ are moreover chances of *effects*. For even if $Tj$ cannot be a sufficient cause of $Hj$, since $ch_{Tj}(Hj)$ is only 1/2, it can be a necessary one, since $j$'s chance of landing heads if it is *not* tossed, $ch_{\sim Tj}(Hj)$, is zero [2.4]. So if causation can be indeterministic, we can and should admit that *one* cause of $j$'s landing heads is that it is tossed, i.e. that

'$Hj$ because $Tj$'

is true. For the link between $Tj$ and $Hj$ satisfies all causation's other connotations as much as $Tj$'s raising $ch(Hj)$ from 0 to 1/2 allows: $Tj$ precedes $Hj$, provides some evidence for it, explains it as well as Bill's smoking explains his getting cancer, and is a moderately useful means to it. Tossing the coin $j$ is in short a reasonably effective cause of the fact that $j$ lands heads [8].

But if '$Hj$ because $Tj$' is true, so too is

'$Hl$ because $Tj$'.

For since $Tj$ raises $ch(Hl)$ more than $ch(Hj)$, it is an even more effective cause of $Hl$ than it is of $Hj$: it provides stronger evidence for $Hl$, explains it better and is a more useful means to it [8]. So if tossing $j$ causes $j$ to land heads, it must also cause the last coin tossed to land heads.

Of course this in itself does not show that causation can be opaque, since replacing '$Hj$' by '$Hl$' in '$Hj$ because $Tj$' does not falsify it. But this is only because $Tj$ happens to raise both $ch(Hj)$ and $ch(Hl)$, which it only does because both these chances will be zero if $j$ is not tossed. But we can easily modify our device, in ways I shall leave readers to work out, to make

$$ch_{\sim Tj}(Hj) = ch_{\sim Tj}(Hl) = 1/2,$$

which, if $j$ lands heads, will make '$H\imath l$ because $Tj$' true and '$Hj$ because $Tj$' false. For then tossing $j$ will raise the chance of the last coin tossed landing heads, but not that of $j$ landing heads:

$$ch_{Tj}(H\imath l) = 3/4 > ch_{\sim Tj}(H\imath l) = 1/2;$$
$$ch_{Tj}(Hj) = 1/2 = ch_{\sim Tj}(Hj).$$

So '$Hj$ because $Tj$' really is opaque for $j$. For even if replacing '$Hj$' with '$H\imath l$' in '$Hj$ because $Tj$' does not in fact alter its truth value, it could do so. Similarly for any $Le$, mental or physical: because $e'=e$ need not entail $ch(Le')=ch(Le)$, any '$Le$ because $Kc$' can be opaque for $e$.

And as for $e$, so for $c$. Consider the fact that the second coin $k$ fails to land heads: $\sim Hk$. This is because $k$ is not tossed, because $j$ lands heads: $Hj$. In other words, $Hj$ is in the circumstances a sufficient cause of $\sim Hk$:

'$\sim Hk$ because $Hj$'

is true. Yet despite the fact that $j$ is $\imath l$, the last coin tossed, $k$ does *not* fail to land heads because the last coin tossed lands heads:

'$\sim Hk$ because $H\imath l$'

is false. To see why, consider $\sim Hk$'s chances with and without $Hj$ and $H\imath l$. If $j$ lands heads and so is the last coin tossed, then $k$'s chance of being tossed and hence of landing heads is 0, so that

$$ch_{Hj}(\sim Hk) = ch_{H\imath l}(\sim Hk) = 1.$$

But if $j$ lands tails, then $k$ will be $\imath l$, the last coin tossed. And then, although $k$'s chance of landing tails if $j$ does so is 1/2, its chance of landing tails if the last coin tossed – namely $k$ itself – does so is obviously 1:

(28)   $ch_{\sim Hj}(\sim Hk) = 1/2;\ ch_{\sim H\imath l}(\sim Hk) = 1.$

But this means that although $Hj$ raises $ch(\sim Hk)$ from 1/2 to 1, $H\imath l$ does not raise $ch(\sim Hk)$ at all. So even when '$\sim Hk$ because $Hj$' is true and $j=\imath l$, '$\sim Hk$ because $H\imath l$' is false, because replacing '$j$' with '$\imath l$' falsifies the true

'$ch_{Hj}(\sim Hk) > ch_{\sim Hj}(\sim Hk)$'

which '$\sim Hk$ because $Hj$' entails. And as in this case, so in general. Because '$ch_{Kc}(Le)>ch_{\sim Kc}(Le)$' can always be opaque for $c$ as well as for $e$, so too can '$Le$ because $Kc$' for any $Kc$ and $Le$, mental or physical.

## 6  Transparent causation

So far so bad. It is true that we need to see, as we now can, how causation can be opaque; and especially how beliefs, desires and other mental states which refer opaquely to particular things or events can be, as they obviously are, causes and effects. On my account all this follows from three simple facts: that 'E because C' entails 'C', 'E' and '$ch_C(E)>ch_{\sim C}(E)$'. These suffice to enable any '$Le$ because $Kc$' to be opaque for both $c$ and $e$.

But this account of causal opacity, however gratifying, only exacerbates the problem posed in §4, because an opaque '$Le$ because $Kc$' cannot entail a transparent '$c$ causes or affects $e$'. Nor can it tell us transparently how $c$ causes or affects $e$. Yet all is not lost: for even if '$Le$ because $Kc$' can always be opaque, it can also always be transparent, as we shall now see.

Consider again Kim's believing that Don is dying because she sees him fall [§5]. So far I have assumed that this belief is opaque for Don, and so it may be. But Kim may also believe *transparently* of Don that he is dying. That is, her belief may be such that, if Don is M, then whether she knows it or not, she also believes of M that he is dying. If so, then if Kim's seeing Don fall causes her to have the first belief, it must also cause her to have the second, because they are one and the same belief. But to make sense of this we need a reading of '$Le$ because $Kc$' that is transparent for $e$; and similarly, obviously, for $c$. How can we get it?

The first point to make is that the need for a transparent reading of '$Le$ because $Kc$' cannot be obviated by denying that beliefs can be transparent. The existence of transparent beliefs is indeed disputed, but we need not dispute it, since we shall need transparent causation anyway. For even if

> 'Kim believes Don is dying'

is opaque for Don, it is obviously transparent for Kim. That is, its truth value cannot be changed by replacing 'Kim' with any co-referring term, such as 'Don's daughter-in-law'. Moreover, and more to the point,

> 'Kim believes Don is dying because she sees him fall', i.e.
> 'Kim's seeing Don fall causes her to believe he is dying',

must also be transparent for Kim, at least when we use it to say how

> Kim's seeing Don fall affects her.

For then it just illustrates the transparent use of (25), '$Le$ because $Kc$', to say how particular events and things affect each other, which gave us our problem in the first place. We cannot therefore blink it more: we must discover how '$Le$ because $Kc$' can be transparent for $c$ and $e$.

To do this we must look more closely at the source of our problem in §4, namely the apparent necessity of the truth of

> 'the $K$ is $K$'.

In fact this sentence is ambiguous. We can indeed use it to say that whatever particular the $K$ is, it is $K$, which is a necessary fact. Here we are using 'the $K$' as a *non-rigid designator* [11.3], since the $K$ in other possible worlds may be a different particular from the $K$ in our world. But we can also use 'the $K$ is $K$' to say of the particular $c$, which happens to be the $K$ in our world, that *it* is $K$, a fact which may be, and usually is, contingent. Here we are using 'the $K$' as a *rigid* designator of $c$, i.e. making it refer to $c$ not only in our world but in all the possible worlds it exists in, including those, if any, where it is not $K$.

This enables us to use 'the $K$ is $K$' to state two different facts, one necessary and the other (usually) contingent. And this in turn makes

'the $L$ is $L$ because the $K$ is $K$'

ambiguous. If 'the $K$' and 'the $L$' refer non-rigidly, it must be false, since the necessary facts, that the $K$ is $K$ and that the $L$ is $L$, which it entails can have neither causes nor effects. If however these terms refer rigidly, 'the $L$ is $L$ because the $K$ is $K$' may well be true and hence entailable by a true '$Le$ because $Kc$' that is transparent for both $c$ and $e$.

Thus, reverting to our earlier examples, if 'the thing that looks like a match' refers rigidly to that very thing, Bill could believe that he has a match because the thing that looks like one looks like one [§4]; just as, if 'Don's painless death' refers rigidly to that event, his painless death could be painless because Kim's injection anaesthetises him [§1].

But how can we make (25), '$Le$ because $Kc$', transparent if, as we saw in §5, it can also be opaque? How in particular can we make a statement of

(26)  $ch_{Kc}(Le) > ch_{\sim Kc}(Le)$,

which (25) entails, remain true whenever we replace '$c$' or '$e$' in it with a co-referring term? How, for example, can we make 'Don's death has a higher chance of being painless if Kim's injection anaesthetises him than if it does not' transparently true for both Kim's injection and Don's death?

To see the answer to this question, let us look again at the coin tossing device of Figure 14. In §5 I used the description '$\imath l$' ('the last coin tossed') to refer non-rigidly to whichever coin would be the last coin tossed in the relevant situation, actual or not. In particular, I had to do this to show that $ch(H\imath l)$ differs from $ch(Hj)$ when $j$ is $\imath l$. For as

(27)  $ch(H\imath l) = ch(Hj) + ch(\sim Hj) \times ch_{Tk}(Hk) = 1/2 + 1/2 \times 1/2 = 3/4$

shows, the difference between $ch(H\imath l)$ and $ch(Hj)$ is the chance that $j$ will land tails, and so *not* be the last coin tossed, multiplied by the chance that $k$, which would then be the last coin tossed, lands heads if tossed.

But if we use '$\imath l$' to refer rigidly to the coin $j$ which is in fact the last coin tossed, then $\imath l$'s chance of landing heads is just $ch(Hj)$: $k$'s chance of landing heads is irrelevant. And then replacing '$j$' in '$ch(Hj)=1/2$' with '$\imath l$', or any other term that refers rigidly to $j$, will not falsify it. Similarly for all other chance statements, and in particular for (26). For if every term '$e''$' which refers to $e$ does so rigidly, then for all such '$e''$'

$$ch_{Kc}(Le') = ch_{Kc}(Le) \text{ and } ch_{\sim Kc}(Le') = ch_{\sim Kc}(Le), \text{ so that}$$
$$ch_{Kc}(Le') > ch_{\sim Kc}(Le') \text{ iff } ch_{Kc}(Le) > ch_{\sim Kc}(Le).$$

In short, (26) will be transparent for $e$.

We can make (26) transparent for $c$ in the same way, as our coin tossing device will again serve to show. Consider the opacity for $c$ shown in §5 by

(28)   $ch_{\sim Hj}(\sim Hk) = 1/2; \ ch_{\sim H\imath l}(\sim Hk) = 1.$

(28) shows that replacing '$j$' with the co-referring '$\imath l$' in '$ch_{\sim Hj}(\sim Hk)=1/2$' falsifies it. But to see *why* it does so, we must unpack (28) as follows. Chapter 2.3 tells us that, for any cause C and effect E,

(5~)   $ch_{\sim C}(E) = (\imath p')(\sim C \Rightarrow ch(E)=p').$

This, for C=$Kc$ and E=$Le$, gives us

$$ch_{\sim Kc}(Le) = (\imath p')(\sim Kc \Rightarrow ch(Le)=p'),$$

which in particular makes (28) say that

$$\sim Hj \Rightarrow ch(\sim Hk)=1/2 \text{ and } \sim H\imath l \Rightarrow ch(\sim Hk)=1.$$

That is, $k$'s chance of not landing heads is 1/2 in the closest worlds to ours where $j$ does not land heads, and 1 in the closest worlds where the last coin tossed does not land heads: because, when $j$ does not land heads, the last coin tossed is not $j$ but $k$. So the reason $ch_{\sim H\imath l}(\sim Hk)$ differs from $ch_{\sim Hj}(\sim Hk)$ even when $j=\imath l$ is that, in '$ch_{\sim H\imath l}(\sim Hk)$', '$\imath l$' refers non-rigidly to the coin – $k$ – which would be the last one tossed if $j$ did not land heads.

But if '$\imath l$' refers rigidly to $j$, which is in fact the last coin tossed, then $ch_{\sim H\imath l}(\sim Hk)$ will equal $ch_{\sim Hj}(\sim Hk)$, and the true '$ch_{\sim Hj}(\sim Hk)=1/2$' will not be falsified by replacing '$j$' with '$\imath l$'. Nor therefore, for the same reason, will it be falsified by replacing '$j$' with any other term that refers rigidly to $j$. Similarly for all other such statements, and in particular for (26). If every term '$c''$' which refers to $c$ does so rigidly, then for all such '$c''$'

$$ch_{Kc'}(Le) = ch_{Kc}(Le) \text{ and } ch_{\sim Kc'}(Le) = ch_{\sim Kc}(Le); \text{ so that}$$
$$ch_{Kc'}(Le) > ch_{\sim Kc'}(Le) \text{ iff } ch_{Kc}(Le) > ch_{\sim Kc}(Le).$$

In short, (26) will be transparent for $c$.

This shows us what it takes to make (26) and hence (25), '*Le* because *Kc*', transparent for both *c* and *e*. How then can we bring this about? The answer is: by fiat. We can make any '*Le* because *Kc*' transparent simply by stipulating that '*c*' and '*e*', and any co-referring terms which may replace them in it, are to refer rigidly to *c* and *e*. This will admittedly falsify

(21)  'Don's fall is the first because his rope is the weakest'

and every other instance of (25), '*Le* because *Kc*', in which '*K*' or '*L*' is an identity predicate: no such instance of (25) that is true can be transparent, which is why it cannot entail (2'), '*c* causes or affects *e*' [§4]. But in any true instance of (25) which obviously does entail (2'), '*K*' and '*L*' will not be identity predicates; and such instances, as we have seen, we can always make transparent. And by so doing we enable them to tell us transparently both that and how any particular *c* causes or affects a particular *e*.

## 7  Transparent and factual causation

So far, at last, so good. But I still need to show *how* a transparent

(25)  '*Le* because *Kc*' entails
(2')  '*c* causes or affects *e*'.

That is the business of this section. But first I must say why I need to show this, by correcting my remark in §4 that, when *c* affects *e*, the particular, *e*, is given. This makes it look as if *c*'s affecting *e* is what makes the factual effect, *Le*, an effect on *e* when it is in fact the other way round; and similarly for *c*.

For example, what makes a factual effect E a fact about Kim is not that Kim is the person thereby affected. On the contrary: what makes Kim the person affected is that E is a fact about Kim, e.g. that she comes to believe that Don is dying. Similarly, what makes a factual cause C of E a fact about a specific particular *c*, e.g. Don, is not that *c* is E's particular cause. It is the other way round: what makes *c* a particular cause of E is the fact that some C, which causes E, is a fact about *c*.

This is why I must derive '*c* causes or affects *e*' from '*Le* because *Kc*'. And that presents a problem, because I have already derived it, in chapter 11.3, from

(22)  '($\exists x)(Lx)$ because $(\exists x)(Kx)$',
(23)  '$c = (\imath x)(Kx)$' and
(24)  '$e = (\imath x)(Lx)$';

a derivation which, as we saw there, already entails its transparency.

This earlier derivation shows that a transparent (2′), '*c* causes or affects *e*', need not follow from a transparent (25), '*Le* because *Kc*'. Yet we still want (25) to entail it, and to tell us transparently how *c* causes or affects *e*, namely by *Kc* causing *Le*. Furthermore, since the truth of corresponding instances of (22) and (25) can hardly be a coincidence, (25) really cannot be logically independent of (22)–(24).

I conclude from all this that (22)–(24) entail not only (2′), '*c* causes or affects *e*', but also (25), '*Le* because *Kc*'. And if they do, then since the proof of transparency given in chapter 11.3 applies here too, the reading of (25) that (22)–(24) entail must be transparent. For suppose '*c*″' and '*e*″' are any other terms referring respectively to *c* and *e*. Then, as before, the transparency of (23) and (24) makes them entail

'$c' = (1x)(Kx)$' and
'$e' = (1x)(Lx)$',

which, together with (22), will then entail

'*Le*′ because *Kc*″'.

I conclude moreover that this entailment, between (22)–(24) and the transparent (25), is mutual. That is, I take a transparent '*Le* because *Kc*' to entail that local circumstances S exist such that, in S, there is an *L* because there is a *K*, *c* is the *K* and *e* is the *L*. Thus if Don's death is painless because Kim's injection anaesthetises him, then it follows that there is a painless death because there is an anaesthetic injection, that Kim's injection is the anaesthetic one and Don's death is the painless one – and hence that Kim's injection causes or affects Don's death. This I maintain is how a transparently true (25), by entailing (22)–(24), entails the transparent (2′), '*c* causes or affects *c*'.

In short, the truth of transparent causal instances of

(25)    '*Le* because *Kc*'

depends only on *c* and *e* being the particulars which, by being *K* and *L* respectively, happen to make true the '$(\exists x)(Kx)$' and '$(\exists x)(Lx)$' in a true

(22)    '$(\exists x)(Kx)$ because $(\exists x)(Lx)$'.

And this, I maintain, is what makes these causal truths transparent for both *c* and *e*: the fact that *c* and *e* need only be referred to in the transparent and non-causal

(23)    '$c = (1x)(Kx)$' and
(24)    '$e = (1x)(Lx)$'.

This completes my case for holding that all causal links between any particulars $c$ and $e$ reduce to causation linking some existential facts, $(\exists x)(Kx)$ and $(\exists x)(Lx)$, which $c$ and $e$ bring about by being $K$ and $L$. And this being so, the evident transparency of many statements saying that or how particulars cause or affect each other provides no reason to suppose that causation is ever a relation between particulars. For even when such statements are transparent for the particulars involved, what the causation involved really links are not those particulars but facts.

May we then conclude that causation is really a relation between facts, as represented by truths of the form

(1′)    'C causes E',

i.e., in full, 'the fact that C causes the fact that E'? No: that conclusion is both premature and wrong. For just as we have seen that '$c$ causes $e$' can be made true without causation relating the particulars $c$ and $e$, so 'C causes E' may be made true without causation relating the facts C and E. And so it is, as we shall now see.

# 13 *Causal relations*

## 1 The case for a relation of causation

We have seen that causation always links facts, in the sense that all causal truths either are or derive from truths of the form

(1)    'E because C'.

Sentences of this form entail the truth of the sentences 'C' and 'E' which they contain and thus, by my definition of 'fact', the existence of the facts C and E [1.2–3]. Hence my alternative form

(1′)    'C causes E',

equivalent by definition to 'E because C', in which 'C' and 'E' occur not as sentences but as abbreviations of 'the fact that C' and 'the fact that E' [1.4]. Moreover, even when 'E because C' is opaque for particulars referred to within the sentences 'C' and 'E', 'C causes E' is always transparent for C and E [9.5]: no true 'C causes E' can be falsified by replacing 'C' or 'E' with any other term referring to the same fact.

All this makes it natural to regard causation as a relation between facts. For consider what it takes to state a relation $O$ between two entities $b$ and $d$, where $b$ and $d$ may be facts, particulars, properties or entities of any other kind, and $O$ may be any relation: being heavier than, a parent of, next to, etc. Then for any sentence '$Obd$' to say that $O$ relates $b$ to $d$, at least two conditions must be met:

(i)    '$Obd$' must entail that $b$ and $d$ exist,

since nothing relates anything to nothing; and, since whether or not $O$ relates $b$ to $d$ cannot depend on what $b$ or $d$ is called,

(ii)    '$Obd$' must be transparent for $b$ and $d$.

For example, 'Bill is heavier than Kim' can only state a relation between Bill and Kim if it entails their existence and is transparent for them, i.e. its truth value would not be changed by replacing 'Bill' or 'Kim' with any other term for Bill or Kim; and similarly in all other cases.

156

'C causes E', as we have seen, meets both these conditions: (i) it entails the existence of the facts C and E, and (ii) it is transparent for C and E. What more does it take to state a relation between C and E – a relation which, to make 'C causes E' the causal statement it undoubtedly is, must be the relation of causing? Arguably nothing. And if nothing, then does not the fact that C causes E entail that a causal relation holds between C and E?

## 2  Properties and relations, predicates and concepts

I agree that meeting conditions (i) and (ii) is all a sentence '*Obd*' needs to do in order to say that a relation *O* links *b* and *d* – *if* such a relation exists. I agree moreover that it must exist if by 'relation' we mean whatever it takes, besides *b* and *d*, to make '*Obd*' true. In this sense of 'relation', '*Obd*' trivially entails the existence of a relation *O* linking *b* and *d*; just as, if we use 'property' to mean whatever it takes, besides *b*, to make '*Kb*' true, '*Kb*' trivially entails the existence of a property *K* which *b* has.

These uses of 'property' and 'relation' are like my use of the term 'fact' to mean an entity corresponding by definition to a true sentence, statement or proposition. In this sense of 'fact' every true statement 'P' entails the existence of a corresponding fact P. But this entailment has a price: ontological vacuity [1.2]. For in this sense 'the fact that P' tells us nothing about what in the world, if anything, makes 'P' true and hence P a fact. Similarly, in the parallel senses of 'property' and 'relation', 'the property *K*' and 'the relation *O*' tell us nothing about what in the world, if anything besides *b* and *d*, makes '*Kb*' and '*Obd*' true and hence gives *b* the property *K* and makes *O* relate *b* to *d*.

But these are the questions we are now to consider. So to pose them properly we need either other senses of 'fact', 'property' and 'relation' or other terms. Specifically, we need terms used as I am already using the term 'particular', namely of entities that exist independently in the world, and not merely of entities defined by linguistic expressions: in the case of particulars, by the names and other terms we use to refer to them. And fortunately we can meet this need by fiat, by simply deciding to use new or existing terms to tell us what in the world, besides particulars like *b* and *d*, it takes to make sentences like 'P', '*Kb*' and '*Obd*' true.

Our ability to do this is shown by the fact that we can and sometimes do think of particulars as I think of facts. That is, we sometimes make our use of names and other terms to refer to particulars entail the existence of those particulars, notably in discussing fiction. Then we make 'Pegasus' refer to Pegasus, and 'King Arthur' to King Arthur, by mere definition. But for this usage we pay the price I pay for my use of 'fact': ontological vacuity. To say in this sense that 'Pegasus' refers to Pegasus is true, but it does not tell us what in the world 'Pegasus' refers to, a question to which the true answer is of course 'nothing'. So when, as here, that is the question which concerns us, we do not think of particulars in this ontologically vacuous way.

In short, when we ask what particulars there are in the world, we mean only those particulars whose existence neither follows from nor depends on our having names for them. In this sense it is by no means vacuous to say that, unlike Pegasus and Hamlet, King Arthur exists in the atemporal sense of 'exists' of chapter 1.2. For now what we are saying, truly or falsely, is that the person we call 'King Arthur' exists, not as a mere definitional consequence of the use of this name by Malory and others, but as a real flesh-and-blood inhabitant of post-Roman Britain.

As for 'King Arthur' and King Arthur (if he exists) or (changing the example to avoid irrelevant controversy) 'Queen Victoria' and Queen Victoria, so for the true 'Don falls' and – what? Not, in my sense, the *fact* that Don falls, an entity whose existence the truth of 'Don falls' entails by mere definition, but whatever in the world, if anything, makes 'Don falls' true. Now I could use the term 'fact' to mean this too; but I shall still need that term for what I have so far meant by it, and these two senses of 'fact', rather like the fictional and historical senses of 'King Arthur', are too easily confounded. So I need another term; and as all existing terms seem to me misleading in various ways, I shall in §4 reluctantly introduce a new one. But that can wait until we have solved the same problem for 'property' and 'relation'.

Here fortunately the problem is easier to solve, because suitable terms already exist. What makes them suitable, however, is not that they have the sense of 'property' and 'relation' that is analogous to our normal non-vacuous sense of 'particular'. On the contrary, they have something like the sense given at the start of this section. And by letting them bear this sense, we can free 'property' and 'relation' for use in the other sense we need. The terms I have in mind are *'predicate'* and *'concept'*.

By 'predicate' I mean a general word or other linguistic expression, like 'falls', 'is red' or 'is heavier than', which can be extracted from a sentence by deleting one or more names or other terms for particulars. By 'concept' I mean the mental counterpart of such an expression, something which we, and perhaps some animals, might apply to particulars even if we lacked a corresponding predicate. There is of course much more to be said about predicates and concepts, especially about which comes first, but nothing that need detain us here. Here all that matters is that between them they allow us to explain away the apparent entailments of $K$ and $O$ by such facts as $Kb$ and $Obd$.

For first, the mere existence of the sentences '$Kb$' and '$Obd$', true or false, obviously entails the existence both of the predicates '$K$' and '$O$' and of the corresponding concepts, which I shall represent in the same way, as '$K$' and '$O$'. Thus for the English sentences 'Don falls' and 'Bill is heavier than Kim' to exist, English must have the predicates 'falls' and 'is heavier than'. And second, anyone who thinks, with or without a language, that Don falls, and that Bill is heavier than Kim, must have the concepts of falling and of being heavier.

Our having these concepts and predicates, together with concepts and terms for the particulars involved, may well suffice for us to think and say 'Don falls' and 'Bill is heavier than Kim'. But they do not suffice to make those thoughts and statements true. Nor does the existence of Don, Bill and Kim, since Don could exist without falling, and Bill and Kim could exist without Bill being heavier than Kim. So the question remains: what more must the world contain, besides Don, Bill and Kim, to make it true that Don falls, and that Bill is heavier than Kim? Whatever it is, it should on the face of it include something general, to make true all true statements of the forms '... falls' and '... is heavier than ...'. In short, it should include so-called *universals*.

From now on therefore I shall mostly restrict 'property' and 'relation' to universals. (When for convenience I use 'property of' in its more usual and ontologically vacuous sense of 'fact about', I shall say so.) Whether there really are universals, and if so what universals there are, are serious questions, but ones we can postpone. Here I need only say that if universals exist, then like particulars such as Don, Kim and Bill, but unlike concepts and predicates, they are parts or aspects of the world which do not depend on anyone using, speaking about or thinking of them. In particular, their existence is not entailed by that of corresponding concepts or predicates. So even if the truth of 'Don falls' and 'Bill is heavier than Kim' does require some properties and relations to exist, these need not include the property of falling or the relation of being heavier than: for there may well be no such property and no such relation.

Similarly with sentences of the form 'C causes E' by which, as we have seen, all singular causation can be stated. I cannot deny that we think and say, using such sentences, that facts cause each other. The existence of these thoughts and statements, and those of the form '$c$ causes $e$', undoubtedly entails that of the concept and predicate 'causes'. But to make such thoughts and statements true takes more than this, and more than whatever it takes to make 'C' and 'E' true. For just as Bill and Kim can exist without Bill being heavier than Kim, so the facts C and E can exist without C causing E.

Don could fall and die and yet not die because he falls, and similarly in other cases.

What more then must the world contain to make 'E because C' true, i.e. make it a fact that C causes E? Must it in particular, assuming for the sake of argument that there are such entities as properties and relations, contain a relation of causation? In other words, is it always the case that when 'E because C' is true, what makes it true is that a causal universal relates whatever entities make 'C' and 'E' true?

## 3  Causation between particulars

How can we answer such a question? If the existence of a relation $O$ does not follow from the truth of '$Obd$', how can we tell whether $O$ exists or not? To see how, let us look first at one of our non-causal examples, 'Bill is heavier than Kim'. Here we know that this, if true, is not made true by a *heavier than* relation between Bill and Kim. For what makes this statement true, on the surface of the earth, is that the earth exerts a stronger gravitational force on Bill than on Kim, since Bill has a greater mass and the earth attracts objects on its surface in proportion to their mass. Out in space, subject to no net gravitational force, Bill would not be heavier than Kim: both would have the same weight, namely zero.

This account of what makes 'Bill is heavier than Kim' true may of course be false. What makes its statements about the gravitational forces on Bill and Kim true may be a local curvature in the geometric structure of spacetime induced by the distribution of matter across space at earlier times. But the issue of what really makes gravitational statements true is not one we need discuss, let alone settle. I raise it only because it shows how we can tell whether a relation $O$ exists, by finding out what in the world makes statements of the form '$Obd$' true. It may turn out to be a relation $O$ holding between $b$ and $d$; but it may not. And if not, then since, if $O$ is anything, it is what, by linking $b$ and $d$, makes '$Obd$' true, it is nothing: there is no such relation.

This test for the existence of a universal is not new. Indeed I have already applied it in concluding that causation is not a relation between particulars. To see this, recall the discussion in chapters 11 and 12 of what makes instances of

(2)     '$c$ causes $e$' and
         '$c$ affects $e$'

true. We know, since many beliefs and statements of these forms exist, that 'causes' and 'affects' exist as predicates and concepts applied to particulars. But this is not enough to make such beliefs and statements true. Nor is the existence of the particulars $c$ and $e$, which can usually exist whether or not $c$ causes or affects $e$: Don's fall need not cause his death, nor need Kim's injection affect it, for those events to be the events they are [12.3]. So something else is needed to make beliefs and statements of these two forms true. And this could be causal relations between $c$ and $e$, since '$c$ causes $e$' and '$c$ affects $e$' always meet the conditions (i) and (ii) of §1: they entail the existence of $c$ and $e$ and are transparent for them. So they could be made true by causal relations holding between $c$ and $e$.

I say 'relations' here because it would take two causal relations between particulars to generate these two kinds of causal fact: *causes*, to make instances of '$c$ causes $e$' true, and *affects*, to make instances of '$c$ affects $e$' true. But as we have seen, there are no such causal universals, since what distinguishes facts of these two kinds is not causation but whether $c$ causes an essential or an inessential fact about $e$ [12.2]. So the only *causal* universal which might relate particulars is one that makes true instances of the disjunctive form

(2′)   '$c$ causes or affects $e$'.

Yet on our account, not even statements of this weak form are made true by a causal relation between $c$ and $e$. What makes them true is that in the relevant local circumstances, for some possible predicates '$K$' and '$L$', $c$ is the $K$, $e$ is the $L$ and there is an $L$ because there is a $K$: $(\exists x)(Lx)$ because $(\exists x)(Kx)$. The particulars $c$ and $e$ which happen to be the $K$ and the $L$ then inherit the causal link between the existential facts $(\exists x)(Kx)$ and $(\exists x)(Lx)$ [11.3].

In short, the burden of chapters 11 and 12 is precisely that what makes '$c$ causes or affects $e$' true is *not* a causal relation between $c$ and $e$. But then since this relation is if anything what, by linking $c$ and $e$, makes '$c$ causes or affects $e$' true, it is nothing. So even if there are universals, there is no such universal as a relation of causation holding between particulars.

## 4  Facts and facta

I conclude that, if causation is a relation at all, it must relate not particulars but the entities, if any, whose existence makes true the sentences 'C' and 'E' entailed by a true 'E because C'. For it to do this there must of course be such entities, and to see if there are we need a word for them. The word 'fact' as I use it will not do, for the reasons given in §2. For in my sense of 'fact', to say that C and E are facts is just to say that the sentences 'C' and 'E' are true, which tells us nothing about what in the world makes them true. And as this sense of 'fact' is too useful, and too entrenched, for me also to use the word to answer the present question without intolerable ambiguity, we need another term.

Unfortunately no other English term I can think of will do. The best candidate, 'state of affairs', I need and am already using to apply even more widely than 'fact': namely, not only to actual but also to merely possible and even impossible facts. That is, to any sentence, statement or proposition 'P', true or false, there corresponds by definition a state of affairs P which, if it obtains, i.e. if 'P' is true, is a fact [1.2]. But then I cannot also invoke the state of affairs P to say what in our world makes 'P' true. For since in my usage this state of affairs exists in our world, as in all others, whether 'P' is true or false, its mere existence in our world cannot be what makes 'P' true. The only thing about it that could make 'P' true is the fact that it obtains. But this fact is no more use to us than the fact that P, with which indeed it is identical. For as the state of affairs P obtains by mere definition iff 'P' is true, 'P obtains' is no answer to the question: what in the world makes 'P' true, i.e. makes P obtain, i.e. makes P a fact.

Since I need 'state of affairs' for this other purpose, and can think of no better English term, I shall use the Latin word *'facta'* (singular *'factum'*), dropping its dictionary restriction to 'things done', for the entities in our world, whatever they may be, whose existence or non-existence makes true statements true. What the facta of causation are, and how they make causal statements true, will become clear as we proceed. But one basic fact about facta I can state at once. Suppose it is not only a fact that P, e.g. that Don falls, but is also a factum, a fact I shall sometimes mark with bold type, thus: **P**. Then ~P would not be a factum even if it were a fact. For all it takes to make 'P' false and so '~P' true is that **P** does not exist – a fact, of course, if 'P' is false, but not a factum.

## 5  Facta as causes and effects

With this preamble, let us return to our question, rephrased as follows: is causation a relation between facta? The considerations of §1 do not show that it is, but equally nothing said in §2–3 shows that it is not. In particular, there is no analogue here of the proof in §3 that causation is not a relation between particulars. For first, all causation between facta could be stated in the same form, 'C causes E': we shall not need two causal relations between facta, corresponding to the causing and affecting of particulars. One causal relation between facta could make true all true instances of 'C causes E'.

Second, a causal relation between facta could generate causal truths of all kinds. For a start, by making statements of the form '$(\exists x)(Lx)$ because $(\exists x)(Kx)$' true, it could also as we have seen account for all transparently true instances of '*c* causes *e*', '*c* affects *e*' and '*Le* because *Kc*': which will cover all truths saying that, and how, particulars cause and affect each other. Next, it could generate all the opaquely true instances of '*Le* because *Kc*' discussed in chapter 12.4–5, including, when '*K*' and '*L*' are identity predicates, causal truths like 'Don's fall is the first because his rope is the weakest'. Finally, by making other instances of 'C causes E' true, it could account for all the singular causal truths that involve no particulars at all.

Even so, no such causal relation exists. To see why not, we must note that, for 'E because C' to be made true by a causal relation between *facta*, it is not enough for it to entail that C and E are *facts*, i.e. that the sentences 'C' and 'E' are true. The 'C' and 'E' which 'E because C' entails must be made true by facta which are themselves related as cause to effect. And as we shall now see, this requirement can often not be met, for one of two reasons:

(a)   one or both of 'C' and 'E' are not made true by facta;
(b)   the facta that make 'C' and 'E' true are not causally related.

Let us take these in turn.

(a) Many 'C' and 'E' such that C causes E may indeed be made true by facta, especially when 'E because C' has the form '*Le* because *Kc*' or '$(\exists x)(Lx)$ because $(\exists x)(Kx)$'. For here the *K*- and *L*-particulars do provide something for a causal relation to link: if *c* is the *K* and *e* is the *L*, then at least for some '*K*' and '*L*', *Kc* and *Le* may well be facta as well as facts.

But what if C and E are negative existential facts: there is *no L*-particular because there is *no K*-particular: $\sim(\exists x)(Lx)$ because $\sim(\exists x)(Kx)$? Thus suppose again that Don, instead of dying because he falls, survives because he holds on [11.2]. Here the causally related facts are that there is *not* a death of Don because there is *not* a fall of Don. What in the world is there for this causation to relate? How can the fact that there is *not* an entity of a certain kind – a fall of Don, a death of Don – be itself a factum, an entity in the world? And if it is not, then whatever this causation is, it cannot be a relation between facta, since there will be no facta for it to relate.

This argument is not of course conclusive. For even if the non-existence of particulars cannot be facta, there may be other facta for this causation to relate. Perhaps for example the facts that Don holds on and that he survives are facta? This is not ruled out by the proof that there are no such negative particulars as Don's holding on or Don's survival [11.2]. 'Don holds on' and 'Don survives' might still be made true by something in the world, namely by a man, Don, satisfying the predicates 'holds on' and 'survives'.

This response will not however do as it stands, since it takes more than Don to make it true that he falls or that he does not fall, and that he dies or that he does not die. For suppose 'Don falls' and 'Don dies' are made true, if they are true, by Don's having the properties respectively of falling and of dying. Then if 'Don does not fall' (and hence 'Don holds on') and 'Don does not die' (and hence 'Don survives') are true, what this means is not that Don has some other properties, but that he does *not* have these ones. This again is not a case of the world containing a man, Don, with certain properties but of its *not* containing such a man. So on the face of it, if Don's falling and his dying are facta, then his holding on and his surviving would not be facta even if they were facts.

Again there is more to be said. First, I have assumed that there are no negative properties, just as there are no negative particulars. For if there were, then the negative properties of not falling and not dying could, if Don survives because he holds on, make facta of the facts that he holds on and survives; just as, if Don dies because he falls, the positive properties of falling and dying can make facta of the facts that he falls and dies. And then there would in either case be facta for causation to relate.

This however will not do: for as we shall see in chapter 15.7, there are no negative properties. Thus if falling and dying are properties, holding on and surviving are not, and Don's holding on and surviving could not be facta even if they were facts. Yet Don could still survive because he holds on; just as, if holding on and surviving were the real properties, and falling and dying were not, he could still die because he falls.

Despite all this, 'Don holds on' and 'Don survives' might still be made true by facta. For although these sentences *mean* only that Don lacks the properties of falling and of dying, they could still be made true by his having other positive properties and relations: such as grasping the cliff, and continuing to think, which entail respectively that he does not fall and that he does not die. So 'Don survives because he holds on' may yet be made true by a causal relation between the facta which in fact make 'Don holds on' and 'Don survives' true.

In many other cases too, the denial that a particular has one property is made true by its having an incompatible one. Thus suppose it is not only a fact but a factum that Kim's temperature is $38.2\pm0.05°C$ [5.2]. This factum makes it true that her temperature is not $100°C$, is less than $40°C$, greater than $35°C$, and so on. Similarly for pressures, shapes, colours and many other families of mutually incompatible positive properties. In each of them a single factum entails a multitude of negative and disjunctive facts, whose causal links might well reduce to a relation between the facta that entail them.

But this will not always work, because some 'C' and 'E' such that C causes E can only be made true by the non-existence of the factum which would make 'C' or 'E' false. Thus suppose that Kim's use of contraception causes her to have no children. This effect is a negative existential fact which cannot be reduced to Kim having negative or incompatible positive properties. That is, the predicate 'has no children' applies to Kim neither because she has the negative property of having no children nor because she has any other positive properties. It applies to her simply because *no* particulars of a certain kind – children of Kim – exist. And that fact is obviously not a factum, since what makes

'Kim has no children'

true is that there are *no* facta about children of Kim. Yet although no factum makes this sentence true, it can still state a cause or an effect, as in:

'Kim has no children because she uses contraception';
'Kim works full time because she has no children'.

This and other such cases show that there are many true instances of 'E because C' which cannot be made true by any relation between the facta that make 'C' and 'E' true, since no such facta exist.

(b) And even when such facta do exist, they may still not be related as cause to effect. For if C is not itself a factum, then the factum that makes 'C' true in a true 'E because C' need not raise the chance that 'E' is true. Take our earlier example of a cause which seems not to raise its effect's chance: Sue's holing out in one, H, when her pulled drive bounces off a tree [6.1]. Suppose H is a factum, **H**. Then the factum, if any, which causes **H** must be **P**, Sue's pulling her drive, since this entails but is not entailed by the fact, D, that she drives. But since **H**'s chance is raised by D but lowered by **P**,

'H because D' and
'H because P'

have opposite truth values: the former being true and the latter false. So although 'D' is made true by the factum **P**, 'H because D' cannot be made true by a causal relation between **H** and **P**, since no such relation exists.

There are, in short, many true 'E because C' which cannot state a causal relation between the facta that make 'C' and 'E' true, since either (a) there are no such facta or (b) those facta are not related as cause to effect. But if there is such a relation then by definition what makes true all true instances of 'C causes E' is that it relates C and E. So since that cannot always be what makes 'C causes E' true, no such relation exists.

## 6  The facta of causation

The arguments of the last section, and in particular its claims about facta, may be disputed in at least two ways. Either the existence of facta, or the distinction between facta and facts, may be denied. Thus *nominalists*, who say that only particulars exist, will deny that there are any facta, just as they deny that there are any universals. However, although I think they are wrong on both counts, here they are on my side, since causation cannot relate facta if there are no facta for it to relate.

Those who admit the existence of facta, but equate them with what I call facts, i.e. with entities trivially entailed by truths, must also be on my side. For as with nominalism, although I reject this equation, it is no threat to my present claim. For equating facta with facts just reduces the idea of a causal relation between facta to the thesis that all causation can be stated by true instances of 'C causes E', i.e. of 'E because C'. With this of course, having been at pains to prove it, I agree. But it does not tell us what in the world makes these causal statements true. Philosophers whose interest in the metaphysics of causation, as in metaphysics generally, begins and ends with the language we use to talk about it, may indeed decline to answer that question. But the fact that others cannot or will not try to say what in the world causation is need not stop the rest of us doing so.

It is not however much of an answer to our question to say what causation is *not*, namely a relation between particulars or between facta. I need to start saying what it *is*, given what we now know about it, and that will be the business of the next chapter. But first we must see what if anything can make both

(1)     'E because C'
e.g.    'Don dies because he falls', and
(1~)    '~E because ~C'
e.g.    'Don survives because he holds on'

true, albeit of course in different circumstances: (1) when C and E are facts, and (1~) when ~C and ~E are. For if a causal relation between facta is not what makes (1) and (1~) true when they are true, then something else must make (1) and (1~), when they are true, not only true but *causal*. In other words, making the causal content of (1) and (1~) explicit, we need something to make both

(1′)     'C causes E' and
(1′~)    '~C causes ~E'

capable of truth.

To see what might do this, consider the fact that causes must raise the chances of their effects [5; 6]. So for any C to cause any E, E's chance in the relevant circumstances with C, $ch_C(E)$, must exceed its chance without C, $ch_{-C}(E)$. Thus not only must C and E be facts, something must make it a fact that

(16)  $ch_C(E) > ch_{-C}(E)$.

Similarly, for ~C to cause ~E, not only must ~C and ~E be facts, something must make it a fact that

(16~) $ch_{-C}(\sim E) > ch_C(\sim E)$.

Hence for both 'C causes E' and '~C causes ~E' to be capable of truth, we must satisfy both (16) and (16~). What I shall now show is how facta which can make (16) hold can also make (16~) hold, and *vice versa*.

Let us start with (16). To make (16) hold, facta must make '$ch_C(E)=p$' and '$ch_{-C}(E)=p'$' true for some $p$ and $p'$ such that $p>p'$. And they must of course do this without entailing '~C' or '~E'. For otherwise (16) would be inconsistent with 'C causes E', which entails 'C' and 'E'. When Don dies because he falls, his chances of dying if he falls and if he holds on must not entail either that he does not die or that he does not fall.

Suppose there are facta which meet these conditions. Suppose moreover that their existence does not depend on whether Don falls or holds on, i.e. that $ch_C(E)$ and $ch_{-C}(E)$ have the same values, $p$ and $p'$, when ~C causes ~E as they do when C causes E. (This need not be so, but since it often is, it must be possible, and we may assume, for simplicity, that it is so.)

Next, since chances are probabilities, ~E's chance must, in any given circumstances, be 1 minus E's chance: $ch(\sim E)=1-ch(E)$ [2.1]. Applying this to the circumstances in which ~C causes ~E gives us:

(29)  $ch_C(\sim E) = 1-ch_C(E) = 1-p$;
(29~) $ch_{-C}(\sim E) = 1-ch_{-C}(E) = 1-p'$.

So when Don survives because he holds on, his chances of *surviving* if he falls and if he holds on must be 1 minus his chances of *dying* if he falls and if he holds on.

Next we note that, for whatever makes '$ch_C(E)=p$' and '$ch_{-C}(E)=p'$' true to make (16) hold, $p$ must be greater than $p'$, i.e.

$p > p'$, so that
$1-p' > 1-p$.

But this, given (29) and (29~), makes $ch_{-C}(\sim E)$ greater than $ch_C(\sim E)$, thus making (16~) hold too. So the facta that make (16) hold when 'C' and 'E' are true can also make (16~) hold when they are false – provided of course they no more entail 'C' and 'E' than they entail '~C' and '~E'.

This reinforces our conclusion in §5 that 'C causes E' is never made true by a relation between C and E, by showing that no factum that makes (16) true can be a relation between the *facts* C and E, let alone between any facta. For (16) could only be a relation between C and E if it entailed their existence, i.e. if it entailed that 'C' and 'E' are true [§1]. But if whatever makes (16) hold can also make (16~) hold when 'C' and 'E' are false, it cannot entail either 'C' or 'E' and so cannot include any relation between the facts C and E.

Nor should it. For regardless of its role in causation, $ch_C(E)=p$ must be logically independent of C and E. For first, it is obvious that, for all $p$,

$ch_C(E)=p$ entails neither C nor ~C.

For example, whatever Don's chance of dying if he falls, it entails neither that he falls nor that he does not.

Second, $ch_C(E)=p$ is also, if less obviously, independent of E, even if $p=1$ or 0. For although

$ch(E)=1$ entails E

[3.1], $ch_C(E)=1$ does not. Only

C&$ch_C(E)=1$ entails E,

by entailing $ch(E)=1$, and, as we have just seen, $ch_C(E)=1$ does not entail C. So Don can always survive a chance of 1 of dying if he falls, simply by not falling. And similarly for $p=0$ and ~E: Don can die even with a zero chance of dying if he falls, again by not falling.

In short, for all $p$,

$ch_C(E)=p$ entails neither E nor ~E.

So if facta can make '$ch_C(E)=p$' and '$ch_{~C}(E)=p'$' true, then by making them true for $p$ and $p'$ such that $p>p'$, they can make both (16) and (16~) hold without entailing either C and E or ~C and ~E. And any facta that can do this can, together with whatever else it takes to make causal statements true, make C cause E when C and E are facts and ~C cause ~E when ~C and ~E are.

Our task then is to discover the facta, if any, which do this, i.e. which make instances of '$ch_C(E)=p$' true. Only now, to cover all cases, we should remove the implication of this notation that C, rather than ~C, is the cause, and that E, rather than ~E, is the effect. For the facta that make '$ch_C(E)=p$' true will not automatically make 'C' or 'E' true, nor will they make $ch_C(E)$

exceed $ch_{\sim C}(E)$. So in order to generalise our question, without wasting the useful connotations of 'C' and 'E', I shall rewrite '$ch_C(E)=p$' as

$$'ch_Q(P)=p',$$

where Q and P are any states of affairs that could, if facts, be causes or effects. This makes our question: what in the world makes instances of '$ch_Q(P)=p$' true?

The facta we are looking for will, if they exist, be the real embodiment of causation. For whatever causation's other features, it is the chances that causes give their effects which give it its major connotations [5; 6; 17]: $ch_C(E)$ and $ch_{\sim C}(E)$ are what make any cause C precede E, explain E, be evidence for E, a means to E and, if C causes E immediately (i.e. without causing it by causing a D that causes it), contiguous to E. This is why, to find out what in the world causation is, we must find out what kind of facta can make it a fact for some $p$ that $ch_Q(P)=p$.

# 14  *Causal facta*

## 1  Propensities and properties

What makes instances of '$ch_Q(P)=p$' true? In chapter 2.3 I provisionally equated $ch_Q(P)$ with the $p$ such that $Q{\Rightarrow}ch(P)=p$, an equation which reduces our question to: what makes '$Q{\Rightarrow}ch(P)=p$' true? And the answer to this question may seem obvious. For, by definition [1.7], '$Q{\Rightarrow}ch(P)=p$' is true iff $ch(P)=p$ in all the closest Q-worlds, i.e. the worlds most like ours where 'Q' is true. Does this not tell us what makes '$Q{\Rightarrow}ch(P)=p$' and hence '$ch_Q(P)=p$' true?

No, because it does not tell us what in *this* world makes '$Q{\Rightarrow}ch(P)=p$' true. Something must do so, because as we can see from Figure 15 (Figure 2 from chapter 1.7 with 'C' and 'E' changed to 'Q' and 'U'), any closest-world conditional '$Q{\Rightarrow}U$' is only a partial truth function of 'Q' and 'U':

| 'Q' | 'U' | '$Q{\Rightarrow}U$' |
|------|------|------|
| True | True | True |
| True | False | False |
| False | True | ? |
| False | False | ? |

Figure 15: Truth table for '$Q{\Rightarrow}U$'

In other words, as Figure 15 shows, when 'Q' is false the truth value – truth or falsity – of 'Q' and 'U' does not settle the truth value of '$Q{\Rightarrow}U$'. So if '$Q{\Rightarrow}U$' is true when 'Q' is false, something else must make it true. This may be something about other possible worlds, but it must also be something about this one. For since by hypothesis '$Q{\Rightarrow}U$' is true in our world, and so states a fact about it, that fact should be entailed by the existence or non-existence in our world of one or more facta. And when 'U' is an instance of '$ch(P)=p$' we have already seen in one case what the facta are.

In chapter 4.4 I called the $p$ such that $Q{\Rightarrow}ch(P)=p$ Q's *propensity* to yield P. ('Yield' here does not of course mean 'cause', since Q will only

170

cause P if $p$ exceeds the $p'$ such that $\sim Q \Rightarrow ch(P)=p'$, i.e. $\sim$Q's propensity to yield P; and $p$ entails nothing about this.) I then noted that

> in this sense of 'propensity', my mass $M$ embodies an infinity of propensities, namely those of all possible net forces $F$ to accelerate me at $A=F/M$. For my having this mass makes '$F \Rightarrow ch(A=F/M)=1$' true of me for all $F$ [4.4].

So if my mass being $M$ is a factum, it can make true not just one but infinitely many instances of '$Q \Rightarrow ch(P)=p$'. And that I say is what it is, and does. Facta like this, which are the core of causation, I shall officially call *singular causal facta*: 'singular' to distinguish them from the laws of nature, some of which are also facta [16.5]; and 'causal' to distinguish them from facta, if any, which are not involved in causation. But since we can always call laws 'laws', and non-causal facta will not concern us, I shall usually call singular causal facta just 'facta'.

Most if not all facta are, like my having mass $M$, particulars with properties – masses, temperatures, durations, etc. – where by 'properties' I mean universals [13.2]. What determines which universals, and hence which kinds of facta, exist in our world we shall see in chapter 15; but first we must see how such facta make instances of '$Q \Rightarrow ch(P)=p$' true.

Suppose then that the factum we need is *Jd*: some particular $d$ having some property $J$. Suppose also that, for some '$K$' and '$L$', '$Q$' is '$Kd$' and '$P$' is '$Ld$', so that '$Q$' and '$P$' are also propositions about $d$. They need not be, of course, since '$Q$' and '$P$' are often about different particulars, as when Q is my bathroom scales reading '73' and P is my coming to believe that my mass is 73 kg [6.3]. But it will simplify what follows, and beg no relevant questions, to assume for the time being that '$Q$' and '$P$' are about the same particular $d$, as they are in the case of mass.

We may therefore take the following as our exemplar:

> *Jd*: a particular thing $d$ has a mass $M$;
> $Q=Kd$: a net force $F$ acts on $d$;
> $P=Ld$: $d$ accelerates at $F/M$.

(To enable $Kd$ to cause $Ld$, we must also take these three supposed facts to be almost but not quite simultaneous, since a cause must be contiguous to but precede its immediate effects. Here however we may for simplicity ignore such niceties, having seen how to accommodate them in the case of radioactive decay [5.2], and take the temporal relations of *Jd*, $Kd$ and $Ld$ for granted.)

Our question then is this: how can a factum like *Jd* make it a fact that $Kd \Rightarrow ch(Ld)=p$? How can the factum that $d$'s mass is $M$ make any net force

*F* certain to accelerate *d* at *F/M*? To answer this question we must look more closely at the connection between properties, like mass, and laws, like the laws of motion, in which they occur.

## 2  Properties and laws

I have already defined mass as the generic property *M* that makes the laws of motion, $F=MA$, and of gravity, $F=GMM'/R^2$, and all the other laws that mass occurs in, apply to any thing that has this property [4.2–3]. However, as I noted in chapter 4.3, this definition does not require any of these laws to be metaphysically necessary, for at least two reasons.

First, no mere definition of a property can entail that any actual property satisfies it. There may well be possible worlds where none of the laws in which mass occurs holds, and in those worlds mass will not exist; just as I would not exist in a world that contained no one with any of my actual properties.

Second, just as I and other particular things and events could exist with somewhat different properties – otherwise we could not be affected, only caused [12.2] – so the property mass may exist in worlds where some of the laws it actually occurs in fail. The property *M* such that $F=MA$ in our world may also exist in worlds where $F \neq MA$. So the existence of the property mass need not on its own entail this law, despite being defined by the fact that, in our world at least, it occurs in it.

Mass is not the only property that is definable in this way by the laws it occurs in. Many properties can be so defined: temperature by the laws of thermodynamics, electric charge by the laws of electrostatics, and so on. So, incidentally, can mental properties, like having a credence, $cr(P)=p$, i.e. a degree of belief, in the truth of a proposition 'P'. For credences are by definition the properties which, with desires of various strengths, make the *expected evaluation principle*, that 'we act in the way we think most likely to realise the objects of our desires', approximately true of those that have them [4.2; 7.2].

Then there are properties defined by indeterministic laws, such as the decay constants λ of radioactive atoms *x*, defined by laws of the form

(15)   $ch(D(x,t)) = 1-e^{-\lambda t}$

[5.1], where $D(x,t)$ is *x* decaying within *t* units of time. Here, since λ is itself a chance (the chance of an atom decaying in a small unit time [5.1]), the property defined by the law is a chance. And this is not an isolated case. On the contrary: all chances are defined by laws, even the chance $ch(Hj)=p$ of a coin toss *j* landing heads. For this too is defined as a property which, among other things, meets the Frequency condition [3.4] – and indeed does so necessarily [4.3]. Thus no toss, in any possible world, can have a chance $p$ of landing heads unless it would make any class of tosses with this chance of landing heads satisfy the laws of large numbers that make $f_\infty(H)$, the limiting frequency with which those tosses will land heads, equal $p$.

Let us assume therefore that $J$ is, by definition, a property such that, among other things, it is a law that, for any $J$-particular $x$, $Kx \Rightarrow ch(Lx)=p$. This may seem to provide the ideal answer to the question posed at the end of §1: namely, that the factum **Jd** makes '$Kd \Rightarrow ch(Ld)=p$' true by entailing it. But unfortunately for us this ideal answer is false: **Jd** does not in fact entail $Kd \Rightarrow ch(Ld)=p$.

To see why not, consider again our example of the property $M$ defined in part by the law that $F=MA$, this time using the following abbreviations:

> $Md=M$: $d$ has mass $M$;
> $Fd=F$: a net force $F$ acts on $d$;
> $Ad=A$: $d$ accelerates at $A$;

where these facts are again almost simultaneous [§1]. Then the factum **Md=M** does *not* entail

> $Fd=F \Rightarrow ch(Ad=F/M)=1$ for all $F$.

That is, it does not entail that if a net force $F$ acts on $d$ it will certainly accelerate $d$ at $F/M$. Why not?

There are two reasons. The first we have seen already: our definition of $M$ lets $M$ exist in worlds where $F \neq MA$. And if it does so, then no **Md=M** can *entail* that $F=MA$ for any $F$, nor therefore that $Fd=F \Rightarrow ch(Ad=F/M)=1$. For facta to entail this, the law that $F=MA$ must also be a factum, **F=MA**, as indeed we shall see in due course that it is [16.5].

Yet even then the entailment fails: even **Md=M&F=MA** does not entail $Fd=F \Rightarrow ch(Ad=F/M)=1$. The reason is that if a net force $F$ *did* act on $d$, its mass might not be $M$: perhaps because $F$ would, literally, knock spots off it. Similarly, for any $J$, if $d$ is $J$ but not $K$: if $d$ *were* $K$, it might not be $J$, perhaps because its being $K$ might cause it not to be $J$. This is why not even the conjunction of **Jd** with the law that $Kx \Rightarrow ch(Lx)=p$ for all $J$-particulars $x$ can entail $Kd \Rightarrow ch(Ld)=p$.

Yet the ideal answer to our question, if not quite right, is nearly right. For even if **Jd** and the relevant law do not entail $Kd \Rightarrow ch(Ld)=p$, they do at least entail

> $Jd\&Kd \Rightarrow ch(Ld)=p$.

For example, given the law that $F=MA$, for $d$'s mass to be $M$ is for $d$ to have a property such that, if any net force $F$ acts on $d$ *and* $d$ still has this property, then its chance of accelerating at $F/M$ will be 1.

Similarly for other properties, including mental ones, like credences. Suppose for example that I want to keep dry and believe I need a coat to do so if I go out when it rains. Suppose also that my beliefs, desires and actions conform to the expected valuation principle. My believing that it's raining ($Jd$) may still not make me take a coat ($Ld$) if I go out ($Kd$), perhaps because if I believe that it's raining I won't go out: $Jd \Rightarrow \sim Kd$. But if I did go out believing it was raining, then I would certainly take a coat: $Jd\&Kd \Rightarrow ch(Ld)=1$. For being disposed to do so, given my other beliefs and desires, is part of what it is to believe that it's raining.

It is important to see that there is no inconsistency here, i.e. that

'$Jd \Rightarrow \sim Kd$' and
'$Jd\&Kd \Rightarrow ch(Ld)=1$'

can both be true. The easiest way to see this is to put it in terms of possible worlds. For '$Jd \Rightarrow \sim Kd$' does not say that '$Kd$' is false in *all* the $Jd$-worlds where the relevant laws hold, only in the closest ones. $Jd$ is after all compatible with $Kd$: I *could* go out believing that it's raining, even if I won't. So there are worlds where I do go out believing that it's raining, and what '$Jd\&Kd \Rightarrow ch(Ld)=1$' says is that, in the closest of these, I will certainly take a coat. But this is quite compatible with my not taking a coat in the even closer worlds where I go out not believing that it's raining.

It is also important to see that it is not viciously circular to define $J$ as the property such that, among other things, it is a law of nature that

$$(x)(Jx\&Kx \Rightarrow ch(Lx)=p),$$

where '$(x)$ ...' is a *first order universal quantifier* meaning 'for all particulars $x$, ...'. We are simply making an existence claim, saying that there is a property, which we call '$J$', such that $(x)(Jx\&Kx \Rightarrow ch(Lx)=p)$ is a law. This, for example, is what my statement, '$F=MA$', of Newton's second law of motion really says:

> there is a family of properties (call them 'masses'), with measure $M$, such that any net force $F$ will, with chance 1, accelerate anything with a mass $M$ at $A=F/M$.

And incidentally, as we shall see in §§4–5, by asserting the existence of these masses, '$F=MA$' asserts also that, if any particular $d$ does have any specific mass $M$, this is not just a fact: it is a factum.

## 3 The facta of propensity

This shows how a law of nature can enable $\mathbf{Jd}$ to make '$Jd\&Kd{\Rightarrow}ch(Ld){=}p$'
true for some $p$. More generally, it shows how a factum $\mathbf{R}$ can make

'$R\&Q{\Rightarrow}ch(P){=}p$'

true, by combining with some law to entail it. But this does not tell us what
we need to know, namely what makes

'$Q{\Rightarrow}ch(P){=}p$'

true. For this, as we have just seen, might be false even if '$R\&Q{\Rightarrow}ch(P){=}p$'
is true, since 'R' might be false if 'Q' were true. What then, besides $\mathbf{R}$,
does it take to make '$Q{\Rightarrow}ch(P){=}p$' true?

As the answer to this question is somewhat complex, let me first answer
the similar but simpler question about deterministic causation. Suppose we
want a factum $\mathbf{R}$ to conjoin with the facts Q and P to make 'Q causes P'
true. Then even when Q is *not* a fact we will want $\mathbf{R}$ to make it true that, if
Q *were* a fact, it would cause P. But this might not be true, since Q might
cause ~R. So something must rule that out: but what?

The obvious answer is a factum $\mathbf{T}$ which would make Q cause R. But
this will not do, since Q might cause ~T, thus starting an obviously vicious
regress which we must stop in some other way – a way which might have
stopped Q causing ~R in the first place. But what is this other way? The
answer is easy: it is not that some factum $\mathbf{T}$ would make Q cause R but that
*no* factum would make Q cause ~R; and similarly at any later stage of the
regress.

In short, what enables $\mathbf{R}$ to make it true, when 'Q' is false, that Q would
cause P is the infinitely disjunctive fact that *either*

no factum exists that would make Q cause ~R,
*or*    a factum $\mathbf{T}$ exists that would make Q cause R and
no factum exists that would make Q cause ~T,
*or*    a factum $\mathbf{T}$ exists that would make Q cause R and
a factum $\mathbf{V}$ exists that would make Q cause T and
no factum exists that would make Q cause ~V,
*or*    ...

Similarly in the general case, as we shall now see. Here our question is
how any factum $\mathbf{R}$, even if it conjoins with a law to entail $R\&Q{\Rightarrow}ch(P){=}p$,
can make '$Q{\Rightarrow}ch(P){=}p$' true if 'R' might be false if 'Q' is true. To see the
answer to this question we must ask what 'might' means here. It cannot just
mean that 'R' might be false 'for all we know': our ignorance cannot be
what stops $\mathbf{R}$ making '$Q{\Rightarrow}ch(P){=}p$' true. Nor can it mean that 'Q' does not

entail 'R', for that we knew already. But then in what sense of 'might' *does* the fact that 'R' might be false if 'Q' is true stop **R** making 'Q⇒$ch$(P)=$p$' true?

I say the answer is that 'might' expresses a contingent possibility of the very kind that chance itself measures [3.1]: to say that 'R' might be false if 'Q' were true is to say that

'Q⇒$ch$(~R)>0'

is true. If so, then for **R** to make 'Q⇒$ch$(P)=$p$' true, something must make this false, the question being what.

The obvious answer, as before, is that something makes 'Q⇒$ch$(~R)=0' true: Q has a zero propensity to make 'R' false. But then, again as before, we need to know what makes *this* true; and the same answer to that question will only start a vicious regress. So again we need another answer, in this case that *nothing* makes 'Q⇒$ch$(~R)=$p$' true for *any p*. But how can that be: how can 'Q⇒$ch$(~R)=$p$' be false for *all p*?

The quickest way to see how is again to put the matter in terms of possible worlds. Recall that any 'Q⇒U' is true in our world iff 'U' is true in all the worlds most like ours where 'Q' is true [§1]. When 'Q' is true there is of course only one such world: ours. But when 'Q' is false, there may be many such worlds, differing from ours equally little but in different ways, e.g. in ways that a force $F$ which does not in fact act on $d$ might do so. But then 'U' may well be true in some of these closest Q-worlds and false in others. And if so, then since neither 'U' nor '~U' is true in all these worlds,

'Q⇒U' and 'Q⇒~U' are both false.

So if the $p$ for which '$ch$(~R)=$p$' is true varies among the closest Q-worlds,

'Q⇒$ch$(~R)=$p$' is false for all $p$.

'Q⇒$ch$(~R)=$p$' can also be, and often is, false for all $p$ because, in some or all of the closest Q-worlds,

'$ch$(~R)=$p$' is false for all $p$,

which of course entails that 'Q⇒$ch$(~R)=$p$' is. In particular, as I noted in chapter 2.1 and will show in chapter 17, for no fact P can any $ch$(P) be a property of any fact later than P. This means for example that after any time $t$ at which $d$'s mass is $M$ there is no such thing, in any possible world, as $d$'s chance of having, nor therefore of not having, mass $M$ at $t$. But then, at all times after ***Md***=$M$, 'Q⇒$ch$(~***Md***=$M$)=$p$' will be false in all worlds for all Q and all $p$; and similarly in other cases.

Suppose then that, for one or other of these reasons, '$Q \Rightarrow ch(\sim R) = p$' is in fact false for all $p$. What factum in our world makes it so? I say none. What makes '$Q \Rightarrow ch(\sim R) = p$' false for all $p$ is simply that no factum makes it true for any $p$. In other words, no factum **T** exists which conjoins with any law to entail, for any $p$, that $T \& Q \Rightarrow ch(\sim R) = p$. And this negative existential fact, conjoined with **R**, then makes it true that

$$Q \Rightarrow ch(P) = p.$$

This is both the simplest and the most usual way in which **R** makes '$Q \Rightarrow ch(P) = p$' true. For example, for many of the net forces $F$ which might act on $d$ at $t$, no factum makes

$$\text{'} Fd = F \Rightarrow ch(\sim Md = M) = p\text{'}$$

true for any $p$. In other words, nothing in the world gives any of these forces any propensity, not even a zero one, to knock any mass off $d$ or add any mass to it. So it is false that if these forces were to act on $d$, its mass might not be $M$. And then the factum $Md = M$ *will* make it true that, if any such force $F$ does act on $d$, $d$ will certainly accelerate at $F/M$. That is, $Md = M$ will after all make it true that

$$Fd = F \Rightarrow ch(Ad = F/M) = 1.$$

Thus, in summary, what makes '$Q \Rightarrow ch(P) = p$' true is, in the simplest case, the fact that, conjoined with the laws of nature,

(a)    some **R** entails $R \& Q \Rightarrow ch(P) = p$ and
(b′)    no **T** entails any $T \& Q \Rightarrow ch(\sim R) = p$.

In more complex cases, what makes it true is the fact that, conjoined with the laws of nature, *either*

(a)    some **R** entails $R \& Q \Rightarrow ch(P) = p$,
(b)    some **T** entails $T \& Q \Rightarrow ch(\sim R) = 0$ and
(c′)    no **V** entails any $V \& Q \Rightarrow ch(\sim T) = p$;
*or*
(a)    some **R** entails $R \& Q \Rightarrow ch(P) = p$,
(b)    some **T** entails $T \& Q \Rightarrow ch(\sim R) = 0$,
(c)    some **V** entails $V \& Q \Rightarrow ch(\sim T) = 0$ and
(d′)    no **W** entails any $Z \& Q \Rightarrow ch(\sim V) = p$;
*or*
(a)    ...

The truth of this infinite disjunction is what makes the factum **R**, by conjoining with some law of nature to entail R&Q$\Rightarrow$ch(P)=$p$, make it true that Q$\Rightarrow$ch(P)=$p$.

This shows how the existence of certain facta, including laws, conjoins with the non-existence of other facta to make instances of 'Q$\Rightarrow$ch(P)=$p$' true. But this does not yet tell us what makes '$ch_Q(P)=p$' true. For as we shall now see, my provisional equation of $ch_Q(P)$ with $(\imath p)(Q\Rightarrow ch(P)=p)$ in chapter 2.3 is after all not quite right.

I said in chapter 2.2 that any fact $ch_Q(P)=p$ is a fact about the local circumstances S. Now that we know what this fact really is, we can (taking the laws of nature for granted) divide it into two facts, $S_1$ and a disjunctive fact, $S_2 \lor S_3$, defined as follows:

$S_1$: (a) S includes a factum **R** that makes 'R&Q$\Rightarrow$ch(P)=$p$' true;

$S_2$: (b') S includes no **T** that makes 'T&Q$\Rightarrow$ch(~R)=$p$' true for any $p$;

$S_3$: S includes *either* (b) a **T** that makes 'T&Q$\Rightarrow$ch(~R)=0' true, and

    (c') no **V** that makes 'V&Q$\Rightarrow$ch(~T)=$p$' true for any $p$;

*or*   (b), (c) a **V** that makes 'V&Q$\Rightarrow$ch(~T)=0' true, and

    (d') no **W** that makes 'W&Q$\Rightarrow$ch(~V)=$p$' true for any $p$;

*or*   ...

The point of dividing the causally relevant facts about S in this way is that, of the three propositions '$S_1$', '$S_2$' and '$S_3$', the only one that links Q to P's chance ch(P) is '$S_1$'. It is therefore with the fact $S_1$ that we should identify the fact that $ch_Q(P)$ exists and has the value $p$. Thus the value of $ch_Q(P)$, and hence of $ch_Q(\sim P)$, should really be given by

(30)   $ch_Q(P) = 1-ch_Q(\sim P) = (\imath p)(R\&Q\Rightarrow ch(P)=p)$,

where **R** is the factum in S which, with some law, entails for some $p$ that R&Q$\Rightarrow$ch(P)=$p$. Similarly, $ch_{\sim Q}(P)$ and $ch_{\sim Q}(\sim P)$ should be given by

(30~)  $ch_{\sim Q}(P) = 1-ch_{\sim Q}(\sim P) = (\imath p')(R'\&\sim Q\Rightarrow ch(P)=p')$,

where **R'** is the factum in S that makes 'R'&~Q$\Rightarrow$ch(P)=$p'$' true for some $p'$. (**R** and **R'** may well be identical: for example, the factum *Md=M* both makes $d$ accelerate at *F/M* when a net force *F* does act on $d$ and makes $d$ *not* do so when it does not.)

(30) and (30~) are my long-promised corrections to the equations

(5)    $ch_C(E) = (\imath p)(C\Rightarrow ch(E)=p)$ and

(5~)  $ch_{\sim C}(E) = (\imath p')(\sim C\Rightarrow ch(E)=p')$

which I have so far used to give the values of $ch_C(E)$ and $ch_{\sim C}(E)$, the chances of an effect E in the relevant circumstances S with and without its cause C. But these corrections, although essential, are really very slight. In particular, as promised in chapter 2.3 and as readers may easily verify, they invalidate none of my earlier arguments. They do not, for example, invalidate my deduction from (5) and (5~) of the fact that, in S, $ch(E)$ is $ch_C(E)$ when 'C' is true and $ch_{\sim C}(E)$ when '~C' is true [2.3]. That still holds. For now, reverting again to our more general 'Q' and 'P', $ch_Q(P)$ is what $ch(P)$ is in the closest world in which 'R' and 'Q' are true, where **R** is the factum that makes 'R&Q$\Rightarrow$ch(P)=p' true. So when 'Q' *is* true in S, then since S includes **R**, this world is our world, so that $ch_Q(P)$ does then, as required, equal $ch(P)$.

In fact, like Newtonian mechanics, the common form of (5) and (5~),

(5') $\quad ch_Q(P) = (\imath p)(Q \Rightarrow ch(P)=p)$,

is so close to the truth that for our purposes we may continue to assume it. For whenever $ch_Q(P)=p$, i.e. whenever 'S$_1$' is true, (5') always holds if 'S$_2 \vee$S$_3$' is true, as it mostly is. And if 'S$_2$' is true, i.e. if no **T** gives Q any propensity, zero or greater, to yield ~R, then, given the laws of nature, 'Q$\Rightarrow$ch(P)=p' is in effect made true by the single factum **R**.

This moreover is not only, as I have remarked, the simplest and most usual case: it is also, as my definition of S$_3$ shows, the one to which, when 'S$_3$' is true, all other cases eventually reduce. We shall therefore lose no real generality by assuming for simplicity that whenever '$ch_Q(P)=p$' and hence 'Q$\Rightarrow$ch(P)=p' are true for some $p$, then – apart from the laws of nature – it is a single factum **R** which makes them so.

## 4  Causal structures

I have so far assumed nothing about the structure of the factum **R** that makes '$ch_Q(P)=p$' true. In the case of mass, **R** is *Md=m*, a factum which contains a particular thing, $d$, and a property $m$ that $d$ shares with all other things of mass $m$. I have written this factum '*Md=m*' to express the fact that $m$ is one of a family $M$ of mutually exclusive properties, the specific masses represented by the different numerical values of $m$. Many other properties – forces, accelerations, temperatures, colours, credences – also form such families. These families are the so-called *determinables*, of which their members – specific masses, forces, accelerations, temperatures, colours, degrees of belief in a given P – are the *determinates* (Johnson 1921 ch. 11).

However, the fact that the mass $m$ is a determinate of a determinable is not immediately relevant. What is relevant is that $m$ is a property, i.e. a universal, so that *Md=m* is an instance of the more general structure *Jd*, where $J$ is a property. But is this structure general enough? Are all facta particular things or events with properties?

One reason for thinking they are not is that some facta seem to include relations, like $b$'s being hotter than $d$, a fact which certainly has causes and effects. (It will, for example, cause $b$ to cool when $b$ comes into thermal contact with $d$.) However, we can ignore relational facta here, for several reasons; the first being that, as everything I have to say about properties will also apply to relations, we may as well stick to the simpler case.

The second reason is that most if not all apparent relations between particulars may really be relations between their properties. Thus it may be that what makes '$b$ is hotter than $d$' true is that $b$'s temperature is $T$, $d$'s is $T'$, and $T>T'$. If so, then this apparent relation between $b$ and $d$ really relates the temperatures $T$ and $T'$. However, to reduce relations between particulars to relations between their properties, we must first discover what relations between properties are, which we can hardly do until we know what properties are and which of them exist to be related. In short, we must walk before we can run; which is my third reason for ignoring relational facta.

My fourth and final reason is that the real question here is not whether facta can contain relations as well as properties but whether they contain either, i.e. whether they contain universals. Two mutually incompatible views appear to deny that they do. One is *nominalism*, the view that only particulars exist, which implies that there are no universals and hence no facta containing them. Now in principle, since nominalists think there are no facta at all, they could be agnostic about the need for facta, if they exist, to contain universals. But in fact most nominalists are tacitly committed to that need, because they argue only against universals, from whose non-existence that of facta will only follow if facta must contain them.

That question therefore comes first. So the view we must tackle first is the one which says that although facta exist, they contain no universals. This is the view that facta are unstructured entities, called *tropes* (Campbell 1990). For trope theorists, a factum like $Md=M$ is a single entity, not a complex of the two entities, $d$ and $M$. On the contrary, it is $d$ and $M$ that are the complexes: '$d$' refers to a bundle of co-located tropes (the mass-trope $Md=M$, a colour-trope, a temperature-trope, etc.), while '$M$' refers to the collection of mass-tropes that exactly resemble $Md=M$. But of course the existence of other members of this bundle $d$ and of this collection $M$, and thus of $d$ and $M$ as distinct entities, is not entailed by $Md=M$. So since, on trope theory, this factum itself entails neither $d$ nor $M$, it does not, as my notation '$Md=M$' implies it does, contain them as constituents.

To see why trope theory is wrong, at least of causal facta, we must look more closely at the structure not just of facta but of all singular causal facts. Suppose then that the 'Q' and 'P' in a true '$Q\Rightarrow ch(P)=p$' are true and so state facts. The facts Q and P need not of course be facta: since what makes 'Q' and 'P' true may well be that certain facta do *not* exist, e.g. facta **Q′** and **P′** such that Q=~Q′ and P=~P′ [13.4]. But since Q and P are at least facts, and so is Q⇒*ch*(P)=*p*, so too is *ch*(P)=*p*.

This chance of P is a fact about Q&S [2.2], where S is the conjunction of relevant facts about the circumstances. Now so far I have just assumed, generalising from the case of mass, that what makes S relevant is that, among other things, it includes a factum **R** which combines with some law of nature to entail R&Q⇒*ch*(P)=*p*. What I shall now show is why this must be so, and why its being so requires **R** to have the structure *Jd*.

First, although *ch*(P)=*p* is really a fact about Q&S, we may, given S, also take it to be a fact about Q. Next, we must recall one of the conditions which this chance, like all others, must meet: the Frequency condition, that

for every *ch*(P), a kind Q* of possible facts, including the fact Q of which that *ch*(P) is a property, yields a collective such that

(11)   *ch*(P)=*p* entails $f_\infty$(P*)=*p*,

for a kind P* of states of affairs that includes P [3.4].

($f_\infty$(P*)=*p* is the limiting frequency with which, in a collective of hypothetical instances of Q*, the corresponding instances of 'P*' are true.) Thus suppose, to revive an earlier example, that Q is a coin *j* being tossed, *Tj*, and that P is its landing heads, *Hj* [3.4]. Then in the circumstances S – how *j* is tossed, the distribution of its mass between heads and tails, etc. – Q* is a hypothetical coin *x* being tossed, *Tx*, and P* is *x* landing heads, *Hx*.

It follows from this that, since causes *must* give their effects chances, any fact Q or P that can be a cause or an effect must instantiate some kind of fact Q* or P*. So too must S, the relevant fact about the circumstances in which Q gives P its chance *ch*(P). For take the hypothetical tossed coins that form *ch*(Hj)'s collective, i.e. the collective whose limiting frequency $f_\infty$(H)=*p* of heads is entailed by *ch*(Hj)=*p*. We need not take these coins to be tossed in the actual circumstances S in which *j* is tossed. Indeed we cannot: since, as we have just noted, S includes how *j* itself is tossed, how its mass is distributed, and so on. But no other coin *x* can be tossed in *those* circumstances, only in circumstances of a kind S* whose instances differ from S, and from each other, by including facts not about *j* but about *x*.

Now in this case the kinds Q*, P* and S* all share the same structure, namely that some particular *x* has a property: being tossed, landing heads, having a certain mass distribution, etc. But this cannot be the only structure which causal kinds of facts can have. For if 'Q' and 'P' can if true state a cause and an effect, then so can '~Q' and '~P' [11.2 ]: if Don's falling can give his dying a chance, then his *not* falling can give his *not* dying a chance. But the kinds which these two states of affairs instantiate have a different structure: namely, that *no* particular has a certain property, such as being a fall, or a death, of Don.

There is thus more than one structure that Q*, P* and S* can have. But each must have *some* structure if it is to be a *kind* of fact; and so then must Q, P and S. For *ch*(P) can only exist and be a fact about Q&S if something about each of Q, P and S defines one or more kinds Q*, P* and S* for which *ch*(P) meets the Frequency condition. Thus Q, for example, may be a coin *j*'s being tossed, *Tj*, which defines a kind *T*, of coin and so of fact, *Tx*: a coin *x* is tossed. P may be Don's surviving, which defines a negative kind, ~*Dx*: a person *x* does *not* die. Or S may be that a matchbox is empty, making Bill's looking in it cause him to believe it's empty, which defines a negative existential kind, ~$(\exists x)(Gx)$: a matchbox with *no* match *x* in it. And so on. But some structure there must be. Every causal Q, P and S needs a structure that it can share with all other instances of some kind Q*, P* or S* which that structure defines.

Q, P and S cannot therefore be the unstructured entities which trope theory says that facta are. But then trope theory must be wrong, since although not all facts are facta, some certainly are. We have already seen, for example, that the relevant circumstances S in which a force *F* causes a thing *d* to accelerate at *F*/*M* includes the factum **Md=M**, that *d*'s mass is *M*. If this factum did not define a kind – namely any thing *x* with mass *M*, **Mx=M** – then S could not define a kind of circumstances S*, as we have seen that it must. **Md=M** must therefore define a kind of factum, as of course it does.

The fact that **Md=M** defines a kind of factum and hence of fact enables it also to be a cause or an effect. Thus a net force *F* could easily cause *d* to have mass *M* at time *t*, i.e. cause **Md=M**, e.g. by knocking spots off the previously more massive *d*. And if **Md=M** can be an effect, it can also be a cause, for example of a less massive object *b* rebounding when it hits *d*.

And so in general: every factum that makes an instance of '$Q \Rightarrow ch(P)=p$' true can also be a cause and/or an effect. But then being such a factum can never stop a fact being causal: i.e. being, for some true '$Q \Rightarrow ch(P)=p$', either Q or P or all or part of the relevant circumstances S. But then every causal factum, whether or not it actually is such a Q, P or (part of) S, needs a structure to define the kinds required for it to yield or have the chances which its being a Q, P or S in a true '$Q \Rightarrow ch(P)=p$' would entail.

## 5 The structure of causal facta

Causal facta cannot then be tropes, since like all other causal facts, they must have a structure which defines a kind. But the structures that causal facta can have are much less varied than those of other causal facts. Indeed, if for the reasons given in §4 we can ignore relational facta, the only structure these facta can have is that exemplified in §1: *Jd*, a particular *d* having a property *J*.

It is quite easy to see why causal facta are restricted to this structure: we need only recall that facta were introduced to be, by definition, the real entities in our world that make true statements true. This is why, if **P** is a factum,

> ~P would not be a factum even if it were a fact. For all it takes to make 'P' false and so '~P' true is that **P** does not exist – a fact, of course, if 'P' is false, but not a factum [13.4].

But if **P** is a real entity, so must its constituents be, starting with whatever *J* defines the causal kind **P\*** that **P** instantiates: a fact about *J* which from now on I shall also mark with bold type: *J*. In short, *J* must be a universal.

This claim is of course contentious and needs more argument, which I shall give in chapter 15. But I need give no argument for the reality of **P**'s other constituent, the one that distinguishes it from other members of **P\***. For this constituent is just a particular, *d*, and no one denies that particulars exist [13.2], another fact that I shall use bold type to mark: *d*.

This is why our reality requirement restricts the structure of the factum **P** in the way it does. For just as there are no negative facta, so there are no negative particulars. Thus suppose that some *d* – the King of Italy, the death of Don – is, if it exists, a real particular, *d*. Then although, if *d* did not exist, we can define ~*d* – the non-King of Italy, the non-death of Don – it cannot, for the reasons given in chapter 11.2, be a real entity.

Nor are there any conjunctive or disjunctive particulars: if *d* and *d'* are real particulars, then *d*&*d'* and *d*∨*d'* are not. Thus suppose for example that Italy does have a King and that Don does die. Then there will be a particular person who is the King of Italy and a particular event which is the death of Don; but there will be no such particulars as the King-of-Italy-*and*-Don's-death or the King-of-Italy-*or*-Don's-death. The reason is that, since wholes

> must be things or events in their own right ... a thing or event must be something more than the so-called *mereological sum* of ... its parts, an entity which exists if they do by mere definition [10.2].

Yet this is precisely what, if they did exist, the particulars $d\&d'$ and $d\lor d'$ would be: entities that exist by mere definition if $d$ and $d'$, or $d$ or $d'$, exist. And this is why I say reality contains no such particulars: we need none to make conjunctive or disjunctive statements like '$Jd\&Jd'$' or '$Jd\lor Jd'$' true, any more than we need negative particulars to make negative statements true. For all it takes to make '$Jd\&Jd'$' true is that $d$ and $d'$ exist and have the property $J$; while all it takes to make '$Jd\lor Jd'$' true is that $d$ or $d'$ exists and has the property $J$.

This is what restricts **P**'s structure to that of $Jd$: the fact that reality contains no negative, conjunctive or disjunctive particulars. For without them, the kind of factum which $J$ defines cannot be that a particular $x$ is *not J*, or that there is *no J*-particular, or that $x\&y$ are $J$ or that $x\lor y$ are, or any combination of these. **P** can only be that some particular – call it '$d$' – is $J$.

The structure $Jd$ is thus quite general enough to cover all singular causal facta (other than relational ones, if any). And the properties $J$ which these facta contain will then determine all the kinds of causal facts which there can be. For those properties are what define the causal kinds of *atomic* facts, $Jx$, of which all the other kinds, including those mentioned above, are complexes: $\sim Jx$, $\sim(\exists x)(Jx)$, $Jx\&Ix$ (where $I$ is another property), $Jx\lor\sim Iy$, and so on. Facts of all these other kinds can also, as we have seen, be Q, P or S in instances of $Q\Rightarrow ch(\text{P})=p$. But what these kinds are depends on what the properties $J, I, \dots$ are. So since all the kinds of causal facts that exist depend on the properties that exist, our next business must be to discover what those properties are. That is the business of the next chapter.

# 15 *Properties*

## 1 Universals

In trying to discover what properties there are we must bear in mind what we are looking for: that is, what kind of entities properties are. Different philosophers use the term 'property' to mean very different things. Some define properties by predicates: if something is red, i.e. if the predicate 'is red' truly applies to it, then, trivially, it has the property of being red. Others identify properties with sets, such as the set of actual and possible particulars to which a predicate applies.

If 'property' had either of these meanings it would not matter to us what properties there are. We want to know what causal kinds of facta, and hence of facts, exist in our world, questions whose answers will not depend on what predicates English and other languages happen to possess. Nor will sets of particulars serve our turn. Of course, for all kinds of facta there will be sets of the particulars which facta of those kinds contain. But this tells us nothing about what kinds there are, since any particulars can form a set, whether or not they all occur in facta of a single kind.

This is why, in putting my question about what kinds there are in terms of properties, I need to mean by 'properties' what I do mean, namely real universals. And what I mean by calling universals 'real' is that they are not like facts (as opposed to facta), whose existence is a trivial definitional consequence of the truth of sentences, statements or propositions [13.2]. Universals are like real particulars, such as Queen Victoria, whose existence depends on more than the use of the name 'Queen Victoria'. Similarly, when I say that properties like masses and temperatures exist, I mean more than that concepts or predicates like 'is $M$ kg' and 'is $T°C$' exist and occur in true thoughts or statements.

Indeed I do not mean that at all. For just as most particulars other than people can and do exist without ever being thought of or talked about, so properties like masses and temperatures could and would exist even if we had no corresponding concepts or predicates. Even mental properties like the credences (degrees of belief) discussed in chapter 3.2 could exist without concepts or predicates like '... believes (to degree $p$) that ...'. For

185

even if believers need concepts which apply to whatever their beliefs are about, they need not have the concept of belief, since they need not have beliefs about beliefs. A cat, for example, can easily have beliefs about mice without it, or any other animal or human thinker, having any concept of, or word for, belief.

## 2  Facta and laws

The existence of properties in any sense relevant to causation cannot depend on the existence of corresponding concepts or predicates. What then does it depend on? The answer is implicit in the case for properties made in chapter 14.4, which required the chance $ch(P)$ in any $Q{\Rightarrow}ch(P)=p$ to meet the Frequency condition [3.4]. Meeting this condition is what requires Q, P and the relevant circumstances S to have a structure that defines kinds Q*, P* and S* of which they are instances. And that, as we then saw, determines what causal properties are: they are the constituents of the facta in any Q, P and S which define the Q*, P* and S* that let the $ch(P)$ in any $Q{\Rightarrow}ch(P)=p$ meet the Frequency condition. So the obvious way to start finding out what properties exist is to look more closely at what the Frequency condition makes causal properties entail.

To simplify matters I shall again assume to start with that Q* and P* have the structure $Kx$ and $Lx$, where $x$ is any particular [14.1]. As before, $K$ and $L$ need not be single properties: Q* and P* need not be kinds of facta as well as of facts. (For example, as we shall see in §3, even if being acted on by a single force $F$ is a single property, being acted on by a net force $F$ that is the resultant of several forces acting at once is not.) The only thing that, as before, I shall assume for simplicity is that 'Q' and 'P' are about the same particular, so that if $Q=Kd$, then $P=Ld$.

Now to make '$Kd{\Rightarrow}ch(Ld)=p$' true, the relevant circumstances S must, as we have seen, include at least one factum **R** [14.3]. This too we may take to be a factum about the particular $d$, e.g. the factum $Md=M$, that $d$'s mass is $M$. If moreover we take the fact that S includes the presence or absence of any other relevant facta **T**, **V**, ... to be another fact about $d$, say $Gd$, we can cover all the complex cases listed in chapter 14.3.

The Frequency condition on $ch(Ld)$ – e.g. $d$'s chance 1 of accelerating at $F/M$ – will then entail the following. Every fact of the kind $Kx$ must, in the circumstances $Gx$, give $x$ the same chance

$$ch(Lx)=ch(Ld)$$

of being $L$. This will make any collective of particulars $x$ that are both $G$ and $K$ have a limiting frequency $f_\infty(L)=ch(Ld)$ of $x$s that are $L$ [3.4]. But for this to be so, it is not enough that every *actual* G&K-particular has the chance $ch(Ld)$ of being $L$. It is not even enough that all actual particulars are such that they would have this chance if they were $G\&K$. For the collective whose $f_\infty(L)$ equals $ch(Ld)$ will have to include *hypothetical* $G\&K$-particulars that need not be actual particulars at all [3.4]: simply because there may be too few actual particulars to form such a collective.

The Frequency condition therefore makes $Kd \Rightarrow ch(Ld)=p$ entail that, however many particulars existed, they would still all have the same chance $ch(Ld)$ of being $L$ if they were $G\&K$. (For example, they would all have the same chance 1 of accelerating at $A=F/M$ if a net force $F$ acted on them and their mass remained $M$.) In other words, the facta that make '$Gd$' true will only make

$$'Kd \Rightarrow ch(Ld)=p'$$

true if '$Gx\&Kx \Rightarrow ch(Lx)=p$' both *is* true of all actual particulars $x$ and *would* be true of all hypothetical ones: in short, if

(31)  '$(x)(Gx\&Kx \Rightarrow ch(Lx)=p)$'

states a law of nature.

## 3  Laws and law statements

The fact that propensities, like $Kd$'s propensity $p$ to yield $Ld$, depend on laws of nature is crucial to what follows. I must therefore make clear what I mean by 'law of nature'. For this expression, like the terms 'event' and 'property', is given very different meanings by different philosophers. In particular, what most of them mean by 'laws' are statements, whereas what I need to mean is whatever makes those statements state laws.

The tradition of taking laws to be statements may stem from taking them to be God's edicts, analogous to those of our legislatures. And even for atheists laws of the land do in some ways resemble laws of nature, for example in applying to merely hypothetical as well as to actual people. Thus the law against murder would still apply to all citizens even if there were more citizens than there actually are.

But this analogy does not really justify calling any statements 'laws'. For even a law of the land needs something more than a statement of it, since it needs something to enforce it, i.e. to try and make all those who violate it pay the prescribed penalty and so make true the legal statement that they will. So even if our laws differ from God's in being less well enforced, there must still be more to them than statements of them.

It is of course true that, in practice at least, a prerequisite of anything's being a law of the land is that someone says it is: nothing can be a law of the land until some authority says so. Hence no doubt the temptation to identify laws with authoritative statements of them. But the temptation should be resisted. For a statement like 'thou shalt not murder' is only called a 'law' in order to make it the case, by telling us, that there *is* such a law, in order to make us obey it. And although the need to do this may well explain why we call statements of the law 'laws', that is no excuse for confounding the two.

In any case this excuse cannot apply to laws of nature, which we and everything else must obey whether or not anyone says what they are. For whatever the laws of mechanics, gravity, electricity, optics, chemistry, biology (and even of psychology and linguistics) may be, they need no statements to enforce them, i.e. to exist. Like particulars and properties, these laws could and would be there even if we lacked the concepts and predicates, and hence the sciences, of mechanics, gravity, etc. which we need to discover and state them.

This is why I shall not only not call statements 'laws', I shall not call laws 'scientific laws', because this term suggests that the existence of laws depends on scientists discovering and stating them, which is absurd. For even if that suggestion is not meant and it rarely matters if law statements are called 'laws', it matters here: because calling these statements 'laws' leaves no obvious term for whatever *makes* them (state) laws. And as that is what concerns us here, that is what I shall henceforth mean by 'laws'.

The other assumptions I need to make about laws, if more substantial, are also more orthodox. But they too need some explanation and defence. First, I shall assume that, in order to be a law, $(x)(Gx\&Kx{\Rightarrow}ch(Lx)=p)$ must hold for all particulars $x$. This means that any statement

'$Gd\&Kd{\Rightarrow}ch(Ld)=p$',

derived from '$Gx\&Kx{\Rightarrow}ch(Lx)=p$' by replacing the variable '$x$' with any singular term '$d$' referring to any particular $d$, must be true. But then any such derived statement must be transparent for $d$. That is, replacing '$d$' in it with another term for $d$ can never falsify it [9.5].

Yet we saw in chapter 12.5 that any true '$ch_{Kc}(Le)=p$' and hence

'$Kc{\Rightarrow}ch(Le)=p$',

can always be opaque for both $c$ and $e$. That is, it can always be falsified by replacing '$c$' or '$e$' with some co-referring '$c''$' (e.g. 'the $K$') or '$e''$' (e.g. 'the $L$'). So, in particular,

'$Gd\&Kd{\Rightarrow}ch(Ld)=p$'

can always be opaque for $d$. But how then can '$(x)(Gx\&Kx{\Rightarrow}ch(Lx)=p)$' entail it?

The answer is that, although any '$Kc \Rightarrow ch(Le)=p$' *can* be opaque, it can also be transparent [12.6]. Furthermore, we can make it transparent simply by stipulating that, in it, '$c$' and '$e$' and any replacements for them are to be read rigidly, i.e. as designating the same particular in any possible world where it exists. This moreover is no arbitrary stipulation but just what we need to make statements of the form '$Le$ because $Kc$'

> tell us transparently both that and how the particular $c$ causes or affects the particular $e$ [12.6].

So the transparent reading of '$Gd\&Kd \Rightarrow ch(Ld)=p$' which is entailed by the law that $(x)(Gx\&Kx \Rightarrow ch(Lx)=p)$ is the very reading our account of causation requires.

However, the fact that law statements entail the transparent singular statements we need will not help us much if law statements can be false. But Cartwright (1983 Essay 3) and others have argued that many of them *are* false, an argument which I must therefore now rebut. In doing so I shall follow Cartwright in using Newton's laws of motion and of gravity to exemplify the argument, as follows.

The argument assumes first that no thing $d$ can be acted on by two or more forces at once, but only by what I have called their 'net force' $F$. If so, my statement of the law of gravity, that

> any two things of the same or different masses $M$ and $M'$ at any distance $R$ attract each other with a force $F=GMM'/R^2$, where G is a constant [4.3],

must be false. For this implies that every thing $d$ with a mass is always attracted by every other such thing, and so is acted on simultaneously by a vast number of forces all satisfying '$F=GMM'/R^2$'. But if the only force on $d$ is the net force $F$ this must be false.

To save the law of gravity – not to mention all the laws linking forces to electrical, magnetic, viscous and other phenomena – we need the far more credible assumption that $d$ can be acted on by many forces at once. But then, to save the law that $F=MA$, $d$ must have as many accelerations at once as there are forces acting on it at once. And that looks far less credible.

But this is because 'acceleration' usually only means *net* acceleration, whereas 'force' does not only mean net force. But what matter here are laws and properties, not statements, predicates or concepts. We should not therefore be impressed by the fact (if it is a fact) that our normal concept of acceleration stops us crediting $d$ with two simultaneous accelerations. This is no reason to deny that $d$ has a determinable property $A$ such that (i)

*F=MA* and (ii) any two facta **Ad**=A and **Ad**=A' have a propensity 1 to give **d** the net acceleration A+A' shown in Figure 16: a fact about **d** which will (a) combine with other such facts in the same way and (b) satisfy the familiar laws linking it to **d**'s net velocity and hence to changes in **d**'s spatial location. This is what matters – not whether, in polite society, it would be thought improper to call the property *A* 'acceleration'.

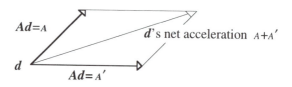

Figure 16: The facta of acceleration

Here I must stress again, as in chapters 4.3 and 14.2, that using the law that *F=MA* to define *A* does not make '*F=MA*' trivially true, any more than using it to define *M* does: for it remains contingent that things have the properties which this law defines. But there is much evidence that they do: namely, all the evidence for Newtonian mechanics, such as the sight of planets moving as predicted by the conjunction of '$F=GMM'/R^2$' with '*F=MA*'. It is of course true that later evidence has made us revise these law statements; but this just proves that their supposed truth was not trivial.

So if, like Cartwright, we assume for the sake of argument that '*F=MA*' does state a law, then it *will* be true, by definition, of the property *A* whose existence it asserts, if not of net acceleration. But then, since we shall need a name for *A*, I shall follow Humpty Dumpty ('when *I* use a word, it means just what I choose it to mean'), and the precedent of 'force', and call *A* 'acceleration' (and net acceleration 'net acceleration').

## 4  Laws and properties

Calling *F=MA* a law thus asserts more than the existence of the property *M* defined by this and other laws. It asserts the existence of the property *A*, similarly defined, which I call 'acceleration', and also of the property *F*, which everyone calls 'force'.

In short, it asserts the existence of three determinables: mass (*M*), force (*F*) and acceleration (*A*), whose measures M, F, and A distinguish their determinates. We can make this explicit by turning the sentence stating the law into its so-called *Ramsey sentence*, got by replacing its three predicates ('… has mass M', 'force F acts on …' and '… accelerates at A') with existentially bound variables. This, expressed in the symbolism of chapter 14.2

with '$Mx=M$', '$Fx=F$' and '$Ax=A$' replaced by the variables '$Xx=M$', '$Yx=F$' and '$Zx=A$', gives us, for all $M$, $F$ and $A$

(32)   '$(\exists X,Y,Z)(x)[(Xx=M \& Yx=F) \Rightarrow ch(Zx=F/M)=1]$',

where '$(\exists X,Y,Z) \ldots$' means 'there are properties $X$, $Y$, $Z$ such that $\ldots$'.

It is however one thing to assert the existence of properties $X$, $Y$ and $Z$, and another to define them, and in particular to distinguish them from each other and from all other properties. Obviously no one law can do that. What can do it is the fact that $X$, $Y$ and $Z$ occur in other laws too, and do so differently. For example, acceleration does not occur in the law that $F=GMM'/R^2$, and mass and force do not occur in the laws, mentioned above, that link acceleration to velocity and location. So between them, the totality of laws of nature in which the properties $X$, $Y$ and $Z$ occur should certainly suffice to distinguish and define them as the properties $M$, $F$, and $A$ which we call 'mass', 'force' and 'acceleration'.

But to state this fact we need more than the Ramsey sentences of all these laws taken separately. Take the Ramsey sentence of $F=GMM'/R^2$,

(33)   '$(\exists X,Y,R)(x,y)[(Xx=M \& Xy=M' \& Rxy=R)$
            $\Rightarrow ch(Yx=G_{MM'}/R^2)=1]$',

where '$(x,y)$' means 'for all particulars $x$ and $y$' and '$Rxy=R$' means '$x$ and $y$ are related by a determinate of measure $R$ of a determinable relation $R$' – i.e. are at a spatial distance $R$.

This Ramsey sentence does do part of what we need: it does say that properties $X$ and $Y$ exist for which it is a law that

$(x)[(Xx\ldots) \Rightarrow ch(Yx\ldots)=1]$.

But this is not enough. For what (33) does *not* say is that these properties $X$ and $Y$ are the very same $X$ and $Y$ whose existence (32) asserts. To say this we need the Ramsey sentence, not of each law taken separately, but of their conjunction: that is, abbreviating (32) and (33) to '$(\exists X,Y,Z)L_1(X,Y,Z)$' and '$(\exists X,Y,R)L_2(X,Y,R)$' respectively,

(34)   '$(\exists X,Y,Z,R)[L_1(X,Y,Z) \& L_2(X,Y,R)]$'.

And so on, adding all the laws in which mass, force and acceleration occur, so that there too they can be identified with the $X$, $Y$ and $Z$ which (34) says exist. But as (34) shows, the Ramsey sentence of that conjunction will also assert the existence of other properties or relations, like $R$, the spatial distance between two particulars. So then, for the same reason, we must add all the other laws in which *these* universals occur. And this of course may bring in yet more properties, thus forcing us to add all the laws *they* occur in; and so on. In the end, we may have incorporated all the laws of nature – or we may not: there may be disjoint groups of laws that share no properties, although I doubt it. But since we may well have to include all the laws, and doing so will do no harm, that is what I shall now do.

Let us therefore call the Ramsey sentence of (the conjunction of) all laws 'Σ'. Σ by definition asserts the existence of all properties and relations which occur in laws of nature. And by so doing, I say Σ answers the question: what causal properties are there? The causal properties (and relations, if any) which exist in our world are the universals over which the Ramsey sentence of all our world's laws must quantify. This, for short, I shall call *Ramsey's test* for the existence of causal properties.

## 5  Nominalism

If Ramsey's test is to tell us what properties exist, it must be rightly understood. In particular, Σ's quantifiers must be rightly read. And the quickest way to see the reading we need is to see why nominalists will object to it, because it means quantifying over universals, whose existence they deny.

Their objection could be met by a so-called *substitutional* reading of the second-order quantifiers in Ramsey sentences. This would make (34) true iff dropping its quantifiers and replacing the variables '$X$', '$Y$', etc., by some predicates yields a true sentence. But this is no use to us. For all this makes (34) say is that for some *predicates*, e.g. '$M$', '$F$', '$A$' and '$D$' ('distance'), the sentences

$$\text{'L}_1(M,F,A)\text{' and 'L}_2(M,F,D)\text{'}$$

state laws. And for this claim to mean anything, it must be restricted to *actual* predicates, with given meanings, not merely conceivable or possible predicates. But as we noted in §1, our question is not what actual predicates occur in law statements but what universals occur in laws, whether or not we have any predicates which we could use to state them. So what makes this reading of Ramsey sentences acceptable to nominalists is precisely what makes it useless to us. For Ramsey's test to tell us what we want to know, we need a so-called *objectual* reading of Σ's second-order quantifiers: that is, we must take them to range over universals, not actual predicates.

And then the nominalist objection to this reading of Σ simply begs the question against universals. Now I cannot here discuss all the nominalist arguments against universals (see Armstrong 1978 vol. 1). I can only assert that they are at best inconclusive, and that the universals we shall need can all be postulated without contradiction. And given this, I can at least rebut the other main objection to them, which is that because 'abstract' entities such as universals play no role in causation, we have no call to postulate them.

But we do, because on my account universals play an indispensable role in causation. Consider the nominalist alternative. Any nominalist version of my account of causation will have to entail that:

(i) all causation can be reported by truths of the forms

(2)    '*c* causes *e*' or
(2′)    '*c* causes or affects *e*',

[1.2], where *c* and *e* are particulars; and

(ii) instances of (2) and (2′) need no universal relation between *c* and *e* to make them true.

Now (ii) is indeed true: (2) and (2′) are never made true by any relation between *c* and *e* [11; 12]. But (i) is false: most causation is not statable by instances of (2) and (2′) [11]. And although instances of the form which we now know we can use to report all causation, namely

(1)    '*E* because *C*',

need no *causal* relation between the facts C and E to make them true, they do, as we have seen, need properties – *if* causation is to exist in the world, independently of our concepts and predicates.

The nominalist then faces the following dilemma: either our world contains universals or it contains no causation that is independent of our concepts and predicates. But this, once faced, is no dilemma at all. For we all rely on causation's connotations, and especially on its provision of means to ends [7], which no one believes always depends on our concepts and predicates: no one thinks, for example, that we cannot be killed by diseases or disasters that no one has any concepts of or words for! In short, the existence of causation as I have described it cannot be seriously disputed. But the existence of universals can. Anyone can hold either that they exist or that they do not – until they see, as we now can, that causation requires them. No one who sees this can remain a nominalist: some universals there must be. The only question is which: the question Ramsey's test is meant to answer.

## 6  Identifying properties

Before showing what Ramsey's test, rightly read, entails, I should perhaps make it more credible by pointing out some implausible things which it does *not* entail. It does not for example entail that we can ever know or even express Σ, merely that the properties our world contains are those which Σ would need to quantify over if it *were* expressed. And this is all we require. We need not meet any of the other conditions necessary for us to know and express $\Sigma$. And this is just as well, since we probably cannot meet them: the number and complexity of nature's laws may well make it impossible for anyone less than God to know or even state all of them. But that does not stop them determining what properties there are.

Nor does Ramsey's test make our failure to know all laws stop us knowing any of them because we do not know which properties they contain. This too is just as well, since although some philosophers feign a scepticism about laws which their obvious reliance on them belies, no one can honestly deny that we know many laws, including most of those cited in this book. But how, given the Ramsey test and the fact that we do not know all laws, can we know what any properties and hence any laws are?

The answer to this question is twofold. First, in order to know that an apparent law statement '$L_1(K,...)$' really does state a law, we do not need to know whether the predicate '$K$' in it corresponds to one property or to several – as it will for example if '$K$' is 'is chlorine', since what we call chlorine is a mixture of several different isotopes.

Second, even if we did need to know whether $K$ is a single property, $K$, we often can and do know this, because we do know enough laws to identify many properties, for example masses and chances [4.3]. And as with those properties, so in general: we need not know *every* law that $K$ occurs in to know enough to distinguish $K$ from all other properties.

But how can we know enough to do even this? Suppose for example we know $n$ laws which we take to define the property we call '$K$', say of being chlorine: $L_1(K,...)$ to $L_n(K,...)$. Then since, by hypothesis, $L_1(K,...)$ to $L_n(K,...)$ really are laws, the Ramsey sentence of their conjunction,

(35)    '$(\exists X,...)[L_1(X,...)\&L_2(X,...)\& \ldots L_n(X,...)]$',

is true. And what (35) says is that there *is* a property $X$ of which everything we believe about what we call '$K$' is true.

So far so good. But it is not far enough, because there may be *two* such properties, $J$ and $J'$: for example, the properties of being different isotopes of chlorine. Both these isotopes obey all the same chemical laws, $L_1(...)$ to $L_n(...)$, but differ in physical ways that show up only in the unknown laws

$L_{n+1}(J,...)$ and $L_{n+2}(J',...)$.

The conjunction of these laws with chlorine's chemical laws will then have the Ramsey sentence

(36)    '$(\exists X,Y,...)[L_1(X\vee Y,...)\&L_2(X\vee Y,...)\& \ldots L_n(X\vee Y,...)\&$
        $L_{n+1}(X,...)\&L_{n+2}(Y,...)]$',

thus showing that what looks to us like one property is really a disjunction of two, so that the laws which our ignorance makes us write '$L_1(K,...)$' to '$L_n(K,...)$' really have the structure $L(J \lor J',...)$.

Does this not show that we can never know if $K$ really is a single property, $K$? No: it only shows that what we take to be a single property may not be, since there may be unknown laws which show that it is not. But equally there may not be, in which case Ramsey's test tells us that $K$ is a single property after all. And we need not know all the laws of nature to know this, i.e. to believe it truly and on good grounds. Thus we may well, as I have claimed, know enough to know that mass is a single determinable. And even when we are wrong, as we were when we thought that being chlorine was a single property, what will show us that is, as Ramsey's test implies, our finding a law to which some but not all otherwise indistinguishable $K$-particulars conform.

So far, again so good for Ramsey's test. But this is still not far enough, since it is hardly news that no property can both occur and not occur in a single law like $L_{n+1}(...)$. The real question is whether two *different* properties can occur in the same way in all the same laws. The closest case I know was put to me by Jeremy Butterfield: two symmetrically related properties $L$ and $L'$ (like being left- and right-handed) which can only be identified by pointing to $L$- and $L'$-particulars. If such properties can exist then not even $\Sigma$ will give either of them a definite description, i.e. one that is true of nothing else: hence the need to identify them by ostension.

But even then Ramsey's test will still work, because $\Sigma$ will still have to quantify over both $L$ and $L'$, even if it cannot tell us which is which. And I cannot see how the test could fail for any other causal properties. For these properties are, by definition, simply what generate the kinds $Q^*$, $P^*$ and $S^*$ that let any $Q \Rightarrow ch(P)=p$ entail the law which the Frequency condition on $ch(P)$ makes it entail [14.4]. That is what makes every causal property not only occur in laws but be, in the way I have outlined, defined by them.

And that is why I say that this is all there is to these universals [14.2]. There is nothing to mass but the laws of mechanics, nothing to temperature but the laws of thermodynamics, nothing to credence but the laws of belief, and so on: a fact which, I must stress yet again, allows each of these laws to be contingent, since it allows each of these properties to exist in possible worlds where some of the laws it actually occurs in fail.

This means in particular that, if the laws $L_{n+1}(J,...)$ and $L_{n+2}(J',...)$ which distinguish our two isotopes of chlorine were to hold only in different possible worlds, then the properties $J$ and $J'$ such that

$$L_1(J,...) \text{ and } L_2(J,...) \text{ and } ... L_n(J,...) \text{ and } L_{n+1}(J,...)$$

are laws in one world, and

$$L_1(J',...) \text{ and } L_2(J',...) \text{ and } ... L_n(J',...) \text{ and } L_{n+2}(J',...)$$

are laws in another, might well be identical. It is only because *J* and *J'* occur in different laws in one and the same world, namely ours, that they must be different properties.

All these implications of Ramsey's test seem to me entirely credible; and I see no other reason to deny that the identity of any causal property depends only on the laws it occurs in: because this is all that such a property's role in causation, which is all there is to it, depends on. And if this is so, then if $\Sigma$ does not distinguish two such properties, nothing will. Whatever world we are in, i.e. whatever $\Sigma$ is, Ramsey's test will tell us what properties our world contains.

## 7  Complex properties

Ramsey's test for what universals there are corresponds closely to a test for what particulars there are which is derivable from Quine's well-known account of *ontological commitment* in his (1948). This, which I shall call *Quine's test*, says that the particulars which exist are those over which our first order quantifiers must range for every fact to be stable without naming any particular.

To see what this means, suppose we want to state any fact *Kd* about any particular *d* without using '*d*' or any other name for *d*. To do this we need a description '*D*' of *d* that is definite, i.e. applies only to *d*, if necessary by definition – like Quine's 'pegasizes', which by definition applies only to Pegasus [12.4]. Then instead of saying '*Kd*', we can say 'the *D* is *K*', which provided we use 'the *D*' as a rigid designator [11.3] will be true for all '*K*' iff '*Kd*' is. But 'the *D* is *K*' can only be true if there *is* a *D* (namely *d*), i.e. if the existentially quantified statement '$(\exists x)(Dx)$' is true. So for any fact about *d* to be stable without naming *d*, our first order quantifiers must range over *d*. Moreover there must, as we shall see in chapter 16.2, be some such fact about every particular: there are no particulars which have no properties at all [16.2]. But then, as Quine's test says, for any *d* to exist, our first order quantifiers must have to range over *d* for every fact to be stable without naming *d*.

Ramsey's test for universals is very like this. For what it says is that the universals which exist are those over which our *second* order quantifiers must range for all laws to be stable without using predicates, i.e. by using the Ramsey sentence $\Sigma$ of all laws. This parallel with Quine's remarkably uncontentious test for particulars is so close that one might expect everyone who accepts universals also to accept Ramsey's test for them. Yet some will not accept it as it stands, because they wish to deny an immediate consequence of it, namely that there are no complex universals. So before we can take Ramsey's test as I have stated it for granted, we must see why it entails this and why that fact should not count against it.

Complex universals are properties or relations which are complexes of other properties or relations. (Here we can ignore relations and consider only properties.) Thus if $J$ and $I$ are simple properties,

> $\sim\!J$ is a *negative* property,
> $J\vee I$ is a *disjunctive* property and
> $J\&I$ is a *conjunctive* property.

If these properties exist, they will generate more complex properties, such as $\sim\!J\vee(I\&\sim\!K)$, where $K$ is another property; and so on indefinitely. But here we may stick to the three simplest cases, which are defined – as their names and symbols suggest – as follows: any particular $x$ is

> $\sim\!J$ iff it is not $J$,
> $J\vee I$ iff it is $J$ or $I$ and
> $J\&I$ iff it is $J$ and $I$.

It is easy to see that all these properties fail Ramsey's test. Suppose for example that $J\&I$ exists. Then, by Ramsey's test, it must be quantified over by $\Sigma$, the Ramsey sentence of all laws. So it must occur in some laws, which must therefore have the form

> L($J\&I,\ldots$).

But for $J\&I$ to exist, $J$ and $I$ must also exist and so, by Ramsey's test, be quantified over in $\Sigma$. But then $\Sigma$ need not quantify over $J\&I$, since the Ramsey sentence of laws of the form L($J\&I,\ldots$) need only quantify over $J$ and $I$. So on Ramsey's test $J\&I$ does not exist after all. And similarly, as readers may easily verify, for all other complex universals: Ramsey's test rules them all out – just, and for the same reasons, as Quine's test rules out complex particulars.

However, the fact that complex particulars and universals fail these tests does not really rule them out, since if we had other reasons to admit them, the tests could be amended quite easily to let them in. Thus Armstrong (1978 chs 14, 15), who accepts conjunctive universals but not negative or disjunctive ones, could say that the universals which exist are all those that $\Sigma$ quantifies over, plus all their conjunctions.

But why should we say this: why should we suppose that any complex universals exist? Well, suppose that one particular, $d$, is $J$ and another one, $b$, is $I$. Then there is something they both are, namely $J$ or $I$. Does this not mean that the disjunctive property $J \lor I$ exists? Not at all: all it means is that the disjunctive *predicate* 'is $J$ or $I$' applies both to $d$ and to $b$. And given what 'property' means here, this gives us no reason to suppose that $d$ and $b$ share a disjunctive *property* $J \lor I$. For that property is certainly not needed to make the corresponding disjunctive statement true: all it takes to make 'is $J$ or $I$' true of both $d$ and $b$ is that each of them is either $J$ or $I$.

Next, let us suppose that $d$ and $b$ are each both $J$ and $I$. Here they really do share a property: indeed two, $J$ and $I$. But this hardly shows that they share a third, $J \& I$. For again, the fact that both $d$ and $b$ are $J$ and $I$ is quite enough to make 'is $J$ and $I$' true of both of them.

So far then I see no reason to accept complex universals; and nor, for negative and disjunctive universals, does Armstrong. But he does produce two arguments for conjunctive universals. First, he notes that a conjunctive fact like $Jd \& Id$ may have effects which are not entailed by those of $Jd$ and $Id$. And so indeed it may. But on our account of causation all this means is that laws of the form

$$L(J \& I, \ldots)$$

need not be entailed by any conjunction of laws of the forms

$$L(J, \ldots) \text{ and } L(I, \ldots).$$

And this, as we have just seen, Ramsey's test can easily allow without allowing $J \& I$.

Armstrong's other argument is his claim that

it is logically and epistemically possible that all properties are conjunctive properties (1978 vol. II p. 32).

The idea here is that nature may be infinitely complex: that, for example, there may be no limit to the small-scale structure of matter. But this possibility needs no complex universals, since there need be no limit to the number or complexity of our laws, nor therefore to the number of properties $\Sigma$ must quantify over. So Armstrong's claim, besides begging the question, is a *non sequitur*.

It is also demonstrably false: since, as we shall now see, it is not possible for any, let alone all, universals to be complex. To see this we must recall again that properties are constituents of facta, the entities in the world which make propositions true: so that if 'P' is made true by a factum **P**, then what would make '~P' true is not that some other factum exists but simply that **P** does not [13.4; 14.5].

Thus, applying this to the simplest case that concerns us, if $d$ is a particular and $J$ is a (simple) property, what makes '~$Jd$' true is that the factum *Jd* does not exist, i.e. that *d* is not *J*. In short, '~*Jd*' is made true by the *non*existence of a factum, not by the existence of one, and so in particular not by the existence of ~*Jd*. But since any factum **P** by definition makes 'P' true, then if ~*Jd* does not make '~*Jd*' true, it does not exist. But it must exist if the negative property ~*J* exists, since *d* exists and, because it is not *J*, is by definition ~*J*. So ~*J* does not exist; and nor, for the same reason, does any other negative property or relation.

Similarly for conjunctive universals. If '*Jd&Id*' is made true by *Jd* and *Id*, it cannot also be made true by *Jd&Id*. But unless *Jd&Id* makes '*Jd&Id*' true it does not exist, which it would do by definition if *J&I* existed, since *d* is *J* and *I*. So neither *J&I* nor any other conjunctive universal exists. Nor, for the same reason, do any disjunctive universals exist. And with no negative, conjunctive or disjunctive universals, there can be no complex universals at all, any more than there can be complex particulars.

So Ramsey's test will after all do as it stands. The causal universals – all simple – which exist in our world are those over which the Ramsey sentence $\Sigma$ of all laws must quantify. These then are all the kinds of causal facta there are, and these in turn define all the kinds of causal facts there are: including ~*J*, *J*∨*I*, *J&I*, and all the other complex kinds mentioned earlier [14.5]. For in denying that they are kinds of facta, I am not denying that they are kinds of fact.

# 16 *Laws*

## 1 Laws and particulars

We have seen how all kinds of singular facta and hence of fact depend on laws. What then are laws? To answer that question we need to recall why and how laws entered our account, in chapter 15.2. We saw there that a statement like '$Kd \Rightarrow ch(Ld)=p$' can be true only in circumstances $Gd$ such that '$Gx \& Kx \Rightarrow ch(Lx)=p$' not only is true of all actual particulars $x$ but would be true of all hypothetical ones. I put this condition by saying that, for '$Kd \Rightarrow ch(Ld)=p$' to be true in $Gd$,

(31)  '$(x)(Gx \& Kx \Rightarrow ch(Lx)=p)$',

must state a law of nature.

This is a natural way to put it because generalisations like 'all $K$s are $L$s' are often held to state (or be) laws only if they meet this condition. If $K$s just happen to be $L$s, the generalisation is said to be only 'accidentally true', whereas a law (statement) must entail that any particular, whether $K$ or not, would be $L$ if it were $K$.

Whether this is precisely what most scientists and philosophers mean by 'law' is a moot point, but not one we need consider. For it is certainly close enough to make asking what makes (31), or the simpler

(37)  '$(x)(Kx \Rightarrow ch(Lx)=p)$',

state a law a not-too-misleading summary of our question: namely, what makes (31) or (37) true of all hypothetical particulars $x$ whether they are actual or not?

What makes this question hard to answer is that it requires laws to be more than facta about actual particulars. This is because the fact that '$Kx \Rightarrow ch(Lx)=p$' is true of all actual particulars $x$ does not entail that it would be true of them all if there were more than there are. Indeed, since this latter fact depends neither on how many particulars exist nor on which they are, the law that $(x)(Kx \Rightarrow ch(Lx)=p)$ cannot depend on *any* factum about *any* given particular.

The law that $F=MA$, for example, does not depend on which or how many things there are, nor on how many of them are acted on by forces. Of course the actual masses and accelerations of things acted on by forces must not refute '$F=MA$' if $F=MA$ is to be a law. But there is more to the law than the fact that '$F=MA$' has no counterexamples: for the law is what deprives this generalisation of counterexamples, and would do so however many things there were. Hence our question: what in the world *is* it that does this? No amount of singular facta about actual things can be the answer to that question.

If $F=MA$, Newton's second law of motion, holds however many things any force $F$ acts on, it must also hold even if $F$ acts on few or no things. Similarly, Newton's first law, that any thing acted on by *no* forces has zero acceleration, must be able to hold even if *no* thing is acted on by no force. And this is just as well, given Newton's law of gravity, that all things attract each other, and the fact (if it is a fact) that our world never has and never will contain just one thing. For this means that every thing is always acted on by some force and hence that Newton's first law of motion has no actual instances. Yet it certainly has actual consequences, for example that any non-zero $F$'s propensity 1 to accelerate any thing $d$ *causes* it to do so: since this law is what makes $F$ *raise* $d$'s chance of accelerating, by making that chance zero, and hence less than 1, if no such force acts on $d$.

## 2 Properties and particulars

This example shows how causation can and does depend on laws which have no instances. Yet the existence of such laws has a very contentious consequence which I must now derive and defend. This is that universals need not have instances: a property can exist which no particular has. To see and solve the problem this seems to pose, we must look more closely at how properties are linked to the particulars that have them.

First, however, I should remark that not all uninstantiated laws entail uninstantiated properties: in particular, Newton's first law of motion does not do so. For if being acted on by a specific force $F$ is a positive property, then being acted on by *no* such force – as opposed to a zero net force – is an infinite conjunction of negative properties; and, as we have seen, no such entities exist [15.7]. So the reason Newton's first law lacks instances is not that any property lacks instances but simply that every thing instantiates Newton's second law.

Other laws however will lack instances iff a property lacks them too. For although the predicate '$K$' in (37), '$(x)(Kx \Rightarrow ch(Lx)=p)$', need not correspond to a single property, $K$, it may do. And if it does, then this property will lack instances if '$K$' does. But if laws do not depend on how many or what instances they have, then (37) could state a law even if nothing has the property **K**.

Yet many philosophers, myself included (1991 ch. 8), have argued that universals must have instances. Why? My main reason was a notorious regress facing the idea of particulars and universals as independent entities constituting facta. Take any such particular **d** and a property **J** that **d** may or may not have. Then since **d** may not be **J**, the mere existence of **d** and **J** cannot entail the existence of the factum

   **Jd**.

For that factum to exist **d** must *have* the property **J**. But this seems to require a 'possession relation' **P** to hold between **d** and **J**, thus making **Jd**'s real structure

   **P(J,d)**.

But what makes *this* a factum? If it takes more than **d** and **J** to constitute **Jd**, it must take more than **d**, **J** and **P** to constitute **P(J,d)**. For if **d** need not be **J**, then **P** need not hold between **d** and **J**. So now we need a 'holding relation' **H** between **P**, **d** and **J**, giving **Jd** the structure

   **H(P,J,d)**.

Yet we are still no better off, since if **d** need not be **J**, so that **P** need not relate **J** and **d**, then **H** need not relate **P**, **J** and **d**. And so on. In short, any attempt to show how **d** and **J** constitute **Jd** only starts a vicious regress (see Bradley 1897 bk I, ch. II).

In my (1991 ch. 8) I concluded for this and other reasons that **d** and **J** can be defined only as parts of **Jd**, a factum that gets its structure by instantiating some general fact, e.g. that all **J**s are **I**s. This means that neither **d** nor **J** can exist on its own: **d** must have some property, and some particular must be **J**, if there are to be facta for **d** and **J** to be parts of.

But now we can see that properties can differ from particulars in this respect, since causal properties are defined, not by the singular facta they occur in, but by the laws they occur in [14.4], and these, as we have just seen, need have no instances. So properties need no instances: *kinds* of singular causal facta can exist even if there are no actual facta of those kinds (see Tooley 1987 ch. 3.1.4). Particulars, on the other hand, still need properties, since the regress argument given above still shows that **Jd**'s constituents cannot both exist on their own. So if **J** can do so, **d** cannot.

Thus the right way to think of particular things and events is this. The basic constituent of the factum **Jd** is **J**: a kind of factum which may or may not have instances **Jd**, **Jd'**, .... These, if they exist, differ only in their particular constituents $d, d', ...,$ which are thereby defined: $d$ and $d'$ are, by definition, what distinguish two different instances, $Jd$ and $Jd'$, of $J$.

More needs saying about particulars; but not just yet. Here we need only note two points about them before seeing how laws relate to universals. First, this definition of $d$ does not make it *necessary* that $d$ is $J$. For $d$ may also provide an instance of some other property, say $Id$. And if $d$ occurs in many such facta, then just as $J$ may survive the loss of a law it occurs in, so $d$ may survive the loss of a factum it occurs in. This is what lets the fact that $d$ is $J$ be contingent.

Second, if there are any causal relations [14.4], all this will apply equally to them. They too will be kinds of facta, whose instances, if any, are differentiated by the pairs, triples, etc. of particulars they contain. Thus suppose the predicate '... is hotter than ...' does in fact correspond to a relation $O$. Then what distinguishes $O$'s instances, the facta $Obd$, $Ob'd'$, ... are the ordered pairs $\langle b,d \rangle$, $\langle b',d' \rangle$, ... such that the first member of each pair is hotter than the second. But what then distinguishes $b$ from $d$? Obviously $Obd$ on its own cannot distinguish them. What can do so are $b$'s and $d$'s other properties, and their relations to other particulars. Thus the sun, which is hotter than the earth, differs from it in composition and mass, and from other stars, which are also hotter than the earth, in size, distance from the earth, and so on.

This suggests that most if not all particulars may well need not just one but many properties; but whether and why this is so are issues we can set aside. Here it suffices that all causal particulars must have at least one property, despite the fact that causal properties may have no instances.

## 3 Nomic relations

Properties may not need instances, but they do need laws; and laws need properties. Just as singular facta must contain particulars, in order to make them singular and to distinguish them from other facta of the same kind, so a law, in order to be a law, and different from other laws, must contain specific properties. Perhaps then, if properties are individuated by the laws they occur in, laws may in turn be individuated by the properties they contain?

Unfortunately not. If it takes more than its instances to constitute a law, it also takes more than the properties it contains. Laws may, as we have seen, entail the existence of properties which they collectively define, but the converse is not true. For if, as I have repeatedly noted, mass may 'exist in possible worlds where some of the laws it actually occurs in fail' [15.6], so may force and acceleration. No single law which these properties occur in is entailed by their mere existence.

If the universals in a law will not entail it, perhaps relations between them will? Perhaps, as Armstrong (1983 pt II) and others argue, this is what a law is: a factum constituted by a special *nomic* relation $N$ holding between the universals it contains. Thus just as a singular factum *Jd*, or *Obd*, comprises one or more particulars *d*, or *b* and *d*, together with a *first order* universal *J* or *O*, so the law that (say) all *J*s are *I*s comprises the first order universals *J* and *I* and the *second order* universal *N*:

$$N(J,I).$$

But this idea will not do either. The first problem it faces is that, as we have seen, it takes more than a generalisation like 'all *J*s are *I*s' to state what I am calling a 'law'. To be relevant to causation, even the simplest of deterministic laws must include a chance, and requires a closest-world conditional to state it: '$(x)(Jx \Rightarrow ch(Ix)=1)$'. But if the structure of this law is $N(J,I)$, what can the structure of the law that $(x)(Jx \Rightarrow ch(Ix)=p)$ be when $p<1$?

This particular problem is easily solved by making $N$ a *determinable* [14.4], with its determinates *p* being the chances *p* of being *I* which a law could make a *J*-particular have. This lets the structure

$$N(J,I)=p$$

cover all laws of the form $(x)(Jx \Rightarrow ch(Ix)=p)$, ranging from the law that all *J*s are *I*s to the law that none are, and every indeterministic law in between. The idea that a law is a second order relation holding between the first order universals it contains can easily cope with indeterminism.

What it cannot cope with is the fact that laws can contain any number of universals, and in any combination. We have seen how seemingly simple predicates in law statements can fail to correspond to universals [15.6]. For example, the antecedent in Newton's first law of motion says that a thing is *not* acted on by any force, which is not a universal but the negation of an infinite disjunction of universals [§1]. Similarly with the chemical laws of chlorine [15.6], whose antecedents are disjunctions, $(x)(Jx \lor J'x \lor ... \Rightarrow ...)$, where $J, J', ...$ are the properties of being different isotopes of chlorine. Similarly with $(x)(Gx \& Kx \Rightarrow ch(Lx)=p)$, apparently the simplest form of law that can make '$Kd \Rightarrow ch(Ld)=p$' true [§1], whose antecedent must be at least a conjunction.

And as for the antecedents of laws, so for their consequents. The seemingly single property $L$ in a law statable by

(37)   '$(x)(Kx \Rightarrow ch(Lx)=p)$'

may actually include any combination of negations (*x* is *not* radioactive), disjunctions (*x* is chlorine, i.e. *J* or *J'* or ...) and conjunctions (*x* is *liquid* chlorine) of properties. And this does not begin to exhaust the possible complexity of laws: consider for example the many laws that involve more than one particular, like the law of gravity, $F=GMM'/R^2$.

Fortunately we need not discuss anything as complex as $F=GMM'/R^2$, since not even all the laws that are stable by (37) can be relations between universals. The reason is that, when *K* and *L* correspond not to single properties but to negations, disjunctions or conjunctions of them, the supposed nomic relation *N* would have to link negative, disjunctive or conjunctive properties. But it cannot link such properties, because no such properties exist [15.7].

However, all may not yet be lost for *N*, since laws linking single properties do entail some laws linking complexes of them. Suppose for example that *J* and *I* are properties such that

$$(x)(Jx \Rightarrow ch(Ix)=p)$$

is a law, which could therefore have the simple structure $N(J,I)=p$. But this, *via* (3), $ch(\sim P)=1-ch(P)$ [2.1], also makes it a law that

$$(x)(Jx \Rightarrow ch(\sim Ix)=1-p),$$

a law containing the negation of the property *I*.

$N(J,I)=p$ could also entail laws with disjunctive antecedents, like the chemical laws of chlorine. For if

$$(x)(Jx \Rightarrow ch(Ix)=p) \text{ and } (x)(J'x \Rightarrow ch(Ix)=p)$$

are laws, so too is

$$(x)(Jx \vee J'x \Rightarrow ch(Lx)=p).$$

All this, however, is not enough, since there are many other laws which no amount of facta like $N(J,I)=p$ can entail, notably laws with conjunctive antecedents. Consider for example our invalid Kim's chance *p'* of being cured if she takes two medicines at once. This is not entailed by her chance *p* of being cured by either medicine on its own, since *p'* can have any value from 1, if the medicines reinforce each other, to 0, if their combination is fatal. And so in general: for as we noted in chapter 15.7, laws of the form

$$(x)(Gx \& Kx \Rightarrow ...)$$

need not, and generally do not, follow from laws of the forms

$$(x)(Gx \Rightarrow ...) \text{ and } (x)(Kx \Rightarrow ...).$$

This means that these and many other laws can neither be, nor be entailed by, any relation *N* between the universals that occur in them. But then a relation *N* between first order universals cannot be what a law is.

Laws might however still *entail* a relation between their universals, a relation we might call 'nomic' and which we might take to embody laws. To see whether laws do entail such a relation, we must recall the discussion in chapter 13.1 of

> what it takes to state a relation *O* between two entities *b* and *d*, where *b* and *d* may be facts, particulars, properties or entities of any other kind, and *O* may be any relation.

I concluded there that for a true sentence '*Obd*' to state this relation it must

(i)     entail that *b* and *d* exist, and
(ii)    be transparent for *b* and *d*.

Can law statements, by meeting these two conditions, state nomic relations between the universals which the law contains?

In most cases the answer to this question must be 'no, not as it stands'. For first, the terms '*K*' and '*L*' in a law statement like

(37)   '$(x)(Kx \Rightarrow ch(Lx)=p)$'

are predicates, applied to particulars. This means that, even when '*K*' and '*L*' do correspond to properties *K* and *L*, then although we *could* use them to refer to *K* and *L*, that is not how we use them in (37). And second, '*K*' and '*L*' may not and often do not correspond to single properties, which is the main reason why not all law statements of this form could state a relation between *K* and *L*.

Yet (37) could state such a relation when *K* and *L are* single properties. And when they are not, we can always envisage recasting (37), in principle if not in practice, using predicates (negated, disjoined and conjoined as required) corresponding to each of the properties in the law which it states. Let us then imagine this done, and suppose the result is our earlier

(31)   '$(x)(Gx \& Kx \Rightarrow ch(Lx)=p)$',

where '*G*', '*K*' and '*L*' now do correspond to single properties *G*, *K* and *L*. Then if we read '*G*', '*K*' and '*L*' not as predicates but as names for *G*, *K* and *L*, can we now take (31) to state a relation between these three properties?

Read in this way (31) certainly meets our condition (i), since by hypothesis '*G*', '*K*' and '*L*' do now correspond to the properties entailed by the law which (31) states. And it can be made to meet condition (ii) by fiat. For just as

> we can make any '*Le* because *Kc*' transparent simply by stipulating that '*c*' and '*e*', and any co-referring terms which may replace them in it, are to refer rigidly to *c* and *e* [12.6],

so we can make (31) transparent for *G*, *K* and *L* by requiring '*G*', '*K*' and '*L*', and any terms used to replace them in (31), to refer rigidly to *G*, *K* and *L*.

But even if (31) does meet conditions (i) and (ii), it can still only entail a nomic relation *N* linking *G*, *K* and *L* if such a relation exists [13.2] – and it does not. To see why not, recall again that by 'a relation *O*' I mean a real universal, an entity whose existence requires more than the presence of the concept or term '*O*' in a true thought or statement. This is why I decline to mean by '*O*'

> whatever it takes, besides *b* and *d*, to make '*Obd*' true [13.2],

since what makes '*Obd*' true is often *not* a relation between *b* and *d* – as we have seen that it is not when '*O*' is 'causes' or 'affects' [11; 12]. But then, since *O* is by definition the relation between *b* and *d* that makes '*Obd*' true, *O* does not exist [13.3], and '*Obd*' cannot, on pain of falsehood, be taken to entail that it does exist. Similarly here: (31) cannot, on pain of falsehood, entail the existence of a nomic relation *N* between *G*, *K* and *L* unless that is at least part of what makes (31) state a law.

But it cannot be. For first, as we have seen, *N* cannot relate *L* to the complex property *G&K*, because no such property exists. So if *N* exists at all, then in order to cover the unlimited complexity of possible laws [15.7], it must be a so-called *multigrade relation N** (Morton 1975), able to relate any number of universals to each other: in this case *G* and *K* to *L*.

But this will not do either, for two reasons. First, a multigrade relation *O** is defined by a simple relation *O*: e.g. two groups of people *fight with** each other iff everyone in each group **fights with** someone in the other. But then multigrade relations are not real universals, merely entailments of the real relations that define them. And second, no real relation *N* can define the multigrade relation *N** we need. For *N* would have to be our original nomic relation between two properties: in this case between *G* and *L* or *K* and *L*. Thus for *G* and *K* to be related to *L* by *N**, either

(37)  '$(x)(Kx \Rightarrow ch(Lx)=p)$' or
(38)  '$(x)(Gx \Rightarrow ch(Lx)=p)$'

would have to state a law for some $p$. Yet we have already seen that such laws, even if they exist, will generally not entail the law that (31) states.

In any case these laws need not even exist, since the fact that (31) states a law for some $p$ does not entail that (37) or (38) do, and mostly they do not. (For example, the fact that $F=MA$ is a law does not even suggest that any law links accelerations to forces or masses alone, and of course none does.) But when they do not, then no real relation $N$ exists to define a multigrade relation $N^*$ that could be entailed by the law which (31) states.

I conclude that laws generally can no more entail nomic relations, simple or multigrade, between the universals that occur in them, than they themselves can be, or be entailed by, such relations. In short, the concept of second order nomic relations between first order universals tells us nothing about what in the world its laws of nature are.

## 4 Determinable universals

This does not however mean that laws entail no second order universals. They do: for that, as I shall now show, is precisely what *determinables* – mass, force, acceleration, temperature, colour, credence in P, etc. – are.

To see why determinables are second order properties we must attend to an obvious fact about them which I have so far ignored. This is that a law like $F=MA$ in which determinables occur must quantify not only over all particulars but also over every determinate $F$, $M$ and $A$ of the determinables it contains. For of course each mass $M$ and force $F$ defines a special case of $F=MA$, a special case which is itself a law. This law may be stated, using the symbolism of chapter 14.3, by

(39)   '$(x)\{(Mx=M \& Fx=F) \Rightarrow ch[(\imath w)(Ax=w)=F/M]=1\}$',

where '$w$' is a variable ranging over accelerations and '$(\imath w)(Ax=w)=F/M$' means that $x$'s acceleration is $F/M$. (Note that here as elsewhere I am for simplicity using each value '$M$' of a suitable measure – e.g. kilogrammes – of the determinable $M$ to name the determinate mass $M$ whose measure '$M$' is, and similarly for $F$ and $A$.)

For our purposes, since we need not consider acceleration as well as mass and force, we can simplify (39) to the more perspicuous

(40)   '$(x)[(Mx=M \& Fx=F) \Rightarrow ch(Ax=F/M)=1]$'.

We can then state the law that $F=MA$ by replacing the constants '$M$' and '$F$' in (40) with variables '$U$' and '$V$' ranging over masses and forces to get

(41)   '$(U,V)(x)[(Mx=U \& Fx=V) \Rightarrow ch(Ax=V/U)=1]$',

where '$(U,V)$' means 'for all masses $U$ and forces $V$'.

But how should we express this limitation of '$u$' to masses and of '$v$' to forces? Every determinate mass and force is after all a universal, and our second order quantifiers should really range over all of them. (Using a so-called *many-sorted* logic, with different quantifiers ranging over different sorts of entity, will not serve our turn: we shall still need to know what in the world these sorts of entity are.) The obvious way is to distinguish first order properties ($u$) which have the second order property **M** of being a mass from those ($v$) which have the second order property **F** of being a force. Writing this '$Mu$' and '$Fv$', we can restate (41), with the variables '$u$' and '$v$' now ranging over all first order properties, as

(42)  '$(u,v)(x)[(Mu\&Mx=u)\&(Fv\&Fx=v)\Rightarrow ch(Ax=v/u)=1]$'.

But if (42) states the law that $F=MA$, then the determinables over which the quantifiers range in its Ramsey sentence that, for all $M$, $F$ and $A$,

(32)  '$(\exists X,Y,Z)(x)[(Xx=M\&Yx=F)\Rightarrow ch(Zx=F/M)=1]$'

[15.4], are second order universals. That is, they are properties of the first order properties over which the quantifiers range in the Ramsey sentence

'$(\exists u,v,w)(x)\{(Mx=u\&Fx=v)\Rightarrow ch[(\imath w)(Ax=w)=v/u]=1\}$',

of the law which (39) and hence (40) states. This, I maintain, is what these determinable properties are: properties of properties of particulars.

This result is interesting for two main reasons. First, it tells us what determinables are. And second, by admitting second order universals, it may let us reduce apparently first order relations between particulars to second order relations between first order properties, so that what makes '$b$ is hotter than $d$' true may really be that $b$ has a temperature $T$ which is *greater than* $d$'s temperature $T'$ [14.4].

Moreover, if apparent first order relations do reduce in this way to first order properties, then our apparent second order determinable *properties* may themselves reduce to *relations*. That is, it may be that what makes $T$ and $T'$ *temperatures* is their being instances of the determinable *hotter than* relation; and likewise for mass, force and acceleration.

Whether the determinable universals in these and other laws really are relations is a question I shall leave readers to answer. For whatever the answer, the Ramsey sentence of any law containing determinables will have to quantify both over second order universals (properties or relations) and over the first order universals that are their determinates. But then so must the Ramsey sentence $\Sigma$ of all laws. From which it follows, by the Ramsey test [15.4], that all these universals, both first and second order, exist.

## 5  Nomic facta and nomic facts

All this however still depends on there being laws of nature, and I have still not said what they are, only what they are *not*: not facta about particulars, not nomic relations between the universals they contain. Nor are they entailed by the existence either of their universals or of the singular facta which are their instances. What then are they?

To answer this question we must first recall from §1 that I am not asking what our *concept* of a law is. I am not even asking what *I* mean by 'law'. That I hope I made clear enough in §1: by 'law' I mean whatever in the world makes something like

(31)  '$(x)(Gx \& Kx \Rightarrow ch(Lx)=p)$' or
(37)  '$(x)(Kx \Rightarrow ch(Lx)=p)$'

true of all hypothetical particulars $x$ whether they are actual or not. And as this is what it takes to make causal statements like '$Kd \Rightarrow ch(Ld)=p$' true, something must do this for there to be causation in the world. The only question is what, i.e. what in the world *are* laws, so understood?

Having found no other answer to this question, I can only conclude that at least some laws are facta in their own right, facta which I shall call *nomic facta*, as opposed to singular facta like *Jd*. There is naturally more to be said, especially about how nomic and singular facta are linked. But before saying it I should try to allay the natural suspicion that invoking nomic facta to make statements like '$(x)(Kx \Rightarrow ch(Lx)=p)$' state laws is vacuous.

I have said that a principal difference between Queen Victoria and Pegasus is that our late Queen's atemporal existence and properties do not depend on anyone's naming or describing her [13.2]. This distinction is not of course vitiated by the fact that we need names and descriptions to say anything about her: e.g. that she exists, who she is and what her properties are. Similarly with the difference between facta and facts. Facts correspond trivially to truths, as Pegasus does to 'Pegasus', whereas facta are the independently real entities that make truths true and facts facts. This difference too is not vitiated by our needing true sentences to say that facta exist, what they are and what facta there are.

Thus invoking nomic facta to account for law statements is no more vacuous than invoking singular facta, particulars and universals to account for singular truths. In both cases the real question is: what entities of the relevant sorts (facta, particulars, universals) actually exist? The answer is, as we have seen, not trivial, since facta, particulars and universals do not correspond one-to-one to the true sentences, names and predicates of any natural language: many facta are never stated, others are stated in many different ways; many particulars have no names, others have many; many universals correspond to no predicates, others to many.

Our questions then are these: what fixes what entities of these sorts exist, and how do they contribute to making causal statements true or false? And since, for the singular facta that make causal statements true, the answers to these questions turn out to depend on laws, I must now answer the same questions for laws.

To do this I note first that just as, in general, different statements like 'P' and 'P∨Q' can be made true by one factum **P**, so in particular different law statements can be made true by one nomic factum. We saw two examples of this in §3. One followed from the logical equivalence of

$$\text{'}ch(P)=p\text{' to '}ch(\sim P)=1\text{-}p\text{'}$$

[2.1] and hence of

$$\text{'}(x)(Kx{\Rightarrow}ch(Lx)=p)\text{' to '}(x)(Kx{\Rightarrow}ch(\sim Lx)=1\text{-}p)\text{',}$$

which means that any factum that makes one of these sentences state a law will make the other do so too.

The other example follows from the fact that if

(37)  '$(x)(Kx{\Rightarrow}ch(Lx)=p)$' and
(38)  '$(x)(Gx{\Rightarrow}ch(Lx)=p)$'

state laws, then so does

(43)  '$(x)(Gx{\vee}Kx{\Rightarrow}ch(Lx)=p)$'.

This is why the chemical laws of chlorine's isotopes entail the chemical laws of chlorine itself: the facta that make (37) and (38) state laws thereby also make (43) state a law.

These examples pose an apparent dilemma. So far I have written as if, when a sentence states a law, what makes it do so is what it states. But we can now see that this need not be so. For although what makes (43) state a law is that (37) and (38) do so, (43) does not say what they say. Which then shall we call the 'law': what (43) *states*, or what *makes* what it states a law?

This however is a false dichotomy, since we can call both of them laws, but of different kinds, by adapting terms used by Ramsey (1990 ch. 7) to express the same distinction. For Ramsey distinguishes

[i] the ultimate laws of nature [from]
[ii] derivative laws of nature, i.e. general propositions deducible from the ultimate laws (p. 142),

where by 'laws of nature' he means law statements. To see how this fits our distinction, consider the Ramsey sentence $\Sigma'$ of the conjunction of all the laws stated by Ramsey's ultimate law statements, i.e. those which entail all others. Then $\Sigma'$ is $\Sigma$, the Ramsey sentence of all laws.

For first, since by definition $\Sigma'$ entails all law statements, the facta that make it true will make all law statements true. Second, $\Sigma'$ and $\Sigma$ quantify over the same universals, since ultimate laws must contain all universals contained in derivative laws if they are to entail them. But if $\Sigma'$ and $\Sigma$ have the same entailments and quantify over the same universals, then they differ not in what they say but at most in how they say it. And then, as it is immaterial to us whether or how $\Sigma$ can be expressed [15.6], $\Sigma'$ *is* $\Sigma$. For while I follow the custom of calling $\Sigma$ a 'Ramsey *sentence*', what I mean by it is what any such sentence would say: i.e. the content, however expressed, of any Ramsey sentence of the conjunction of everything that makes any statement state a law [15.4].

Laws in *this* sense we may thus, following Ramsey, call *ultimate laws*: the nomic facta that make all law statements state laws. *Derivative laws*, which are what Ramsey's derivative law statements *state*, are not facta at all but mere entailments of them, which we may call *nomic facts*. Where the facta are what matter, they are what I shall mean by 'laws'; elsewhere I may also apply the term to nomic facts, distinguishing the facta only when I need to.

How then shall we represent our ultimate laws, our nomic facta? Take the statement in §3 that '$(x)(Jx{\Rightarrow}ch({\sim}Ix)=1\text{-}p)$' [is] a law containing the negation of a property $I'$. This is the same *factum* as $(x)(Jx{\Rightarrow}ch(Ix)=p)$, in which only $I$ occurs: here the distinction lies only in how the factum is stated, not in the factum itself.

Not so, however, with Newton's first law of motion, that things acted on by no forces do not accelerate. This factum has, as we have seen, an inherently negative antecedent [§2]. Similarly, if

(31)  '$(x)(Gx\&Kx{\Rightarrow}ch(Lx)=p)$'

is *not* entailed by

(37)  '$(x)(Kx{\Rightarrow}ch(Lx)=p)$' or
(38)  '$(x)(Gx{\Rightarrow}ch(Lx)=p)$',

i.e. if the law it states is a nomic factum, then this factum too contains an inherently complex antecedent.

Given these and many other, far more complex, structures which nomic facta may have, I can see no simple way of showing their structure, let alone that of all nomic facts. But this does not matter, since what matter here are not laws themselves but the singular causal statements that need laws to make them true. All that matters here is that *some* facta make the statement (31), '$(x)(Gx\&Kx\Rightarrow ch(Lx)=p)$', which '$Kd\Rightarrow ch(Ld)=p$' entails, state a law [§1]. Whether or not (31) shows the structure of the factum or facta that do this, i.e. whether the law it states is ultimate or derivative, is immaterial. But then, since for our purposes we can ignore the structure of whatever makes (31) state a law, we can simply call it '**N**'.

## 6 Nomic and singular facta

There is however one aspect of **N** we must consider. This is its relation to the singular facta that I shall call **N**'s *instances*. These are not the facts, if any, that instantiate (31)'s antecedent and consequent: facts like *Gd*, *Kd* and *ch(Ld)=p*. Such facts must of course conform to **N**: i.e. if a particular *d* is *K* in circumstances of kind *G*, then there must be a chance *p* that *d* is also *L*. Otherwise '$Gd\&Kd\Rightarrow ch(Ld)=p$' will be false, and then so will (31). That is obvious and unproblematic.

What is less obvious is how **N** relates to what I mean by its instances. These are the singular facta **R** that are needed to make '$R\&Q\Rightarrow ch(P)=p$', and hence '$Q\Rightarrow ch(P)=p$', true [14.3]. Here '*Q*' is '*Kd*', '*P*' is '*Ld*', and **R** is a factum included in the relevant circumstances *Gd*, in which *d* may or may not be *K* or *L*. So for **N** to make '$Kd\Rightarrow ch(Ld)=p$' true it must entail the existence of some such factum **R** whether *d* is *K* or not. How can it do this, and what then is **R**?

My answer to the second question has so far been that **R** is some factum about *d*: *Jd* [14.1]. But this answer will no longer do, for two reasons. First, we now need an answer for *all* instances of $Q\Rightarrow ch(P)=p$, not just for the special case where '*Q*' and '*P*' are about the same particular *d*, which often they are not. Indeed, as we have seen, they may not be about specific particulars at all: there are many other kinds '*Q\**' and '*P\**' of which '*Q*' and '*P*' may be instances. They may be conjunctions, disjunctions or negations of any number of statements about any number of particulars. They may even be irreducibly negative existential statements, saying for example that *no* one falls off Castle Rock on 4 June 1988, and that no one dies there then [14.4].

We cannot therefore rely on '*Q*' and '*P*' to provide a particular for **R** to contain. And even if we could, that would not be enough, since to make '$Kd\Rightarrow ch(Ld)=p$' true, our factum **N** must entail an **R** not only for every *actual* particular *x* but for every hypothetical one [§1]. So we cannot restrict **R** to facta about actual particulars. Yet that is what a singular factum is: a factum *Jd* about some actual particular *d* [14.5]. How can we square this circle ?

## 7  Laws and spacetime

To square it we must first recall from chapter 1.2 how a fact P can be located in space and time even when it is tenseless, i.e. such that 'P' is true everywhere and always. Suppose, to vary the example, P is the fact that one Lee Harvey Oswald kills President John F. Kennedy of the United States. The tenseless statement 'P' of this fact is true at all places and times, as are 'Oswald kills Kennedy in Dallas', 'Oswald kills Kennedy in 1963' and 'Oswald kills Kennedy in Dallas in 1963'; whereas 'Oswald kills Kennedy in New York', 'Oswald kills Kennedy in 1964' and 'Oswald kills Kennedy in New York in 1964' are all false. All this follows from P's location – a small part of a street in Dallas, and a short interval of time in 22 November 1963 – i.e. from the smallest $s$ and $t$ for which 'P at $s$ at $t$' is true [1.2].

But not all tenseless facts are located in this sense. For some P, 'P at $s$ at $t$' is true for *all* places $s$ and times $t$, and if 'P' states a law, it must be. For

(31)   '$(x)(Gx\&Kx \Rightarrow ch(Lx)=p)$'

can only state a law if

'$(x)(Gx\&Kx \Rightarrow ch(Lx)=p)$ at $s$ at $t$'

does so too for all $s$ and $t$. This is because, for (31) to state a law,

'$Gx\&Kx \Rightarrow ch(Lx)=p$'

must be true of *all* hypothetical particulars $x$ [§1], whether actual or not, including therefore particulars $x$ at any $s$ and $t$. This is why no law, including **N**, can have a restricted location. But how then can **N** entail the local factum **R** which '$Kd \Rightarrow ch(Ld)=p$' or, in general, '$Q \Rightarrow ch(P)=p$' needs to make it true?

The answer lies in the fact that **N** lacks location only because it makes

'N at $s$ at $t$'

true for all $s$ and $t$. Yet 'N at $s$ at $t$' states different facts for different $s$ and $t$, since although **N** entails them all, most of them do not entail each other. In particular, 'N at $s$ at $t$' states a different fact for every $s$ and $t$ that is a *point* in spacetime.

The importance of these point facts is that conjunctions of them will entail all other instances of **N**: for if 'N at $s$ at $t$' is true for every point within spatial and temporal regions $s$ and $t$ it will also be true for $s$ and $t$. In other words, spacetime regions are mere conjunctions of spacetime points and hence, because there are no complex particulars [14.5], not real entities at all. The real entities are the points, which I shall write '$st$', writing spacetime regions '[*st*]', so that 'N at *st*' states not only a fact but a factum: **N***st*. And this I maintain is the factum **R** for which we are looking:

> **R** is a point factum **N***st*.

This claim needs both qualification and defence. First the qualification. To make '$Q \Rightarrow ch(P)=p$' true, the relevant **N** must be instantiated by all the spacetime points in the relevant circumstances S, e.g. all round Castle Rock as the climber Don falls off it on 4 June 1988. This of course presents no problem, since **N**, like all laws, is instantiated everywhere. It will however usually require S to include not just one factum **R** [14.3] but an infinite conjunction of them. So since a conjunction of facta is not itself a factum [15.7], we should really reword the condition $S_1$ of chapter 14.3 as

$S_1$: (a) S includes a fact $\Pi R$ such that '$\Pi R \& Q \Rightarrow ch(P)=p$' is true,

where $\Pi R$ is a conjunction of facta **R**, namely of as many point facta **N***st* as are needed to make true

> '$\Pi R \& Q \Rightarrow ch(P)=p$' and hence
> '$Q \Rightarrow ch(P)=p$'.

$\Pi R$ is the local fact on which even a *total* cause Q of P depends, a total cause being one that does not depend for its efficacy on any other local facts [2.2]. For example, a *Kd* that causes *Ld* will be a total cause of *Ld* if the relevant laws are not, for some $p>p'$,

> $(x)(Gx\&Kx \Rightarrow ch(Lx)=p)$ and
> $(x)(Gx\&{\sim}Kx \Rightarrow ch(Lx)=p')$,

as assumed in chapter 15.2, but

> $(x)(Kx \Rightarrow ch(Lx)=p)$ and
> $(x)({\sim}Kx \Rightarrow ch(Lx)=p')$.

For then the relevant circumstances S in which *Kd* causes *Ld* simply comprise the conjunctive fact $\Pi R$ that these laws hold throughout some sufficiently large region of spacetime containing *Kd*.

So much for my qualification. It means that, in principle, we should replace '**R**' with '$\Pi R$' wherever it occurs from chapter 14 on. In practice however, now we have seen what $\Pi R$ is, because the difference between **R** and $\Pi R$ makes no odds to any of our arguments, I shall for simplicity stick to **R** and the original wording of $S_1$.

Next, I need to defend and explain my invoking of spacetime points. First, as we have seen, we need them to provide the local instances of nomic facta that we need to make causal statements of all kinds true. In so doing, points enable causation to link all kinds of singular facts, including many, like negative existential facts, which cannot themselves be facta.

Second, points embody the facts about *hypothetical* particulars of all other kinds which we have seen that singular causation entails. This they do by providing the locations whose instantiation of our ultimate laws makes all such particulars, wherever they may be, conform to those laws. Without spacetime points there would be nothing in reality to do this.

But why can our nomic facta not do this? If **N**, by definition, makes '$Gx\&Kx{\Rightarrow}ch(Lx)=p$' true of all hypothetical particulars, why do we need spacetime points as well? The reason lies in the contingency of most if not all laws, i.e. in the fact that **N** may not exist in all possible worlds. Suppose for example that there were more $G\&K$-particulars $x$ than there actually are. Then for '$Kd{\Rightarrow}ch(Ld)=p$' to be true for any actual $d$, **N** must make

(31)  '$(x)(Gx\&Kx{\Rightarrow}ch(Lx)=p)$'

true of all these non-actual $x$s [15.2]. But to do this **N** must exist not only in our world, where these $x$s do not exist, but in at least the closest worlds where they do exist. But if **N** is contingent, what in *this* world stops these being worlds where **N** does not exist?

The answer lies in **N**'s instantiation by every point in spacetime. This is what lets **N** make (31) true of all these non-actual $G\&K$-particulars $x - if$ we confine them to actual locations. And as for these particulars, so for hypothetical instances X of all kinds Q*, P* and S* of facts such that, in S,

'$Q{\Rightarrow}ch(P)=p$'

is true. Provided all these instances X make 'X at [$st$]' true only for actual places $s$ and times $t$ which instantiate **N**, then **N** can make

'$S^*\&Q^*{\Rightarrow}ch(P^*)=p$'

true of all of them, as the truth of '$Q{\Rightarrow}ch(P)=p$' requires.

If this shows why **N** needs spacetime points to do its causal job, it also shows why they need **N**. For like other particulars, a point $st$ will occur in many facta N$st$, N'$st$, ... instantiating different ultimate laws **N**, **N'**, .... And just as other particulars may survive the loss of any one property, so $st$ may survive the loss of any one law. In other words, a particular point $st$ may exist in worlds where **N** does not exist and where for that reason '$Kd{\Rightarrow}ch(Ld)=p$' would be false. So to make it true in our world we need more than our spacetime points: we need the point facta in which they occur, and hence the nomic factum **N** of which those facta are instances. In short, what singular causation requires is *laws embodied in spacetime*.

## 8 Points and other particulars

The fact that points instantiate facta rather than properties makes them differ from other particulars in two ways that call for further comment. First, laws cover only actual points, not ones that are merely hypothetical. This does not of course entail that the universe cannot expand as cosmologists say it does: for all they mean is that its spatial volume increases with time, which is if true just a fact about the shape of space-time. Nor does it entail that spacetime itself could not be larger than it is, only that nothing in our world entails that our laws would then exist, although of course they could.

The other peculiarity of points is that they occur in facta like **N**$st$ with *nomic facta* like **N**, whereas other particulars like **d** occur in facta like **J***d* and **O***bd* with *universals* like **J** and **O**. But is this difference real, or only terminological? Why not classify our ultimate laws with other universals, which also have many instances and no locations? The reason is that, as we shall now see, laws differ from (other) universals in too many other ways.

The main way is that laws and universals lack locations for completely different reasons. **N** lacks location because it has instances everywhere: '**N** at [$st$]' is true for every [$st$]. **J** and **O**, on the other hand, need not have *any* instances; and they lack location because, although '$K$[$st$]' is true for some '$K$' (e.g. 'is a spacetime region'), when **J** and **O** are universals '**J** at [$st$]' and '**O** at [$st$]' make no sense. Given these differences, calling nomic facta 'universals' is positively misleading, which is why I reserve 'universal' for unlocated entities that do not correspond to truths: properties and relations.

The difference between points and other particulars does not however stop us letting the quantifiers in law statements like

(37)  '$(x)(Kx{\Rightarrow}ch(Lx)=p)$'

range over points too. This is because, since the predicates '$K$' and '$L$' in (37) cannot be true of points, the hypothetical $K$-particulars $x$ for which $ch(Lx)$ must be $p$ if (37) is to state a law include no points. So provided (37) is true of all particulars that are *not* points, it will also be true of all points: because, by definition [1.7], '$Kx{\Rightarrow}ch(Lx)=p$' is true for all $p$ for any '$Kx$' that is false in all possible worlds, which it will be if $x$ is a point. This means that we shall not need a many-sorted logic to distinguish points from other sorts of particulars [§4]: a standard single-sorted logic will do.

This is why, despite differing in so many ways, points and other causal particulars are far more alike than laws and universals are. They are all real entities corresponding only to singular terms, not to whole truths. They are all located – points *are* locations – in spacetime. None can exist on its own: each is just what distinguishes a singular factum of one or more kinds **J** or **N** from other facta of the same kinds. And our first order quantifiers can range over all of them alike. This is why I call points 'particulars'.

However, despite these fundamental similarities, points do differ greatly from things and events. The most important of these differences is that points constitute the four-dimensional manifold that is spacetime, one of whose dimensions is closely related to causation in a way we have still to explain. The dimension of course is *time*, and its relation to causation the major but still contentious connotation of causation that 'causes generally precede their effects' [5.4]. Now at last it is time to see what makes this true.

# 17 *Time*

## 1 The precedence of causes

'All singular causation either is or reduces to causation between facts' [11.4]. And the location of all causes and effects also is or reduces to that of facts, since particular causes and effects must be wherever the relevant facts about them are: for Don to fall off Castle Rock on 4 June 1988, both Don and his fall must be there then. We can thus locate all causes and effects by locating facts, as in chapter 1.2: the location of any factual cause Q being the smallest spacetime region $[st]$ for which 'Q at $[st]$' is true, and similarly for any effect P.

This lets us define the time order of all causes and effects by that of the locations of facts: if $t$ and $t'$ are the temporal locations of Q and P, Q precedes P iff $t$ precedes $t'$. But what makes $t$ precede $t'$? As most Q and P are extended in time, $t$ and $t'$ are mostly intervals of instants. So let $[t]$ and $[t']$ be two such intervals containing any instants $t$ and $t'$. Then whatever makes $t$ precede $t'$ will determine whether $[t]$ precedes $[t']$, as follows.

First, obviously, $[t]$ precedes $[t']$ if all instants in $[t]$ precede all instants in $[t']$. But $[t]$ may also precede $[t']$ if they overlap, as we saw in chapter 5.2 with the half-open interval $[t_0,t_0+1)$ including $t_0$ but not $t_0+1$, which precedes the half-open interval $(t_0,t_0+1]$ that includes $t_0+1$ but not $t_0$. Here $[t]$ precedes $[t']$ because *some* instant in $[t]$ precedes all instants in $[t']$ but not *vice versa*; and similarly in other cases.

In short, we can define the time order of all facts, and thus of all causes and effects, if only we can say what makes one *instant* precede another. And there is an obvious answer to that question: namely, that precedence is a primitive relation, a temporal universal (which I shall write '«') that we already know a lot about – for example, that it is transitive (if $t$ precedes $t'$, and $t'$ precedes $t''$, $t$ must precede $t''$), irreflexive (no $t$ can precede itself) and asymmetrical (no $t'$ can precede any $t$ that precedes it).

But this answer, however obvious, must be wrong, because it makes causation's temporal connotation, that causes generally precede their effects, a sheer coincidence. If precedence is a primitive relation, it should be as conceivable that effects generally precede their causes as that causes precede their effects. But it is not: not even those who think that some effects could precede their causes think that all or even most of them could.

But if this is inconceivable, can we not rule it out by *defining* a cause as the earlier of two causally related facts? Unfortunately not. That will only work if causation's other connotations [5.4] do not distinguish causes from effects, as indeed its contiguity and evidential connotations do not: since contiguity is symmetrical, and effects can be as good evidence for their causes as causes can be for their effects [5.5]. If these were causation's only other connotations, a primitive relation « might well serve to make causes precede their effects by definition.

But they are not: causation has other connotations, the explanatory [5.4] and means–end [7.1] ones, which do distinguish causes from effects. For while causes explain their effects and are means of bringing them about, effects do not explain, and are not means of bringing about, their causes. And this is what stops us making causes precede their effects by definition.

For since these connotations also distinguish causes from effects, they too could be used to define a cause: namely, as whichever of two causally related facts *explains* or is a *means* to the other. But then we must ask why these two definitions always pick out the same member of a pair of causally related facts. But no definition can explain that. What explains it is a consequence of these differences between cause and effect, namely that any cause C must raise the chance of any effect E: for otherwise C can neither explain E [6.5] nor be a means to it [7.5]. This is what makes it more than a coincidence that causation satisfies both these connotations.

Similarly, defining a cause as the earlier member of any cause–effect pair would only prompt the query: what makes this definition give the same result as our other definitions? Again no definition can explain that. What explains it is the fact that this difference between cause and effect also depends, as we shall see in §3–6, on all effects having, in the relevant circumstances, chances both with and without their causes.

## 2  Simultaneous causation

But if that is the explanation, then since, as we have seen, effects *must* have chances with and without their causes [2; 5], causes must precede their effects not just generally but always. Yet there are many apparent cases of simultaneous causation, which we must therefore explain away. Kant even claims that 'the great majority of efficient natural causes are simultaneous with their effects' (1781 A203), giving as an example that

> if I view as a cause a ball which impresses a hollow as it lies on a stuffed cushion, the cause is simultaneous with the effect.

Yet of this, our first example, he adds at once that

> I still distinguish the [cause and effect] through the time relation of
> their dynamical connection. For if I lay the ball on the cushion, a
> hollow follows upon the previous flat smooth shape; but if (for any
> reason) there previously exists a hollow in the cushion, a leaden ball
> does not follow upon it.

This illustrates his immediately preceding conclusion that although

> the time between the causality of the cause and its immediate effect
> may be a vanishing quantity, and they may thus be simultaneous ...
> the relation of the one to the other will always still remain determin-
> able in time.

And so it will, as we can see by looking more closely at Kant's cushion,
which I shall call '$c$'.

Suppose first that $c$ is *elastic*, so that removing the ball, $b$, will cause $c$
to change its determinable shape, $S$. But not of course instantly: $S$ will not
change until after $b$ is gone. But then $b$'s being on $c$ at $t$ cannot be a cause
of $c$'s having its determinate shape $s$ at the same instant $t$. The cause of that
fact must be $b$'s being on $c$ during a half-open interval $[t',t)$ from some
earlier instant $t'$ up to but not including $t$. This is why the cause must
precede its effect in this case.

But what if $c$ is *inelastic*, so that removing $b$ will not cause $c$'s shape to
change? $b$'s being on $c$ in $[t',t)$ cannot now cause $c$ to be $s$ at $t$: for $c$'s
chance of being $s$ at $t$ will now be 1 whether this is so or not. So now the
only immediate cause of $c$'s being $s$ at $t$ is the fact that $c$ is $s$ during $[t',t)$:
since if it were not, $c$'s chance of being $s$ at $t$ would be 0. This does not of
course make $b$'s being on $c$ irrelevant: for the fact that $b$ was put on $c$
earlier, by causing $c$ to be $s$ thereafter, also causes $c$ to be $s$ at $t$. But both
of these causes of the fact that $c$ is $s$ at $t$ still precede that fact.

So Kant's cushion, elastic or not, will not after all give us causes that do
not precede their effects. But perhaps its failure to do so follows from the
causal asymmetry that Kant mentions: the fact that the ball affects the
cushion but not *vice versa*. Perhaps if the causation went both ways, it
would have to be simultaneous. Not so: but to see why not, we must turn to
a second, simpler example of seemingly simultaneous causation.

Consider an ideal gas, which at any constant temperature conforms to
Boyle's law, linking its determinable pressure $P$ to its volume $V$ so that in
equilibrium, i.e. when $P$ and $V$ are unchanging, $PV=K$ ($K$ is a constant).
This makes the causation go both ways: e.g. halving $V$ in a cylinder causes
$P$ to double, and doubling $P$ in a balloon under pressure causes $V$ to halve.

Now imagine a sample **g** of this gas in equilibrium during a time interval containing **t**, with a determinate volume *v* and pressure *p*. Which causes which: does *v***g** at **t** cause *p***g** at **t** or *vice versa*? And either way would not the causation have to be simultaneous?

To see why this does not follow, we must look more closely at **g**, which for simplicity we may imagine contained in a transparent spherical balloon, as shown below in Figure 17.

(The figure also shows how to accommodate Einstein's special theory of relativity, which makes simultaneity across space arbitrary within limits set by the speed of light. This makes us take *p***g** and *v***g** not at an instant but over intervals [$t'$,$t$] and [$t$,$t''$] long enough for light to cross **g** to and from any spacetime point *st* on its surface. It also stops instants being the real particulars which in §1, for the sake of argument, I took them to be, a fact I shall mark by no longer using bold type for them: *t*. For what relativity tells us is that the set of spacetime points in the instant *t* are simultaneous in only one of many equally valid so-called *reference frames*. And although this fact rarely matters in practice, I shall use this example to show how to represent temporal links between causes and effects which, like *p***g** and *v***g**, because they are extended in space, must also be extended in time.)

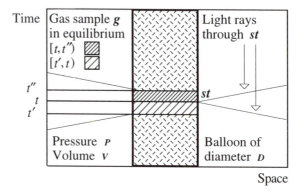

Figure 17: Causation in equilibrium

Consider then the half-open intervals shown in Figure 17: the interval [$t'$,$t$), including $t'$ but not $t$, and the interval [$t$,$t''$), including $t$ but not $t''$. Then in the circumstances – the temperature is constant and Boyle's law holds throughout this region of spacetime – both

P:      *p***g** during [$t$,$t''$) and
P′:     *v***g** during [$t$,$t''$)

are caused both by

Q:     *pg* during [*t'*,*t*) and by
Q':    *vg* during [*t'*,*t*).

For given Q, the chances both of P and of P' are 1 with Q' and 0 without; just as, given Q', their chances are 1 with Q and 0 without.

This presents no problem. P and P' simply have two causes, Q and Q', each depending on the other for its efficacy, just like the three causes – the existence of a spark, inflammable gas and oxygen – of an explosion in a car engine's cylinder [6.2]. The symmetry in the present case no more stops Q and Q' preceding P and P' than it stops a car engine cylinder's spark, gas and oxygen preceding the explosion each of them causes.

My third apparent example of simultaneous causation also fails to entail it, but for a different reason. The example goes as follows. Imagine a rigid front-engined train moving off. If the train is perfectly rigid, it cannot expand. But if the front moves off before the rear does, it must expand. So front and rear must move as one: the rear's movement must be simultaneous with the movement of the engine at the front that causes it.

To this I reply that nothing can be, in this sense, perfectly rigid: nothing can be *completely* inelastic. However, like the time between a cause and its effect, a thing's elasticity can be, in Kant's phrase, 'a vanishing quantity'. This follows from the denseness of time and space [5.2], which stops any spacetime point being next to any other. Thus suppose (ignoring relativity) that the front of the train moves off at an instant *t* and the rear at a later instant *t'*. Then however long the train, and however close *t'* is to *t*, there are infinitely many instants between *t* and *t'*, at each of which an intermediate point on the train moves off. So even if relativity limits the speed of causal propagation, the temporal connotation of causation does not. Nor therefore does it set any limit, short of perfection, to the rigidity of things.

My fourth example involves fields: electrical, gravitational, etc. Take for example a point particle *q* whose electric charge $E$ at a spacetime point *st* affects the electrostatic field at all points absolutely later than *st*. But how can it do this without affecting the field at *st* where $E$ itself is, i.e. without a simultaneous effect? Would that not mean acting immediately at a distance, thus violating causation's contiguity connotation [5.4]?

The answer to this question again lies in the denseness of spacetime. For no one denies that $Eq$ at *st has* effects at remote places and times: what causation's contiguity connotation says is not 'no action at a distance' but 'no *unmediated* action at a distance'. And since spacetime is dense, the effect of $Eq$ at *t* at any later time, however close, can always be mediated by effects at intermediate times. So the most that causation's contiguity and temporal connotations can make a dense spacetime imply is that *all* causation is mediated; and as we shall see in §4, they do not even do this.

But what then of Newton's theory of gravity, which says that any two things with any determinate masses $M$ and $M'$ at any distance $R$ exert a force $F=GMM'/R^2$ on each other [4.3]? Does this not entail unmediated action at a distance? No: for as Newton (1713) says, although by his theory

> we have explained the phenomena of the heavens and of our sea by the power of gravity, [we] have not yet assigned the cause of this power. ... Hitherto I have not been able to discover the cause of those properties of gravity from phenomena, and I frame no hypotheses (Book III, General Scholium).

But nothing in Newton's theory stops such a hypothesis – e.g. that gravity is mediated by a gravitational field – satisfying the contiguity requirement. Nor does his theory entail simultaneous causation, as my treatment of the gas and train examples above should enable readers to see for themselves.

So much for simultaneous causation: one way and another I can explain away all the apparent cases I know of. But this no more proves me right to do so than my ability to explain away causes which seem not to raise their effects' chances proved I was right to do that [6.1]. For here, as there, others may reject my explanations and insist in some or all of these cases that the causation really *is* simultaneous. And

> if so, then at the level of intuitions about cases, we shall reach a stand-off, no doubt because our intuitions are affected by the theories we use them to support. Intuitions about cases can therefore no more settle this question than they could settle the question of whether causation can be indeterministic [6.1].

So again we need an argument to settle the question; and again there is one. For the mere fact that any effect E must in the relevant circumstances have chances both with and without any cause C [2.2] entails, as we shall now see, that C precedes E.

## 3  Causal loops

To see how causation relates to time, we must first notice that it relates also to space. Its contiguity connotation, for example, relates it to distance in space as well as in time: requiring the first effects of Don's falling to be where he falls, not ten miles away; explosions in engine cylinders to be caused by sparks in those very cylinders; and so on.

Causation is also our criterion for applying the core concept of space-time: spatiotemporal *coincidence*. For any two facts to coincide is for them to be able to interact immediately, as the pressure $P$ and volume $v$ of our gas sample $g$ seem to do [§2]. And on such facts of coincidence all other facts about spacetime depend, such as how many dimensions it has. For the dimensions of spacetime are simply determinable ways in which facts (and thus things and events) can fail to coincide – just as, for example, the 'dimensions' of colour are the ways in which colours can fail to match.

Thus, just as colour 'space' has three dimensions because colours can fail to match in three ways (brightness, saturation and hue), so spacetime has four dimensions because there are four ways in which facts can fail to coincide. This is why we always do, and can only, contact others at the same *latitude, longitude, altitude* and *time* as them. To meet someone is to share his or her determinates of all these determinables; to differ in any of them is not to meet, and so to be unable to interact immediately.

But causation does more than make spacetime a multi-dimensional causal manifold. It also makes one of its dimensions differ from the rest as time does from space, by being necessarily linear and having a direction, as I shall now show.

I start by defining a concept that I shall call *causability*, weaker than causation, as follows. Recall that for Q to *cause* P, Q and P must be facts, and $ch_Q(P)$, P's chance with Q in the relevant circumstances S, must exceed $ch_{\sim Q}(P)$, its chance in S without P [1; 2; 6].

P can be *causable* by Q, by contrast, even if Q and P are not facts and $ch_Q(P)$ does not exceed $ch_{\sim Q}(P)$. For by definition, for any states of affairs P and Q in any circumstances S,

P is causable by Q iff $ch_Q(P)$ and $ch_{\sim Q}(P)$ exist in S,

i.e. iff S includes facta **R** and **R'** (which for simplicity I shall hereafter take to be identical [14.3]) which for some $p$ and $p'$ ($p$ need not exceed $p'$) entail

R&Q$\Rightarrow$ch(P)=$p$ and R'&~Q$\Rightarrow$ch(P)=$p'$.

And since, given (3), $ch(\sim P)=1-ch(P)$ [2.1], $ch_Q(\sim P)$ and $ch_{\sim Q}(\sim P)$ exist iff $ch_Q(P)$ and $ch_{\sim Q}(P)$ do, if P is causable by Q, then so too is ~P, and P and ~P are causable by ~Q. In short, as I shall sometimes put it,

P/~P is causable by Q/~Q iff $ch_Q(P)$ and $ch_{\sim Q}(P)$ exist.

Causability, because it depends only on the facta that make $ch_Q(P)$ and $ch_{\sim Q}(P)$ exist, is the central causal concept [13; 14]. For if P/~P is causable by Q/~Q, then whether Q or ~Q causes P or ~P depends only on whether 'Q' or '~Q', or 'P' or '~P', is true and whether $ch_Q(P)$ and $ch_{\sim Q}(P)$ differ and if so how. In all these cases what really embodies the causation is the same: the facta that make P/~P causable by Q/~Q.

With causability so defined, the next step is to show why there can be no *causal loops*. By a 'causal loop' I mean a chain of facts $Q_1 \ldots Q_n$, where $n > 2$, such that

$Q_{i+1}$ is causable by $Q_i$ for all $i$ from 1 to $n$ and $Q_n = Q_1$.

For $n > 5$ I depict this below in Figure 18, together with the facta $\mathbf{R}_i$ that make each $Q_{i+1}$ causable by $Q_i$. (The figure must not be taken to show the layout of these facts and facta in spacetime, since I do not assume, and have not yet shown, that they must have different locations.)

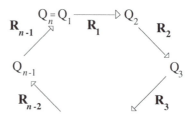

Figure 18: Causal loop

By calling these loops 'causal' I do not of course mean that any of these facts $Q_i$ *does* cause its successor, $Q_{i+1}$: for that will be so only if $ch_{Q_i}(Q_{i+1})$ exceeds $ch_{\sim Q_i}(Q_{i+1})$, which it may not do. But it could, even if it does not, because the values of $ch_{Q_i}(Q_{i+1})$ and $ch_{\sim Q_i}(Q_{i+1})$ are logically independent. So $Q_i$ always *could* cause $Q_{i+1}$ for all $i$ from 1 to $n$ (and so to 1 again) if, but only if, there can be what I am calling 'causal loops'. Loops which are causal in this stronger and more common sense will therefore be possible iff causal loops in my sense are possible.

Although no one really believes in causal loops, the obvious objection to them has convinced few philosophers. This is the 'I could kill my granny' objection to the most familiar kind of loop, entailed by backward time-travel. Thus suppose $Q_1$ is my leaving in 2001, $Q_2$ my landing in 1901, and $Q_3 \ldots Q_{n-1}$ a causal chain linking $Q_2$ to my leaving, $Q_n = Q_1$. The objection is that if this could happen, then $Q_3 \ldots Q_{n-1}$ could include a fact, like my killing my grandparents before my parents are conceived, that would cause $\sim Q_1$, and this, given $Q_1$, is impossible. So any causal loop, if possible, could be impossible; so since what is possible cannot be impossible, causal loops can never be possible.

The stock reply to this is that of course stories about time travel, like all other stories, must be consistent to be capable of truth. And as consistency is possible – I *can* travel and not kill my grandparents, every $Q_i$ *can* cause

$Q_{i+1}$ and not $\sim Q_{i+1}$ – the possibility of inconsistency cannot show that causal loops are impossible. Indeed not; but they may still *be* impossible, and some consequences of Figure 18 show that they are.

To see why, we must recall that for $Q_{i+1}$ to be causable by $Q_i$, the states of affairs $Q_i$ and $Q_{i+1}$ need not be facta, or even facts. The only facta our causal loops need are the facta $\mathbf{R}_i$ that make each $Q_{i+1}$ causable by $Q_i$. Given these facta, the causal structure of Figure 18 would be the same even if none of $Q_1$ to $Q_n$ were facts. It is the facta $\mathbf{R}_i$, not the actual causes and effects $Q_i$, that make this causal structure a loop.

Next, we must note that all these $\mathbf{R}_i$ are logically independent of each other [16.7]. So if any of Figure 18's loops is possible, so too is any loop got from it by keeping $\mathbf{R}_1$ and changing the other $\mathbf{R}_i$s, e.g. by reducing them to one, $\mathbf{R}_2$, thus making $n=3$. In other words, any causal loop is possible iff the simplest one is: the loop shown below in Figure 19, where $Q_1=Q$, $Q_2=P$ and S is the relevant circumstances, a conjunction of facts including both $\mathbf{R}_1$ and $\mathbf{R}_2$.

$$Q \quad \underline{\quad S \quad} \quad P$$

Figure 19: Simplest causal loop

To see why this is impossible, consider the two pairs of logically independent chances needed to make P/~P and Q/~Q causable by each other:

$$ch_Q(P)=p \text{ and } ch_{\sim Q}(P)=p';$$
$$ch_P(Q)=q \text{ and } ch_{\sim P}(Q)=q'.$$

The Frequency condition on these four chances makes each of them entail a corresponding limiting frequency in a collective of hypothetical instances of kinds Q\*, ~Q\*, P\*, ~P\* and S\* defined by S, Q and P [14.4], as follows.

First, in any circumstances of kind S\* an instance either of kind Q\* or of kind ~Q\* will be accompanied by an instance of P\* or of ~P\*. For example, every person like Don who climbs something like Castle Rock (S\*) will either fall (Q\*) or not (~Q\*) and either die (P\*) or not (~P\*).

Then in any finite class {S\*} of hypothetical instances of kind S\*, the following frequencies, i.e. fractions, will exist:

$f$(P\*/Q\*): the fraction of Q\*s accompanied by P\*s;
$f$(P\*/~Q\*): the fraction of ~Q\*s accompanied by P\*s;
$f$(Q\*/P\*): the fraction of P\*s accompanied by Q\*s;
$f$(Q\*/~P\*): the fraction of ~P\*s accompanied by Q\*s.

Then what the Frequency condition on the corresponding chances entails is that, as the number of S*s in {S*} increases without limit, so:

(44a) $f(P^*/Q^*) \rightarrow f_\infty(P^*/Q^*) = ch_Q(P) = p$,
and   $f(P^*/\sim Q^*) \rightarrow f_\infty(P^*/\sim Q^*) = ch_{\sim Q}(P) = p'$;
(44b) $f(Q^*/P^*) \rightarrow f_\infty(Q^*/P^*) = ch_P(Q) = q$,
and   $f(Q^*/\sim P^*) \rightarrow f_\infty(Q^*/\sim P^*) = ch_{\sim P}(Q) = q'$.

So for the basic causal loop shown in Figure 19 to be possible, our class {S*} of hypothetical instances of S* must satisfy (44a) and (44b) for all individually possible values of the logically independent $p, p', q$ and $q'$. But it cannot, as we shall now see.

Consider first the chances,

$$ch_Q(P)=p \text{ and } ch_{\sim Q}(P)=p',$$

of any Q* and ~Q* in {S*} being accompanied by a P*. Suppose that

$$p = 0.4 \text{ and } p' = 0.8,$$

and that {S*} has as many Q*s as ~Q*s: $10 \times 10^{100}$, i.e. ten googolplexes or, for short, 10Gs. Then (44a) and the laws of large numbers [3.4] leave

$$f(P^*/Q^*) \text{ and } f(P^*/\sim Q^*)$$

almost no chance – to put it mildly – of differing by more than (say) 0.1% from $p$ and $p'$, i.e. from 0.4 and 0.8. But then the numbers of Q*s and ~Q*s in {S*} accompanied by P*s and by ~P*s have almost no chance of differing by more than 0.1% from those shown in Figure 20:

| Numbers in Gs | Total | P*s | ~P*s |
|---------------|-------|-----|------|
| Q*s           | 10    | 4   | 6    |
| ~Q*s          | 10    | 8   | 2    |
| Total         | 20    | 12  | 8    |

Figure 20: Numbers of Q*s and ~Q*s accompanied by P*s and by ~P*s

In short, as Figure 20 shows, it is almost certain that {S*} contains a total, ±0.1%, of

12G P*s and 8G ~P*s.

This follows from {S*}'s containing 10G Q*s, each with a chance 0.4 of being accompanied by a P*, and 10G ~Q*s, each with a chance 0.8 of being accompanied by a P*. And if P/~P is causable by Q/~Q, this must be possible.

Now consider the chances of each of these 12G P*s and 8G ~P*s being accompanied by a Q*. If Q/~Q is causable by P/~P, these chances,

$$ch_P(Q)=q \text{ and } ch_{-P}(Q)=q',$$

must exist and be logically independent both of each other and of $ch_Q(P)=p$ and $ch_{-Q}(P)=p'$. So we may consistently suppose, for example, that

$$q = 0.25 \text{ and } q' = 0.5.$$

But then (44b) and the laws of large numbers leave the numbers of P*s and ~P*s in {S*} accompanied by Q*s and by ~Q*s almost no chance of differing by more than 0.1% from those shown in Figure 21:

| Numbers in Gs | Total | Q*s | ~Q*s |
|---------------|-------|-----|------|
| P*s | 12 | 3 | 9 |
| ~P*s | 8 | 4 | 4 |
| Total | 20 | 7 | 13 |

Figure 21: Numbers of P*s and ~P*s accompanied by Q*s and by ~Q*s

But this flatly contradicts Figure 20: the fact that {S*} contains

10G Q*s and 10G ~Q*s

cannot possibly make it almost certain that it contains

7G Q*s and 13G ~Q*s!

Yet if all four of the logically independent chances entailed by a causal loop between Q and P can exist, this must be possible. So, since it is not possible, not all of these chances can exist: i.e.

Q cannot be causable by P if P is causable by Q.

So the causal loop of Figure 19 cannot exist; and nor therefore can any other causal loop.

## 4 Contiguity

This argument against causal loops assumes nothing about the locations of Q and P. It applies to all facts however large or small, near or far apart, they may be. No causal loop, of any size, is possible. But if the proof of this is independent of where Q and P are, what can it tell us about their relative locations?

The answer lies in our causal criterion for spatiotemporal coincidence [§3]: 'for any two facts to coincide is for them to be able to interact immediately'. Yet we have just seen that no two facts can *inter*act at all, let alone immediately. So if P is causable by Q, then since Q cannot also be causable by P, Q and P cannot coincide.

But what then of our example of immediate interaction in §3? If facts cannot interact, how can the pressure *p* of a gas sample *g* interact with its volume *v*? Easily. For the fact that the later

P:      *pg* during $[t,t'')$ and
P′:     *vg* during $[t,t'')$

cannot cause each other does not stop them both being caused by the earlier

Q:      *pg* during $[t',t)$ and by
Q′:     *vg* during $[t',t)$.

Neither of these two pairs of coincident facts, P and P′, and Q and Q′, need form a causal loop to do this, since neither member of either pair need be causable by the other.

This shows how *pg* and *vg* can interact without causal loops – and, as I remarked in §3, do so immediately. For in this case the two causes, like the two effects, coincide in space, and *t* is the first instant after $[t'',t)$. *pg* and *vg* during $[t,t')$ can therefore be immediate effects of *pg* and *vg* during $[t'',t)$. So even in a dense spacetime a cause Q can have an effect P with no D such that Q causes D and D causes P [5.4]: causation's contiguity connotation does not in fact rule out immediate causation.

But this still does not tell us why causation must satisfy this connotation, i.e. why action at a distance *must* be mediated. 'No action at a distance' is of course an old and still widely held maxim, but that does not prove it: so after all is causal determinism, which modern physics, among other things, shows to be false [5.1–3]. Whether modern physics also threatens causal contiguity is still disputed, partly because different authors mean different things by 'causes'. I think it only threatens the contiguity of something weaker than causation, e.g.

> the sense of locality that requires that correlation between spacelike separated events always be factorable-out by a common cause (Skyrms 1980 IIB2).

Whether modern physics really violates locality in this sense I cannot say. But I do not need to. For unless and until physics violates something that includes what I mean by 'causation', which locality does not, it is not my business – which is simply to show why, whatever physics says, a causation that makes causes evidence for, explain and provide means to their effects [5.4; 7.1] will also make them contiguous to their immediate effects.

If causation were a relation between facts or particulars, unmediated action at a distance might well be possible, even given what I have argued elsewhere, namely that

> the principal function of the maxim 'no action at a distance' ... is to use their effects to identify, and to locate in spacetime, events in general and changes in particular (Mellor 1981 p. 125).

This I believe is what underlies our causal test for coincidence, which says that, if P and Q interact immediately, they coincide. But it does not entail that test, since a fact may have more immediate causes and effects than are needed to locate it. Why then can some of them not be remote in space or time? If causation is a relation I know of no good answer to that question.

But causation is not a relation [11; 13]; and now we know what it is we can see why causes must be contiguous to their immediate effects. To do this we must start from the fact that, by definition, any P is causable by any Q iff P has chances, $ch_Q(P)=p$ and $ch_{\sim Q}(P)=p'$, with and without Q [§3].

Next, we must recall that these chances are facts about circumstances S which are located not where P is but where Q is [2.2]. Specifically, as we saw in chapter 14.3, the fact that $ch_Q(P)=p$ is the fact

$S_1$: S includes a factum **R** that makes '$R\&Q \Rightarrow ch(P)=p$' true

(or, more generally, to let Q be extended in spacetime,

$S_1$: S includes a fact $\Pi R$ such that '$\Pi R\&Q \Rightarrow ch(P)=p$' is true,

where $\Pi R$ conjoins as many point instances **R** of some law **N** as are needed to make '$\Pi R\&Q \Rightarrow ch(P)=p$' true [16.7]).

Similarly, the fact that $ch_{\sim Q}(P)=p'$ is the fact

$S_1'$: S includes a factum **R'** that makes '$R'\&\sim Q \Rightarrow ch(P)=p''$' true,

where **R'** may be **R**, as for simplicity I am assuming that it is [§3].

It follows that, as chapter 14.3's equations (modified by setting R'=R)

(30) $\quad ch_Q(P) = 1-ch_Q(\sim P) = (\imath p)(R\&Q \Rightarrow ch(P)=p)$ and
(30~) $ch_{\sim Q}(P) = 1-ch_{\sim Q}(\sim P) = (\imath p')(R\&\sim Q \Rightarrow ch(P)=p')$

show, the existence of **R** is enough to give P and ~P the chances, with and without Q, that make P/~P causable by Q/~Q.

But **R**'s existence is not enough to make P/~P *immediately* causable by Q/~Q. That takes two more facts about S derived from chapter 14.3:

$S_2$: S includes no **T** that makes '$T\&Q \Rightarrow ch(\sim R)=p$' true for any $p$;
$S_2'$: S includes no **T** that makes '$T\&\sim Q \Rightarrow ch(\sim R)=p$' true for any $p$.

As we saw in chapter 14.3, what these facts do is ensure, by depriving Q and ~Q of any propensity to yield ~R, that if **R** entails

$$R\&Q \Rightarrow ch(P)=p \text{ and } R\&\sim Q \Rightarrow ch(P)=p'$$

then it will also be true that

$$Q \Rightarrow ch(P)=p \text{ and } \sim Q \Rightarrow ch(P)=p'.$$

Now, as we also saw, there are other possible facts, besides $S_2$ and $S_2'$, which can do this job. In particular, it can also be done by the incompatible

$S_3$: S includes *either* (b) a **T** that makes 'T&Q$\Rightarrow$ch(~R)=0' true and
(c') no **V** that makes 'V&Q$\Rightarrow$ch(~T)=p' true for any p;
*or*  (b), (c) a **V** that makes 'V&Q$\Rightarrow$ch(~T)=0' true and
(d') no **W** that makes 'W&Q$\Rightarrow$ch(~V)=p' true for any p;
*or*  ...,

and its obvious counterpart for ~Q, which I shall call '$S_3'$'. But there is one crucial difference: whereas $S_3\&S_3'$ can only ensure that

$$Q \Rightarrow ch(P)=p \text{ iff } R\&Q \Rightarrow ch(P)=p \text{ and}$$
$$\sim Q \Rightarrow ch(P)=p' \text{ iff } R\&\sim Q \Rightarrow ch(P)=p'$$

indirectly, by giving Q a propensity – a zero propensity – to yield ~R, $S_2\&S_2'$ does the job directly. And this, as we shall now see, is what makes P *immediately* causable by Q.

$S_2\&S_2'$ entails that no factum gives Q or ~Q any propensity, not even a zero one, to yield either R or ~R. That is,

R/~R is not causable by Q/~Q.

This matters because not only, by definition of **R**, is 'R&Q$\Rightarrow$ch(P)=p' true, but

'~R&Q$\Rightarrow$ch(P)=p'''

may also be true for some p''. And if so, then given Q, P will have chances

$$ch_R(P)=p \text{ and } ch_{\sim R}(P)=p'',$$

and may therefore, if p>p'', be caused by **R** as well as by Q. But even if it is, $S_2\&S_2'$, by entailing that R is not causable by Q, entails that

Q cannot cause P by causing **R**,

so that **R**, despite being what *makes* Q cause P, cannot in the relevant sense *mediate* this causation: that is, **R** cannot be a D such that Q causes D and D causes P [5.4].

And if **R** cannot mediate this causation, then nothing can. For if anything did, then whether Q causes P would depend on that too, and '$S_2\&S_2'$' would be false. Similarly if Q causes ~P, or ~Q causes P or causes ~P. In each case it is $S_2\&S_2'$ that makes the causation immediate. In short, if

$S_1\&S_1'$ is what makes P/~P *causable* by Q/~Q,
$S_2\&S_2'$ is what makes P/~P *immediately* causable by Q/~Q.

This then tells us for all Q and P, without invoking their locations, what it is that makes P immediately causable by Q. So suppose it is, and suppose that Q and P are facts. To see what this says about their relative locations, recall that any $ch_Q(P)=p$ in any relevant circumstances S entails that there are kinds Q*, P* and S* such that, in any S*, any hypothetical Q* has the same chance $p$ of being accompanied by a P* [15.2; §3]. But what does 'accompanied by' mean here? In other words, *which* P* does a given Q*, say Q, have this propensity $p$ to yield? As we shall now see, the only possible answer to this question is: a P* that is contiguous to Q.

First, we must realise that this question needs an answer, since $ch_Q(P)=p$ is not a chance that *some* instance of 'P*' is true: for that chance, if $0<p<1$, depends on how many Q*s there are, which $ch_Q(P)$ does not. Don's chance of dying if he falls, for example, is not the chance that *someone* who falls as he does dies, which depends on how many such people there are: it is the chance that *he* dies. So $ch_Q(P)$ must measure Q's propensity to yield a specific P*, or at least one associated more closely with Q than with any other Q* – namely P.

How can it do this? If 'P' and 'Q' are about the same particular the answer may seem obvious: the dying that is causable by Don's falling is *Don*'s dying. But this answer is not always available, since 'P' and 'Q' need not be about the same or indeed any particular [14.4]. Sharing a particular could not for example be what makes the fact P, that *no* one dies at Castle Rock on 4 June 1988, causable by the fact Q, that *no* one falls there then. What then could make this P the instance of P* – of people not dying – which this Q has a propensity to yield?

Again the answer is obvious: proximity. It is no one's dying *near* Q, i.e. near Castle Rock on 4 June 1988, which is causable by Q. And this answer, unlike any other, *is* always available, because all singular causes and effects have locations. Of course the answer only really works for immediate causation, since chains of causes and effects can make P causable by a very remote Q*: as when my view of the night sky is affected by facts about galaxies millions of light-years away. Yet even this depends indirectly on proximity, because galaxies will only affect those who are linked to them by chains of contiguous causation embodied in the photons they emit.

And as in this case, so in general. No P is causable by a distant Q unless it is also causable by a proximate P′ which is similarly causable by Q. This I maintain is a necessary fact. Every P must be contiguous to any Q by which it is immediately causable, simply because contiguity to Q is what makes P the P* that Q and ~Q have immediate propensities to yield. This is why causes must be contiguous to their immediate effects.

But if this is what makes causation satisfy its contiguity connotation, one last question remains: why *contiguity* rather than *coincidence*, which would get P even closer to Q? Because a P that is causable by Q cannot coincide with Q? But why not, provided Q is not also causable by P, thus ruling out the impossible causal loops of §3? Why in short must §3's causal test for coincidence require facts to be able to *inter*act, which we know they cannot do?

The answer is that we cannot meet the proviso needed to rule out causal loops, because Q and P often instantiate the same kind of fact, so that

$$Q*=P*.$$

Take the gas example from §3, where

P = *pg* during [*t,t″*) and
Q = *pg* during [*t′,t*).

Here, because P and Q are of the same kind (*pg*), if the P* which Q causes coincided with Q, it would *be* Q. But P cannot be Q, because

'Q causes Q'

must be false for all Q [1.6], since it lacks all causation's connotations [5.4]: no fact can be evidence for, explain or be a means to itself. Moreover, if the P* that Q causes could be (and so was) Q, Q could not cause any *other* P*, like the later P, *pg* during [*t,t′*), that Q does cause; which is absurd.

So neither in this case nor in any other can a P* that is immediately causable by Q coincide with Q: which is why contiguity to Q is as close to Q as anything causable by Q can get.

## 5 Causability and precedence

We have seen that there can be no causal loops [§3] and that causally linked facts cannot coincide [§4]. This makes causation pick out a single linear dimension of spacetime with a direction given by the asymmetry of

P/~P is causable by Q/~Q

(Reichenbach 1956 ch. II.5). So if that dimension *is* time, this fact shows why any possible spacetime, however many spatial dimensions it has, can have only one time dimension. More: it shows that any possible world with laws, and hence chances and causability, must have at least one dimension, that of time, even if it has no space.

Furthermore, if time is the dimension of causation, causation's temporal connotation [5.4] follows at once: causes *must* precede their effects. And this, since the past precedes the present, which precedes the future, and our perceptions are effects of what we perceive (or misperceive), shows why we can never perceive the future or affect the past. All this is explained if time is the causal dimension of spacetime. How then can we show that it is?

First, we must show how, if precedence is entailed by causability, it can be transitive, irreflexive and asymmetrical, as we know it is [§1]. The last two we have shown already: Q's inability to cause itself, either immediately or *via* a causal loop, will make precedence *irreflexive*; and the fact that no Q is causable by a P that is causable by Q will make it *asymmetrical*. It is less obvious why a causally defined precedence should be transitive, since

> 'P is causable by Q'

need not and often does not follow from

> 'P is causable by a D that is causable by Q'.

Consider for example our smoker Bill's chances of expiring soon (E). Suppose E is causable by Bill's getting cancer (C), which is causable by his smoking (B). That is, E has chances if Bill gets cancer and if he does not, as C has if Bill smokes and if he does not: $ch_C(E)$, $ch_{-C}(E)$, $ch_B(C)$ and $ch_{-B}(C)$ all exist. Yet Bill's dying may still not be causable by his smoking, since he may still not have a chance, high or low, of dying if he smokes: $ch_B(E)$ may not exist.

For suppose Bill's chance of dying if he gets cancer, $ch_C(E)$, depends on whether he gets another illness (J). If so, his chance of dying if he smokes, $ch_B(E)$, depends on his chance of getting this illness if he smokes: $ch_B(J)$. But if no law links Bill's properties, including his smoking, to his getting this other illness, $ch_B(J)$ will not exist. But then J will not be causable by B; and nor then will E, since $ch_B(E)$ will not exist either, even though C is causable by B and E is causable by C.

Causability then, unlike precedence, is not transitive. But it can still entail precedence. For since precedence *is* transitive, then

> *if*    'P is causable by Q' entails 'Q precedes P'
> *then*   'P is causable by a D causable by Q' and
>         'P is causable by a D causable by a D′ causable by Q' and
>         etc.

entail it too. So if Q precedes any P that is causable by Q, it will also precede any P linked to Q by a causal chain, even if P is not causable by Q.

Causability can therefore fix the precedence of facts. But to make time the dimension of causation, it must also fix the precedence of spacetime points. To see how it does this, recall that any pair of law statements, like

(37)   '$(x)(Kx \Rightarrow ch(Lx)=p)$' and
(37~)   '$(x)(\sim Kx \Rightarrow ch(Lx)=p')$',

must be true of all hypothetical particulars $x$ – and thus of $K$-particulars at any point or region that can be the location of a $K$-particular [16.1,7].

So then, if causability entails precedence, any such region [$st$] at which a hypothetical $x$ is $K$ must precede every [$s't'$] at which that $x$ is $L$. But *every* point will either be in such an [$st$] for *some* hypothetical $Kx$ or in such an [$s't'$] for some other hypothetical $Lx$ – and all but the first and last points of spacetime (if any) will be in both. The causability entailed by the laws that (37) and (37~) state will therefore fix, for every pair of spacetime regions and hence of points, which if either precedes the other.

But this account of how laws fix the precedence of spacetime points raises a serious question. For if one pair of laws can fix the time order of all points, so can other, logically independent, pairs of laws. But what makes all these orders consistent? What for example stops laws stated by

(38)   '$(x)(Gx \Rightarrow ch(Lx)=p)$' and
(38~)   '$(x)(\sim Gx \Rightarrow ch(Lx)=p')$',

making $s't'$ precede $st$ when (37) and (37~) make $st$ precede $s't'$?

To answer this question we must recall that '$st \ll s't'$' does *not*, as for the sake of argument I assumed in §1, state a relation « between independently existing entities $st$ and $s't'$: an assumption which is false on both counts.

First, no such universal « exists: what makes any

'$st \ll s't'$'

true is not a factum $st \ll s't'$ but the fact that for some Q at $st$ and P at $s't'$,

       P is causable by Q
*or*    P is causable by a D causable by Q
*or*    P is causable by a D causable by a D' causable by Q
*or*    …

Second, $st$ and $s't'$ do not exist independently of the facts and facta located at them: they merely distinguish different instances of the laws of nature which, among other things, fix their time order [16.7]. And since those laws must be compatible to coexist, they cannot impose incompatible orders on the points that instantiate them. That is why all laws must impose the same time order on all pairs of points and regions in spacetime.

## 6  The causal form of inner sense

We have seen how causability can fix the time order of all spacetime points. Why then should anyone deny that it does so? Why indeed should we not make it do so by definition, giving causation its temporal connotation by defining time as the causal dimension of spacetime?

The reason is that time has another, *experiential*, connotation, relating it to our experience of it. And just as it takes more than a definition to make causation's connotations go together [§1], so it takes more than a definition to make time's causal and experiential connotations go together.

What is time's experiential connotation? It is not simply the fact that

> of any two elements of time of which I am directly conscious one is after the other (Robb 1914 p. 4),

for to know this I must also be aware of this fact about them, as I often am: I am often aware not only of the temporally ordered elements of my experience but also of their order.

This is what I mean by time's experiential connotation, which could be used to define time as, in Kant's words,

> nothing but the form of inner sense (1781 B50).

But this will not do, because it will not explain why causes precede their effects. It might do so if causation and time were merely the inevitable figments of our minds that Kant says they are (1781 B124). But no such view can explain causation's other connotations, notably the means–end one [7.6], and the laws and chances they entail. This is why, like Reichenbach (1956 pp. 13–15), I take it for granted that our world's apparent causal and temporal order is more than a Kantian presupposition of experience.

This is not to deny that time's experiential connotation needs accounting for: it does. And part of it we have accounted for already, by showing that causation would exist even in a one-dimensional spacetime. For this, if time is the dimension of causation, at once explains

> the fact that time order is possible in a realm which has no spatial order, namely the world of the psychic experiences of an individual human being (Reichenbach 1928 §16).

What it does *not* explain is why the time order we perceive our experiences to have is that given by time's causal connotation. To explain this we must see how we perceive time order, in our own experiences and in other facts.

We perceive time order all the time, whenever we see motion or any other change: thus to see that a clock's second hand is moving clockwise is to see for example that it passes the figure '1' on the clock face *before* it passes the figure '2'. Similarly when, with any of our senses, we perceive changes in colours, temperatures, pressures, sounds, tastes, etc. We are constantly perceiving time order in the world around us, as well as in our own experiences. And it is the causal structure of these perceptions that makes the perceived time order of our experiences coincide with that given by causation, as I shall now show.

To show this I must start by making two points about what I shall mean here by 'perception'. First, I shall include misperception: perceptions need not be true. Second, as we need not believe what we see, I shall distinguish perceptions from the beliefs they usually cause. In short, I shall take

'*x* perceives P'

to entail neither

'P' nor '*x* believes P'.

Thus suppose that Bill, an astronomer, sees a solar flare occur, Q', just after hearing a clock strike one, Q. He knows that, as it takes longer for light to come from the sun than for sound to come from the clock, Q' actually precedes Q. So he does not believe what his senses tell him, namely that Q precedes Q'. But they do still tell him this. There is an obvious sense in which Bill perceives this without believing it, the sense in which I see without believing that a conjurer's rabbit comes out of an empty hat. This illustrates what I shall mean hereafter by 'perceive', 'see', 'hear', etc.

The causal structure of Bill's perception of the time order of Q and Q' is shown below (not to scale!) in Figure 22. The thick line represents Bill's so-called *world line*, i.e. where he is at any time or rather (so as not to beg the present question) his location in the non-causal dimensions of spacetime at any location in the causal dimension.

The next thing to note about Figure 22 is that, because its vertical axis represents this causal dimension of spacetime, any 'P' in it that represents a fact P which is causable by a given Q must be placed above 'Q'. Hence the figure's layout, in which

Q is the clock's striking one,
P is Bill's hearing Q,
Q' is the sun's flaring,
P' is Bill's seeing Q', and
P'' is Bill's thereby seeing Q«Q', i.e. that Q precedes Q'.

The arrows show the relevant causal links between these facts, namely that

Q causes P, Q′ causes P′, Q′ causes P″ and P causes P″.

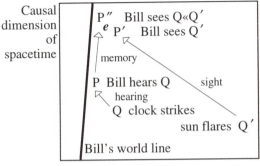

Figure 22: Perception of time order

Three more points about Figure 22 must also be noted before we go on. First, I have assumed that P is caused by Q, and P′ by Q′, i.e. that Bill's perceptions that Q and that Q′ are true, even though P″, his perception that Q«Q′, is false. This assumption is made only to simplify the ensuing argument, which does not really need it. All the argument really needs is the fact that P″ is caused by P as well as by Q′, as of course it is: for of course Bill cannot perceive that Q precedes Q′ unless he perceives Q.

Second, I shall assume for simplicity that P′ and P″ *coincide* in space-time, although of course if

P″ is causable by P′,

they can at best be *contiguous* [§4]. In fact they can be either, as we can see by distinguishing the *fact* that Bill sees something from the *event* which is his seeing of it – the former being an existential fact about the latter [11.3]. Then if P′ is the fact that Bill has a perception of Q′, and similarly for P″ and Q«Q′, then for P′ and P″ to *coincide* these must be the same event:

e = Bill's perception that Q′ = Bill's perception that Q«Q′.

But while P′ may well be essential to *e*, P″ is not: Bill's perception of Q′ would obviously exist even if he never noticed whether Q«Q′. So even if

Q′ causes *e*,
P only *affects e*

by causing P″, an inessential fact about *e* [12.2]. Moreover P can only have this effect on *e* if P′ is also a fact about *e*, since P can obviously not make Bill see Q«Q′ unless he also sees Q′. In short, P can only cause P″ if Q′ does so too, either directly – as I am assuming – or *via* P′. And either way P″ will be another example, to add to those given in §2, of an effect with two causes P and Q′, each of which depends on the other for its efficacy.

Third, despite calling the link between P″ and P 'memory' in Figure 22, there are three common assumptions about memory that I must disown in this case: (i) what we remember must precede our remembering it (which would beg the present question); (ii) P″ includes remembering P as well as Q (it need not); (iii) Bill is aware of P″ as a memory of Q (he need not be).

Yet even without these assumptions, 'memory' is the best word for the link between P and P″, since it does memory's main job: it lets a perception cause its content to be embodied at another time in another state of mind. Here it makes Bill's perception P cause its content, Q, to occur again in the content, Q«Q′, of P″ – and to do so as *preceding* Q′, not as succeeding it.

In short, this link makes the *causal* order of P and P″ fix the *time* order which Bill thereby perceives Q and Q′ to have. For obviously, if Bill's perception of Q′ had affected his perception of Q and not *vice versa*, he would have perceived that Q′«Q. And as for Bill, so for everyone:

> the causal order of our perceptions of facts is the time order we thereby perceive those facts to have.

This I say is what makes the dimension of causation satisfy time's experiential connotation. But it must be rightly understood; and two points especially need making to meet two obvious objections to it. First, I do not of course deny that Bill can see Q and Q′ without seeing whether Q«Q′: i.e. that P and P′ (and hence *e*) can exist without P″. All I am claiming is that

> *if* we see time order in the way I have described, the time order we see will be the causal order of the perceptions we see it by.

This also meets the other objection, that unconscious perceptual processing may make Bill see Q′«Q instead of Q«Q′ (Dennett 1991 p. 149). So it may, but then the causal structure of this perception will be more complex than that shown in Figure 22. This possibility does not refute my claim that

> if we see time order *in the way I have described*, the time order we see will be the causal order of the perceptions we see it by.

This I maintain is a necessary truth: not because it is what we *mean* by 'time order' but because it is what enables us, when we perceive any pair of facts, to perceive their time order in this way.

Now let us apply all this to Bill's perceptions not of outside facts, like the sun flaring or a clock striking, but of his own conscious experiences, as shown below in Figure 23. Here the horizontal axis need not represent non-causal dimensions of spacetime: this can be Reichenbach's

> realm which has no spatial order ... the psychic experiences of an individual human being.

But these experiences will still have a causal order, as when a smell like cigar smoke, Q, gives Bill a sudden craving, Q', for tobacco. Our question then is this: how do Bill's perceptions of Q and Q' make him perceive their time order – and, unlike those shown in Figure 22, make him do so truly?

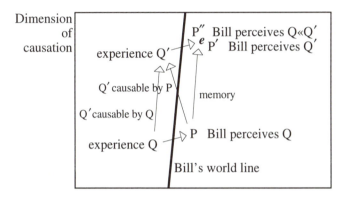

Figure 23: Perceiving the time order of experiences

First, in Figure 23, unlike Figure 22, we can be sure that P and P' are true, simply because conscious experience is, by definition, self-intimating. So whatever kind of experience Q is, to be *conscious* it must be a virtually deterministic cause of P – $ch_Q(P)\approx1$ and $ch_{\sim Q}(P)\approx0$ – as Q' must be of P'. But even if consciousness guarantees Bill true perceptions of Q and Q', it will not guarantee the truth of his perception P'', that Q precedes Q'. What will?

The short answer is 'nothing': for as Q«Q', unlike Q and Q', may not be self-intimating, Bill may not perceive this time order at all. And even if he does he may, if he does it by further processing, perceive it falsely. But not if he does it as depicted in Figure 23. For then, as in Figure 22, the causal order of his perceptions, P and P', of his experiences Q and Q', will be the time order he thereby perceives Q and Q' to have. That is, the fact that

> Bill's perception of Q affects his perception of Q',

rather than the other way round, makes Bill perceive, truly or falsely, that

(45)   Q precedes Q′

rather than the other way round. And if time *is* the dimension of causation, then the following two arguments show that this perception will be true.

(i) Since P causes P″, P precedes P″and hence the coincident P′. And as memory spans time, we may take it that, for some modest time interval [*t*],

(46)   P precedes P′ by [*t*],

i.e. that Bill perceives Q′ some time after he perceives Q.

On the other hand, we may assume that Q and Q′ intimate themselves to Bill, if not immediately, then at least practically instantaneously, i.e. in a time interval very much less than [*t*], so that

> Q is practically simultaneous with P, and
> Q′ is practically simultaneous with P′

– facts which, with (46), entail (45) and hence that Bill's perception P″, that Q precedes Q′, is true.

(ii) I have assumed that Q′, Bill's sudden craving, is caused by Q, his experiencing a cigar-like smell; and even if Q does not in fact cause Q′ (say because Q′'s chance is as great without Q as with it), it always could: i.e., as shown in Figure 23,

> Q′ is causable by Q,

But this itself entails, if time is the dimension of causation, that

> Q precedes Q′,

and hence that Bill's perception P″, that Q precedes Q′, is true.

Moreover, Bill's craving Q′ could also have been caused by P, i.e. by his *perceiving* that he was experiencing a cigar-like smell, so that

> Q′ is causable by P,

as is also shown in Figure 23. And what this means is that Bill's perception that Q precedes Q′ *must* be true. For now, as we can see at once from Figure 23, neither of the relevant causal links, namely that

> Q′ is causable by Q and
> P″ is caused by P,

can be reversed without creating a causal loop, which is impossible [§3]. But then the first link must entail the same time order of Q and Q′ that the second link makes Bill perceive, namely that Q precedes Q′.

This shows how, if time is the causal dimension of spacetime, we can know the time order of our own experiences. It explains, as promised at the start of this section, why the dimension of spacetime that satisfies time's causal connotation will also satisfy its experiential one. And this is enough to show that time must indeed be the dimension of causation. For while, as we have just seen, time's experiential connotation is derivable from its causal one, the converse is not true. No Kantian form of inner sense can entail the other asymmetrical connotations of causation: that causes explain and are means to their effects. But then no experiential definition of time can tell us why a fact Q which explains and is a means to a fact P must also precede it. The only answer to that question is the answer given here: the form of inner sense is causation.

# Bibliography

Works referred to are listed below together with some recent and relevant works in English (articles in listed collections are not listed separately).

Anscombe, G. E. M. (1971) 'Causality and determination', *Causation*, ed. E. Sosa and M. Tooley (1993), Oxford: Oxford University Press, 88–104.

Armstrong, D. M. (1978) *Universals and Scientific Realism* (2 volumes), Cambridge: Cambridge University Press.

(1983) *What is a Law of Nature?*, Cambridge: Cambridge University Press.

(1989) *Universals: An Opinionated Introduction*, Boulder, Colorado: Westview Press.

Armstrong, D. M. and Heathcote, A. (1991) 'Causes and laws', *Noûs* **25**, 63–73.

Ayer, A. J. (1956) 'What is a law of nature?', *The Concept of a Person and Other Essays* (1963), London: Macmillan, 209–34.

Bacon, J. *et al.*, eds (1993) *Ontology, Causality and Mind*, Cambridge: Cambridge University Press.

Bealer, G. (1993) 'Universals', *Journal of Philosophy* **90**, 5–32.

Bennett, J. (1988) *Events and Their Names*, Oxford: Clarendon Press.

Bigelow, J. and Pargetter, R. (1991) *Science and Necessity*, Cambridge: Cambridge University Press.

Braddon-Mitchell, D. (1993) 'The microstructural causation hypothesis', *Erkenntnis* **39**, 257–83.

Bradley, F. H. (1897) *Appearance and Reality*, 2nd edn, Oxford: Clarendon Press.

Brown, B. (1992) 'Defending backwards causation', *Canadian Journal of Philosophy* **22**, 4, 429–43.

Butterfield, J. (1985) 'Spatial and temporal parts', *Philosophical Quarterly* **35**, 32–44.

(1992) 'Bell's theorem: what it takes', *British Journal for the Philosophy of Science* **43**, 41–83.

Campbell, K. (1990) *Abstract Particulars*, Oxford: Blackwell.

Carnap, R. (1955) 'Statistical and inductive probability', *The Structure of Scientific Thought*, ed. E. H. Madden, Boston: Houghton Mifflin, 269–79.

(1962) *Logical Foundations of Probability*, 2nd edn, Chicago: University of Chicago Press.

Carroll, J. W. (1991) 'Property-level causation?', *Philosophical Studies* **63**, 245–70.

(1993) *Laws of Nature*, Cambridge: Cambridge University Press.

Cartwright, N. (1983) *How the Laws of Physics Lie*, Oxford: Clarendon Press.

Castañeda, H.-N. (1984) 'Causes, causality and energy', *Midwest Studies in Philosophy* **9**, 17–27.

Clendinnen, F. J. (1992) 'Nomic dependence and causation', *Philosophy of Science* **59**, 341–60.

Cohen, L. J. and Hesse, M. B., eds (1980) *Applications of Inductive Logic*, Oxford: Oxford University Press.

Crane, T. (1991–2) 'Mental causation and mental reality', *Proceedings of the Aristotelian Society* **92**, 185–202.

Cross, C. B. (1992) 'Counterfactuals and event causation', *Australasian Journal of Philosophy* **70**, 307–23.

Daly, C. (1994) 'Tropes', *Proceedings of the Aristotelian Society* **94**, 253–61.

Davidson, D. (1980) *Essays on Actions and Events*, Oxford: Clarendon Press.

de Finetti, B. (1937) 'Foresight: its logical laws, its subjective sources' (transl. H. E. Kyburg Jr), *Studies in Subjective Probability*, ed. H. E. Kyburg Jr and H. E. Smokler (1964), New York: Wiley, 93–158.

Dennett, D. C. (1991) *Consciousness Explained*, London: Penguin.

Dowe, P. (1992) 'Process causality and asymmetry', *Erkenntnis* **37**, 179–96.

Dretske, F. (1977) 'Laws of nature', *Philosophy of Science* **44**, 246–68.

Ducasse, C. J. (1926) 'On the nature and the observability of the causal relation', *Causation*, ed. E. Sosa and M. Tooley (1993), Oxford: Oxford University Press, 125–36.

Dudman, V. H. (1991) 'Interpretations of "if" sentences', *Conditionals*, ed. F. Jackson, Oxford: Oxford University Press, 202–32.

Dummett, M. (1964) 'Bringing about the past', *Truth and Other Enigmas* (1978), London: Duckworth, 333–50.

Dupré, J. (1984) 'Probabilistic causality emancipated', *Midwest Studies in Philosophy* **9**, 169–75.

——— (1993) *The Disorder of Things*, Cambridge, Mass.: Harvard University Press.

Dupré, J. and Cartwright, N. (1988) 'Probability and causality: why Hume and indeterminism don't mix', *Noûs* **22**, 521–36.

Earman, J. (1989) *World Enough and Space–Time*, Cambridge, Mass.: MIT Press.

Eells, E. (1982) *Rational Decision and Causality*, Cambridge: Cambridge University Press.

——— (1990) *Probabilistic Causality*, Cambridge: Cambridge University Press.

Ellis, B. and Lierse, C. (1994) 'Dispositional essentialism', *Australasian Journal of Philosophy* **72**, 27–45.

Ellis, R. D. (1992) 'A critique of concepts of non-sufficient causation', *Philosophical Inquiry* **14**, 1–10.

Fales, E. (1990) *Causation and Universals*, London: Routledge.

Faye, J. *et al.*, eds (1994) *Logic and Causal Reasoning*, Berlin: Akademie Verlag.

Fetzer, J. H., ed. (1988) *Probability and Causality*, Dordrecht: Reidel.

Fisher, R. A. (1959) *Statistical Methods and Scientific Inference*, 2nd edn, Edinburgh: Oliver and Boyd.

Gasking, D. (1955) 'Causation and recipes', *Mind* **64**, 479–87.

Glymour, C. *et al.* (1991) 'Causal inference', *Erkenntnis* **35**, 151–89.

Harman, G. (1973) *Thought*, Princeton: Princeton University Press.

Hausman, D. M. (1992) 'Thresholds, transitivity, overdetermination, and events', *Analysis* **52**, 159–63.

——— (1993) 'Why don't effects explain their causes?', *Synthese* **94**, 227–44.

——— (1993) 'Linking causal and explanatory asymmetry', *Philosophy of Science* **60**, 435–51.

Heil, J. and Mele, A., eds (1993) *Mental Causation*, Oxford: Clarendon Press.

Hempel, C. G. (1965) 'Aspects of scientific explanation', *Aspects of Scientific Explanation and Other Essays in the Philosophy of Science*, New York: The Free Press, 331–496.

Hitchcock, C. R. (1993) 'A generalized probabilistic theory of causal relevance', *Synthese* **97**, 3, 335–64.

Honderich, T. (1988) *A Theory of Determinism*, Oxford: Oxford University Press.

Horwich, P. (1987) *Asymmetries in Time*, Cambridge, Mass.: MIT Press.

Hume, D. (1748) *An Enquiry concerning Human Understanding, Enquiries concerning the Human Understanding and concerning the Principles of Morals*, ed. L. A. Selby-Bigge (1902), Oxford: Clarendon Press, 5–165.

Humphrey, P. (1989) *The Chances of Explanation*, Princeton: Princeton University Press.

Jeffrey, R. C. (1969) 'Statistical explanation *vs* statistical inference', *Essays in Honor of Carl G. Hempel*, ed. N. Rescher, Dordrecht: Reidel, 104–13.

—— (1983) *The Logic of Decision*, 2nd edn, Chicago: University of Chicago Press.

Johnson, W. E. (1921) *Logic, Part I*, Cambridge: Cambridge University Press.

Kant, I. (1781) *Critique of Pure Reason*, English edn, 2nd impression, transl. N. Kemp Smith (1933), London: Macmillan.

Keynes, J. M. (1921) *A Treatise on Probability*, London: Macmillan.

Kim, J. (1976) 'Events as property exemplifications', *Action Theory*, ed. M. Brand and D. Walton, Dordrecht: Reidel, 159–77.

—— (1993) *Supervenience and Mind*, Cambridge: Cambridge University Press.

Kingman, J. F. C. and Taylor, S. J. (1966) *Introduction to Measure and Probability*, Cambridge: Cambridge University Press.

Kripke, S. A. (1980) *Naming and Necessity*, Oxford: Oxford University Press.

Krips, H. (1987) *The Metaphysics of Quantum Theory*, Oxford: Clarendon Press.

Kvart, I. (1991) 'Counterfactuals and causal relevance', *Pacific Philosophical Quarterly* **72**, 314–37.

—— (1994) 'Causal independence', *Philosophy of Science* **61**, 96–114.

Le Poidevin, R. (1991) *Change, Cause and Contradiction*, London: Macmillan.

LePore, E. and McLaughlin, B., eds (1985) *Actions and Events*, Oxford: Blackwell.

Leslie, J. (1989) *Universes*, London: Routledge.

Levi, I. (1990) 'Chance', *Philosophical Topics* **18**, 117–49.

Lewis, D. (1973) *Counterfactuals*, Oxford: Blackwell.

—— (1986) *Philosophical Papers Volume II*, Oxford: Oxford University Press.

Lipton, P. (1991) *Inference to the Best Explanation*, London: Routledge.

Lombard, L. B. (1986) *Events: A Metaphysical Study*, London: Routledge & Kegan Paul.

Lowe, E. J. (1989) *Kinds of Being*, Oxford: Blackwell.

Luce, R. D. and Raiffa, H. (1957) *Games and Decisions*, New York: Wiley.

Mackie, J. L. (1974) *The Cement of the Universe*, Oxford: Clarendon Press.

Mackie, P. (1992) 'Causing, delaying, and hastening: do rains cause fires?', *Mind* **101**, 483–500.

McTaggart, J. McT. E. (1908) 'The unreality of time', *Mind* **18**, 457–84.

Mellor, D. H. (1971) *The Matter of Chance*, Cambridge: Cambridge University Press.

—— (1980) ed., *Prospects for Pragmatism: Essays in Memory of F. P. Ramsey*, Cambridge: Cambridge University Press.

—— (1981) *Real Time*, Cambridge: Cambridge University Press.

—— (1991) *Matters of Metaphysics*, Cambridge: Cambridge University Press.

—— (1998) *Real Time II*, London: Routledge.

Menzies, P. (1988) 'Against causal reductionism', *Mind* **97**, 551–74.

Menzies, P. (1989) 'A unified account of causal relata', *Australasian Journal of Philosophy* **67**, 59–83.

—— (1989) 'Probabilistic causation and causal processes: a critique of Lewis', *Philosophy of Science* **56**, 642–63.

Menzies, P. and Price, H. (1993) 'Causation as a secondary quality', *British Journal for the Philosophy of Science* **44**, 187–203.

Morton, A. (1975) 'Complex individuals and multigrade relations', *Noûs* **9**, 309–18.

Nelson, A. (1985) 'Physical properties', *Pacific Philosophical Quarterly* **66**, 268–82.

Newman, A. (1992) *The Physical Basis of Predication*, Cambridge: Cambridge University Press.

Newton, I. (1713) *Mathematical Principles of Natural Philosophy*, Revised English translation of 2nd edn, transl. A. Motte, ed. F. Cajori (1934), Berkeley: University of California Press.

Newton-Smith, W. H. (1980) *The Structure of Time*, London: Routledge & Kegan Paul.

Oaklander, L. N. and Smith, Q., eds (1994) *The New Theory of Time*, New Haven: Yale University Press.

Oddie, G. (1991) 'Supervenience and higher-order universals', *Australasian Journal of Philosophy* **69**, 20–47.

Olson, K. R. (1987) *An Essay on Facts*, Chicago: University of Chicago Press.

Owens, D. (1992) *Causes and Coincidences*, Cambridge: Cambridge University Press.

Papineau, D. (1986) 'Causal factors, causal inference, causal explanation II', *Aristotelian Society Supplementary Volume* **60**, 116–36.

—— (1990) 'Why supervenience?', *Analysis* **50**, 66–71.

—— (1991) 'Correlations and causes', *British Journal for the Philosophy of Science* **42**, 397–412.

Peacocke, C. (1979) *Holistic Explanation*, Oxford: Clarendon Press.

Pettit, P. *et al.*, eds (1987) *Metaphysics and Morality: Essays in Honour of J. J. C. Smart*, Oxford: Blackwell.

Pollock, J. L. (1990) *Nomic Probability and the Foundations of Probability*, Oxford: Oxford University Press.

Popper, K. R. (1990) *A World of Propensities*, Bristol: Thoemmes.

Price, H. (1991) 'Agency and probabilistic causality', *British Journal for the Philosophy of Science* **42**, 157–76.

—— (1992) 'Agency and causal asymmetry', *Mind* **101**, 501–20.

Quine, W. v. O. (1948) 'On what there is', *From a Logical Point of View*, 2nd edn (1961), Cambridge, Mass.: Harvard University Press, 1–19.

—— (1960) *Word and Object*, Cambridge, Mass.: MIT Press.

—— (1985) 'Events and reification', *Actions and Events*, ed. E. LePore and B. McLaughlin, Oxford: Blackwell, 162–71.

Ramsey, F. P. (1990) *Philosophical Papers*, ed. D. H. Mellor, Cambridge: Cambridge University Press.

Ray, C. (1991) *Time, Space and Philosophy*, London: Routledge.

Ray, G. (1992) 'Probabilistic causality reexamined', *Erkenntnis* **36**, 219–44.

Redhead, M. (1987) *Incompleteness, Nonlocality and Realism*, Oxford: Clarendon Press.

Reichenbach, H. (1928) *The Philosophy of Space and Time*, English transl. (1958), New York: Dover.

—— (1956) *The Direction of Time*, Berkeley: University of California Press.

Robb, A. A. (1914) *A Theory of Time and Space*, Cambridge: Cambridge University Press.

Rosenberg, A. (1992) 'Causation, probability, and the monarchy', *American Philosophical Quarterly* **29**, 305–18.

Ruben, D.-H., ed. (1993) *Explanation*, Oxford: Oxford University Press.

Salmon, W. C. (1984) *Scientific Explanation and the Causal Structure of the World*, Princeton: Princeton University Press.

—— (1979) ed., *Hans Reichenbach: Logical Empiricist*, Dordrecht: Reidel.

Sanford, D. H. (1984) 'The direction of causation and the direction of time', *Midwest Studies in Philosophy* **9**, 53–75.

—— (1994) 'Causation and intelligibility', *Philosophy* **69**, 55–67.

Shalkowski, S. A. (1992) 'Supervenience and causal necessity', *Synthese* **90**, 55–87.

Simons, P. (1987) *Parts: A Study in Ontology*, Oxford: Clarendon Press.

Sklar, L. (1985) *Philosophy and Spacetime Physics*, Berkeley: University of California Press.

Skyrms, B. (1980) *Causal Necessity*, New Haven: Yale University Press.

Skyrms, B. and Harper, W. L., eds (1988) *Causation, Chance and Credence*, Dordrecht: Kluwer.

Sober, E. (1986) 'Causal factors, causal inference, causal explanation I', *Aristotelian Society Supplementary Volume* **60**, 97–115.

Sosa, E. and Tooley, M., eds (1993) *Causation*, Oxford: Oxford University Press.

Strawson, G. (1991) 'The contingent reality of natural necessity', *Analysis* **51**, 209–13.

Strawson, P. F. (1959) *Individuals:*, London: Methuen.

Swinburne, R. (1981) *Space and Time*, 2nd edn, London: Macmillan.

—— (1983) ed., *Space, Time and Causality*, Dordrecht: Reidel.

Swoyer, C. (1982) 'The nature of natural laws', *Australasian Journal of Philosophy* **60**, 203–23.

Taylor, B. (1985) *Modes of Occurrence*, Oxford: Blackwell.

—— ed. (1987) *Michael Dummett: Contributions to Philosophy*, Dordrecht: Nijhoff.

Taylor, R. (1966) *Action and Purpose*, Englewood Cliffs, New Jersey: Prentice–Hall.

Thalberg, I. (1980) 'Can we get rid of events?', *Analysis* **40**, 25–31.

Thompson, I. J. (1988) 'Real dispositions in the physical world', *British Journal for the Philosophy of Science* **39**, 67–79.

Tooley, M. (1987) *Causation: a Realist Approach*, Oxford: Clarendon Press.

Urbach, P. (1988) 'What is a law of nature? A Humean answer', *British Journal for the Philosophy of Science* **39**, 193–210.

Vallentyne, P. (1988) 'Explicating lawhood', *Philosophy of Science* **55**, 598–613.

van Fraassen, B. C. (1989) *Laws and Symmetry*, Oxford: Clarendon Press.

van Inwagen, P., ed. (1980) *Time and Cause*, Dordrecht: Reidel.

Vermazen, B. and Hintikka, M. B., eds (1985) *Essays on Davidson: Actions and Events*, Oxford: Clarendon Press.

von Mises, R. (1957) *Probability, Statistics and Truth*, 2nd English edn, London: Allen and Unwin.

von Wright, G. H. (1974) *Causality and Determinism*, New York: Columbia University Press.

Wilson, R. A. (1992) 'Individualism, causal powers, and explanation', *Philosophical Studies* **68**, 103–39.

Woodward, J. (1990) 'Laws and causes', *British Journal for the Philosophy of Science* **41**, 553–73.

—— (1992) 'Realism about laws', *Erkenntnis* **36**, 181–218.

# Index